D1713412

Inventing retirement

The development of occupational pensions in Britain

Inventing retirement

The development of occupational pensions in Britain

Leslie Hannah
Professor of Business History, London School of Economics

WITHDRAWN

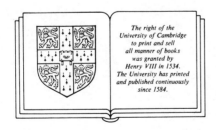

The right of the
University of Cambridge
to print and sell
all manner of books
was granted by
Henry VIII in 1534.
The University has printed
and published continuously
since 1584.

CAMBRIDGE UNIVERSITY PRESS
Cambridge
London   New York   New Rochelle
Melbourne   Sydney

Published by the Press Syndicate of the University of Cambridge
The Pitt Building, Trumpington Street, Cambridge CB2 1RP
32 East 57th Street, New York, NY 10022, USA
10 Stamford Road, Oakleigh, Melbourne 3166, Australia

First published 1986

Printed in Great Britain at the University Press, Cambridge

British Library cataloguing in publication data

Hannah, Leslie
Inventing retirement: the development of
occupational pensions in Britain.
1. Pension trusts – Great Britain – History
I. Title
331.25′2′0941   HD7106.G8

Library of Congress Cataloguing in Publication Data

Hannah, Leslie.
Inventing retirement.
Bibliography: p.
Includes index.
1. Pensions – Great Britain – History. I. Title.
HD7165.H36 1986   331.25′2′0941   85-18970

ISBN 0 521 30361 3

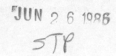

Contents

vi *Contents*

Tables and figures

Preface

Retirement was not invented in the twentieth century; but it did then become the eventual lot of the majority of British employees and its terms were then fundamentally rewritten. This book is about the way that occupational pension schemes have shaped these profound changes. In recent years, economists and others have come to appreciate the important role of pension schemes in employment contracts, in the distribution of wealth, in social welfare policy, and in the capital markets; but historians have not explicitly addressed their studies to the origins and purpose of our pensioning system. Why do employers, rather than individuals, or, as was once the case, trade unions, now organize old age saving? Why do employees have less control of the resulting pension funds than they used to? Why do most people now retire, often compulsorily at a fixed age? Why has Britain paid such poor state pensions and depended so heavily on occupational pensions? Why are pension rights protected well against inflation for workers who remain with one employer but miserably for those who change jobs or for most occupational pensioners after retirement? These questions address issues which in one way or another have concerned employers and employees for a century or more. I hope that the historical perspective provided by this book will enable those who are attempting to answer them now to understand better the constraints and opportunities which the legacy of the past provides.

This work was commissioned by the Legal & General Group, the market leader in private occupational pension provision for the last fifty years.

Their gift to the Business History Unit of the London School of Economics which supported the research was part of a programme designed to celebrate their 150th anniversary in 1986. It was agreed that the author would be completely free to publish his own conclusions without any strings. In acknowledging this support, I have to acknowledge more than financial sponsorship. The managers of the Legal & General were generous with their own time and helpful in introducing me to many organizations and individuals in the pension industry. Without this help, the task of writing this book, based as it is on private archive material much of which is not in the public domain, would have been difficult if not impossible. I am particularly grateful to Sir James Ball, Alan Bland, C. S. S. Lyon, John MacCarthy, T. J. Palmer, P. W. Simon and J. M. Skae of the Legal & General for their support and encouragement as the work progressed, and also to a number of former Legal & General staff: P. Cahill, the late T. A. E. Layborn, G. W. Pingstone and R. H. Peet. I am also grateful to the staff of: Bacon & Woodrow, the Chartered Insurance Institute, Clerical, Medical & General Assurance, the Department of Health and Social Security, the Eagle Star Group, the Industrial Society, the Institute of Actuaries, the Labour Party, the Life Offices' Association, the National Association of Pension Funds, the Occupational Pensions Board, the Prudential Group, the Registry of Friendly Societies, the Superannuation Funds Office of the Inland Revenue, and the Trades Union Congress, as well as to the staff of the many self-administered pension funds listed in the note on sources at the end of the book. Their generous gift of time as well as access to material was a useful aid to abstracting the relevant information from the large quantities of documentation in their possession, and their patience at what must often have seemed rather bizarre questions about the distant past was particularly appreciated. Archivists, pension managers, and other practitioners in the field who generously gave their time to discuss these issues include: R. W. Abbott, Sir Alec Atkinson, P. Atteridge, F. Bacon, T. Baker-Jones, R. Barker-Jones, P. Basten, S. Bird, Revd A. H. Birtles, M. Bonavia, Lord Boyd-Carpenter, J. Bretherick, R. H. Clutton, C. Coates, C. N. Coles, R. J. W. Crabbe, M. Crawley, G. Desmons, H. Edwards, F. P. Farncombe, J. Frith, N. Glass, R. A. Golding, E. Green, D. H. Hallam, W. C. Harvey, H. J. Hazell, E. Higgs, R. E. Holt, K. Howells, H. James, D. Jarratt, M. Jubb, J. M. Keyworth, R. J. Kirton, Sir Arthur Knight, G. A. Knight, Colin R. Lowndes, N. MacDonald, B. Murray, H. Nabb, R. Neale, Donald A. Odell, T. H. M. Oppé, M. Pilch, C. Pratt, R. H. Rawlinson, the late F. M. Redington, M. Robbins, E. F. Rogers, A. Roper, M. Roper, G. Ross Goobey, W. A. L. Seaman, A. Selman, R. Standring, J. Stern, H. Stevenson, R. A. Storey, A. Sutcliff, H. Ward, S. Ward, R. Weit, A. H. Wilcock, M. Wilks, and N. Wratten.

In conducting this research I was ably assisted by a team of research assistants, who contributed beyond their allotted tasks to a constructive dialogue on the interpretation of quite new and difficult archival evidence. Sarah Silcox managed the project office, undertook the bulk of the research in pension fund archives, and checked all the references. I would simply not have completed the writing of this book to deadline without her help over the whole two years of the project. Hugh Woolhouse, Judy Slinn and Nuala Zahedieh each worked for about a year producing invaluable research reports on pension topics.

John Kay and Paul Johnson read the final version of the manuscript and rescued me from many remaining errors. I also found discussions with a wide range of academic colleagues helpful, and I shall particularly thank Tony Atkinson, Charles Baden-Fuller, Theo Barker, B. Benjamin, John H. Boyes, D. Brooke, John Butt, Sir Alec Cairncross, Hugh Cockerell, Donald Coleman, Richard Davenport-Hines, Michael Elliott, David Galenson, Howard Gospel, Francis Green, Dulcie Groves, José Harris, Eddie Hunt, Geoffrey Jones, Heather Joshi, Bill Kennedy, Mervyn King, Peter Laslett, Jay Light, Sir Douglas Logan, Tony Lynes, Joe Melling, Charles Munn, Chris Napier, Richard Nobles, Richard Portes, Angela Raspin, Michael Reddin, Stephen Sass, Tom Schuller, Barry Supple, Pat Thane, Keith Thomas, Carol Watson, Ron Weir, Noel Whiteside, Tom Wilson, and Jay Winter.

Finally, a year as Thomas Henry Carroll Ford Foundation Visiting Professor at the Harvard Graduate School of Business Administration enabled me to complete the writing of the book. To my hosts there, Dean John McArthur and Professors Gordon Donaldson, Alfred Chandler, Jr and Tom McCraw, I owe not only the writing opportunity, but the memory of a very happy year of collegial academic interaction within a stimulating research community of scholars.

The customary disclaimer applies: no individuals or organizations, save the author named on the title page, should be held accountable for the book's contents.

Leslie Hannah
Soldiers Field, Boston, Massachusetts
March 1985

Part I *The rise of pensioning*

1 Savings, work and old age in Victorian Britain

> The practice of viewing the aged as a separate class is modern . . .
> G. R. Porter and F. W. Hirst, *The Progress of the Nation*, 1912, p. 76

Behind contemporary man's age-old fears of personal ageing, behind the anger of social critics at our treatment of the old, or behind the sociologist's analysis of the decay of family mutuality, there often lies a mental image of the golden age past. In this picture, much favoured by politicians and the media, the old were revered; their wisdom and experience were shared with youth; family hearths extended generous welcomes to grandmothers and grandfathers; and, in rural society, especially, family support and household production enabled the old to adapt to increasing infirmity with dignity and at their own pace. In recent years, historians have been able to show that such rose-coloured views of old age in the world we have lost are largely myth. Over twentieth-century lifetimes, our typical experience of old age and our ideas about retirement have both undergone profound changes, and they are not uniformly happy innovations. If we are to analyse them, it will be as well to start off with an understanding of the social and economic experience of old age in the society which gave birth to them, rather than with myths of lost joys and innocence.

Pessimism about old age is not, of course, new. As long ago as 1776, Adam Smith was bemoaning the decline in respect for the old and observing that advanced nations treated their aged citizens badly.[1] Historical demographers have shown clearly that the residence of old people with their children was never in modern, recorded history the norm in Britain.[2] Financial support for the old by their offspring, though welcomed by the poor law authorities, was by no means universal.[3] Old people wishing to live

3

with their children and grandchildren were as likely then as now to encounter resistance and emotional strains.[4] Poverty in old age was, then as now, likely to be blamed on the supposed long-run decline of filial piety.[5] Such reciprocity as existed between young and old in family life may have been developed in some pre-industrial villages, but it probably developed further in booming factory towns: where women could get jobs and welcomed a grandmother at home in the child-caring role.[6] Similar instrumental ties, reinforcing emotional attachments, were no less necessary in the higher reaches of society. Any man of means contemplating retirement in the nineteenth century was well advised to hold on to his fortune and position, remembering that wealth and power, not age as such, were the source of much of the respect he would enjoy, just as had been the case in pre-industrial England.[7] If there had been a golden age for the old, then, it was more in the realm of imagination than in the everyday experience of the old in the Victorian period.

Yet, undeniably, there was in nineteenth-century Britain less differentiation of people by age than has since become the norm. Sixty or sixty-five did not then mark the rite of passage for individuals which they have since become, and there was also much less contemporary awareness of the old generally as a social 'problem'. Why were the old less visible? In part it was that there were fewer of them: the population over sixty-five (now 15% of the total) never exceeded 5% of the Victorian population as a whole.[8] Victorian Britain was a youthful society, with the burden of dependent children taxing the incomes of families far more than the dependent old. The demographic transition to the small families of the twentieth century reduced that problem, while increased longevity has greatly increased the older population. In the last century, fewer people expected to survive to old age. The expectation of life of twenty-year-olds did not reach sixty-five years of age until the twentieth century:[9] most nineteenth-century Englishmen entering the adult work force thus might not expect to survive to the age recognized as a watershed marking old age.[10] Those who did reach sixty-five were, moreover, not likely to stop work on account of it: in the closing decades of the nineteenth century around two-thirds of people aged sixty-five and over who had been in the work force were still working.[11] The problem of financing old age – smaller though it was than present day problems – was, none the less, one of which Victorians of all social classes were well aware. Their perceptions and preconceptions produced a range of individual and collective responses which were profoundly to influence future developments.

Among the business and professional classes it was not uncommon to follow the classic behaviour posited in life-cycle theories of savings: people borrowing to establish a family in early adulthood, and then in their forties beginning to accumulate *rentier* investments by saving and inheritance (the latter coming earlier than it typically now does) to finance a slow withdrawal from business in their fifties and sixties.[12] Amongst the wealthy (to whom income tax was then confined), the tax reliefs introduced by Gladstone in 1853 on premiums for insurance policies increased the incentive to provide for widowhood and old age by this means, and the insurance companies assiduously courted this custom.[13] Only about a fifth of taxpayers availed themselves of the relief, but those who did commonly devoted 5% or more of their income to this form of saving by the turn of the century.[14] Gladstone also extended the system of government annuities to make small annuities available at post offices, but this failed to widen the annuity market beyond the affluent. Even they found that buying an annuity – at age sixty-five this typically meant exchanging a lump sum of £1,000 for an annual income of £100 ceasing on death – was unattractive given the tax discrimination against it. Most of the affluent preferred to manage their old age investments directly, spending capital (which, unlike the capital element in annuities, was not taxed) and income as they needed it. This could leave someone who lived a long time short, and those who were unwilling to take this risk stimulated the gradually growing market for both government annuities and insurance company annuities.[15] The affluent who had provided in these ways could afford to withdraw gradually from work if they were self-employed (or resign if they were employees), and enjoy in retirement those other pursuits which they found congenial. With continually rising living standards in the later nineteenth century more people were able to do so. The lower middle classes certainly aspired to building up a nest egg for old age, and those who succeeded accounted for part of the increase in the proportion of the aged who retired in the later-nineteenth-century decades.

There were, however, real limits to the extent of such savings. The industrial insurance companies, selling on a door-to-door basis to a mainly working-class market, made large advances in the late nineteenth century, but little of this was for old age saving, rather than for short-term contingencies and burial insurance. The savings ethos of the mass of the population remained quite sharply differentiated from the patterns established by the Victorian bourgeoisie,[16] and this severely constrained their retirement options. Smilesian critics pointed out that for threepence a week from age twenty – less than the cost of twenty cigarettes – a man could save enough to buy an annuity of five shillings a week (about a quarter of average wage earnings by the turn of the century) from age sixty-five.[17] There were, of course, still some people who could not afford even that,[18] but, more importantly, even the many who could probably felt (and if they did they were right) that a man of twenty was more likely to be dead than alive at sixty-five. For the poorer workers, moreover, life expectation was lower than for the population as a whole, so the disinclination to save for an uncertain eventuality could be quite rationally justified in the light of more real demands on the meagre budget. Household creation, and child rearing – not to speak of the enjoyment of beer or the benefits of gambling – all had higher priorities than retirement saving in the forty or so years of adult working life which the poor could expect.[19] Working-class thrift tended to take the form of friendly society or trade union subscriptions, designed more to deal with unemployment or sickness, both of which were more certain for the typical worker than old age, as well as more likely to occupy a larger portion of their lives. It was only among the better-off workers that such mutual savings funds developed far in the direction of financing old age pensions. Trade unions sometimes paid sickness and unemployment benefits to their older members which were in effect retirement pensions, and a few extremely well-paid trade societies, such as the London Compositors, had generous pension benefits, but these were exceptional; moreover, only a small minority of the working population were members of trade unions in the nineteenth century.[20] Friendly societies achieved more widespread coverage and also provided *de facto* pension benefits for long-standing members. However, these liabilities were already causing serious problems for the societies by the end of the nineteenth century and members were reluctant to increase their subscriptions to the level necessary to finance old age more securely.[21]

Only one such working man's society – the Northumberland and Durham Miners' Permanent Relief Society – appears to have developed successfully an adequate regime of provision for old age in the nineteenth century.[22] Its achievements have been curiously neglected by historians, though it was for many years the largest private occupational pension scheme in Britain in terms of the number of contributing members: there were 140,000 members at the turn of the century, and nearly 4,000 pensions were being paid. These benefits were popular among the members, and as the local coal industry expanded and wages rose, membership was still growing fast. The Society had started as an accident compensation fund in 1862 following the Hartley Colliery disaster, with some support from the employers, and developed its modest pension benefits gradually. The support from employers tailed off in the late nineteenth century, and the members' committee determined benefits and fixed subscriptions as was usual in friendly societies. The majority of miners in the prosperous north-eastern coal fields chose to join. In 1899, when coal hewers earned about thirty shillings a week, members paid $1\frac{1}{2}$d. a week for superannuation benefits, and the total subscription of four pence, including the accident fund, absorbed little more than 1% of earnings. After ten years, those over sixty became eligible for a four shillings a week pension if they could produce a medical certificate of inability to work and were not earning more than five shillings a week from light work. There was no formal retiring age, and most miners preferred to work if they could (coming on the fund on average seven years after the minimum retiring age). This preference for remaining in employment (hardly surprising in the light of the severe drop in income which the pension represented for the high-earning miners), together with the low life-expectancy of miners, enabled the fund to honour its commitments and improve benefits, gaining the confidence of members for several decades.[23] The friendly societies organized by railway workers – though with rather more help in that case from employers – also provided explicit pension benefits for large numbers of railwaymen.[24] However, such collective initiatives by workers for explicit provision for old age were confined to relatively affluent groups such as miners and railwaymen, and were very much the exception rather than the rule.

For the mass of workers without such coverage (and indeed for many in these collective schemes providing only low levels of benefits), staying on the job was the normal, accepted practice in old age until incapacity intervened to force retirement. This did not mean that incomes could be maintained at a high level into old age. It was quite normal for older employees, whose productivity was reduced by declining physical strength or mental vigour, to have their pay reduced, or to be asked to leave strenuous employment and find lighter work elsewhere. The wage data and the practices of employers who did require retirement of ineffective workers both suggest that physical and mental powers declined at an earlier age than is now the case.[25] In many manual occupations earnings peaked at age forty-five and after that it was increasingly difficult to find new employment; from age fifty-five men frequently had to drop skilled occupations entirely. A minority were able to stay on with the same firm in lighter work: a furnaceman earning two or three pounds a week might be offered a position as a weighman at little more than a pound a week; miners would cease to work underground and take a lighter job at the pit head; a deserving employee 'past his job' at the Reading biscuit makers, Huntley & Palmer, could expect a light job at a reduced wage.[26] Frequent sickness absences and long periods of unemployment also reduced the incomes of the elderly, and technical changes in industry may have had the effect of reducing their job opportunities since employers preferred to train younger workers in new methods.[27] Some employers would keep on old, unproductive workers with long service for charity's sake,[28] but for many of the redundant old, the end of working life might involve menial work at very low wages. An old couple might finally work as night-watchman and self-employed washerwoman, or simply earn money on the side by growing vegetables or letting a vacant room.

When self-help failed, sons and daughters might provide assistance in kind or cash,[29] but the major recourse, particularly of the very old and the incapacitated, was the poor law. The tradition of community support for the elderly was unusually well developed in Britain; and, while the poor law had been tightened up in the nineteenth century to prevent malingering, the aged were usually subjected to rather less harsh treatment than the sturdier unemployed. These traditions did, however, come under increasing pressure, with attempts to force families to pay a larger share of the costs of maintaining the old, and a disinclination to offer 'outdoor relief' (rather than the deterrent compulsory residence in a workhouse). From 1870 onwards, some scholars are now suggesting, there was in many areas a conscious effort to make the relief unpalatable to the old, and to encourage them to rely on themselves or their families rather than the community for old age income.[30] The later Victorians may, then, have the distinction of being the only generation in Britain in modern decades which, though itself enjoying comfortably improving real living standards, refused to share them more than proportionately with the aged needy.[31] This was only possible in an underdeveloped democracy with an unusually acute sense of the virtues of self-help among the limited electorate. The overwhelming majority of the aged poor, even at the end of the nineteenth century, did not have the vote, and if they did, for many years lost it on entering the workhouse. But the growing power of organized labour, the widening franchise and the liberal populist tradition were eventually to coalesce and to demonstrate the political viability of a wider community conception of the responsibilities of the state towards the aged, on the national rather than local level on which the poor law operated.

In the Victorian period, despite increasing signs of these new possibilities, the central government kept out of income maintenance for the old. But there were other communities which had the organizational and financial muscle to provide some assistance to the old. There was a long tradition of employers, large and small, rewarding long-serving employees of all ranks with an *ex gratia* pension. Examples of this can be found as widely in modern industries as in the traditional rural communities with which such paternalism is usually associated.[32] Such payments were in the nature of a charitable gift, but the local employment nexus of which they were a culmination was, of course, strengthened by knowledge of their existence. In communities where the tradition was particularly well developed, the employer, though he had discretion in individual cases, could no more have generally and unilaterally stopped such pensions than he could have ceased contributing to the local church and reading room, or refused to sponsor public or works events. These pensions were part of a system of reciprocal obligations well understood by the members of the communities where the institution flourished. Indeed, local poor law guardians occasionally requested employers to pay such pensions,[33] and former employees themselves did not baulk at writing to request pensions.[34] The extent of *ex gratia* pension entitlement was undoubtedly small and the practice was explicitly outlawed by some firms.[35] Others argued that such provision discouraged private thrift,[36] though, in view of their selective and conditional nature, few could *reliably* count on such a pension. Many employers did, however, directly encourage thrift among their work force by sponsoring works savings banks, provident funds, or friendly societies: often covering administrative expenses, paying the interest (sometimes at privileged rates) on money deposited with the firm, or declaring bonuses on pay and encouraging employees to deposit them rather than spend them.[37] The origins of many modern pension funds can be traced back to the attempts of such paternalistic firms to encourage the habit of thrift among their employees. The amounts typically accumulated in these funds were inadequate to buy a reasonable pension annuity in old age. Nonetheless, they did offer employees a convenient way of building up a nest egg for periods of unemployment and sickness, and such a lump sum provided some supplement to declining income from employment as old age or incapacity approached.

One very large, bureaucratic employer – the state – had gone very much further than this in providing pensions for its employees, who then accounted for only a small proportion of the labour force (less than 3% in 1891). In the civil service, especially, various pension systems were already well developed by the early nineteenth century.[38] Some pensions were a survival from the days when Samuel Johnson had defined them as 'pay given to a state hireling for treason to his country': that is to say for political, sexual, or other favours.[39] In the army and navy, and the customs service, offices were sometimes bought from their previous incumbents by offers of a lump sum or annual payment by somebody wishing to succeed to the post. (This practice survived, and in some cases still survives, as a method of financing retirement well into the twentieth century in the sale of professional practices by, for example, architects, solicitors and doctors.) In the mid nineteenth century, reformers, building on earlier attempts to systematize state employees' pensions, introduced new schemes for both the civil service and the armed forces. The civil service scheme was to become an important model for the clerical and executive ranks in other sectors, offering, as it did, a particularly generous level of benefits.[40] In 1859 earlier civil service schemes were replaced by a non-contributory one providing pensions of one-sixtieth of final salary for each year of service (with a maximum of forty-sixtieths) from age sixty or later. (Compulsory retirement at sixty-five was not imposed until the 1890s.)[41] This generous level of provision became the target for other groups in the public sector, and by the end of the nineteenth century some teachers and local government employees also had won pension rights by statute or by local management agreement. The Treasury and local ratepayers were, however, cautious about extending schemes, and the few early local schemes involved a contribution from the staff and provided less opulent levels of pension than the civil service scheme.[42]

The largest organizations with bureaucratic features outside the state sector in nineteenth-century Britain were the railways, the nation's first big business. Their predecessors, the inland waterways, had produced the first examples of formal pension schemes in the private sector,[43] and the early railways soon developed savings clubs, employee friendly societies, and *ex gratia* pensions. The London and Birmingham Railway (later part of the London and North Western Railway) offered old age allowances in the 1840s of from five to twenty shillings a week, financing these, esoterically, from the sale of lost luggage and newspapers.[44] A more formal scheme for LNWR clerical staff followed in 1853, with the staff contributing $2\frac{1}{2}$% of wages and the company guaranteeing 4% interest on accumulating funds and additional company contributions.[45] Membership was compulsory and for those with ten or more years' service pensions could be drawn on retirement at age sixty or later. Pension levels were fixed at $22\frac{3}{4}$% of average salary after ten years' service and 109% of average salary after forty-five years' service. Other railway companies followed with similar schemes. Less popular variants were 'money purchase' schemes (in which the pensions depended on the accumulated contributions by employer and employee, and interest earned) and 'final average salary' (in which the pensions were related to salary in the last five or seven years preceding retirement rather than the average salary of a whole working life).

By the 1880s most railways had evolved well-defined pension schemes for their management and clerical staff. In the typical scheme the employee paid $2\frac{1}{2}$% of his salary into the fund, which was matched by the company; the company guaranteed the rate of interest, and the funds were placed on deposit with the firm, or in fixed interest securities. Membership was compulsory, and both employees and employer were represented on the committee of management, though with employer interests playing the leading role in determining policy. Pensions were based on years of service and average salary in that period: a typical level was 25% of average salary after ten years' service and 67% after forty-five years. The funds were usually administered by a staff of three to four clerks, though they increasingly relied on professional actuaries for advice on more complex questions of determining rates of funding and levels of benefits. The actuaries were usually moonlighting from or retired from insurance companies, whose business was based on similar actuarial problems.[46]

The railway funds were not quite like the pension schemes which came to dominate the private sector in the first half of the twentieth century: in particular, the special parliamentary acts required to set them up seemed unfamiliar and expensive to many businesses, whereas to railways (or municipalities which also regularly promoted private bills) it was a simple matter to tack a pension fund clause on to their bills. A parliamentary act provided a legal basis for a separately constituted fund, but did not guarantee the success of schemes unless they had a solidly established employer behind them. There had, for example, been a remarkably early statutory scheme for merchant seamen: the Act for the Relief and Support of Mariners and Disabled Seamen, and the Widows of Such as Shall be Killed, Slain or Drowned in the Merchants' Service was passed in 1749. It required most seamen to pay sixpence a month, and for over a century provided a modest level of benefit to large numbers of aged seamen. It was, however, underfunded, and ships' masters seem to have benefited from it more than ordinary sailors (perhaps because of their more stable employment and comparative longevity). Agreements on necessary reforms in funding proved impossible and the scheme collapsed in 1852, existing pensions continuing to be paid, but many contributors losing their accumulated rights. A voluntary scheme which replaced it was taken up by only 5% of those eligible, most of them ships' masters, but attempts to produce wider schemes for the industry failed.[47]

The statutory schemes for railways usually excluded the manual or weekly paid employees – 'servants' rather than 'officers' in contemporary railway parlance – but the companies did contribute generously to a variety of friendly society schemes for these workers. Sometimes membership in such schemes was made compulsory, and railway employers found it increasingly difficult to avoid close involvement in the management of the funds and the development of the benefit structure.[48] The LNWR inaugurated a scheme for manual workers in 1883, initially making only a small contribution, though in subsequent decades this substantially increased.[49] A major factor was the railways' desire to counteract the growing influence of trade unionism. The Great Western Railway Enginemen and Firemen's Mutual Assurance, Sick, and Superannuation Society had been founded in 1865, and the company had compelled workers to join. By the 1890s, however, the Fund, run by the men themselves, was paying benefits which could not be supported by the contributions and was hopelessly in deficit. Having compelled their workers to join, the company felt some responsibility. But they were unwilling to bail out the scheme without taking greater control. They employed an actuary, who not only computed a deficit of £1,250,000 in the scheme, but pointed out the benefit to the company of controlling pensions and improving their level to 'take the fire out of the Socialist cause'.[50] After years of negotiations with the men, the GWR agreed in 1901 to subsidize more generous pensions through a new statutory scheme for manual employees over which the company had greater control.[51]

Developments in railways were paralleled in the other large-scale Victorian public utilities, the gas companies. The largest, the Gas Light &

Coke Company, introduced a scheme for staff in 1842 and for manual workers in 1870;[52] and many other large gas undertakings had schemes by the turn of the century.[53] Financial institutions also commonly made some provision for pensions and in a few banks towards the end of the century the traditions of informal *ex gratia* pensions were giving way to more formal schemes, with set levels of benefits. For example, the directors of the London Joint Stock Bank, founded in 1836, had rejected the idea of a pension fund in the early years, but by 1871 were setting aside funds in their accounts for superannuation.[54] This method of establishing a scheme – by balance-sheet reserve – did not, of course, provide a segregated fund safe from creditors in the event of bankruptcy (as the railway funds did), but for safe financial institutions (and bankruptcies among them were rare after 1870) this was a relatively low risk for employees to bear. In the 1880s there was pressure from clerks for an extension of pensions beyond the few banks that provided them,[55] and Lloyd's Bank, for example, introduced a non-contributory scheme with compulsory retirement at sixty-five and a pension proportional to final salary.[56] Formal schemes were also established by a few large insurance companies in the later decades of the nineteenth century, the Prudential in 1872 and the Royal Exchange in 1880 being among the first.[57] However, many banks and insurance companies, particularly the smaller ones, preferred to maintain an informal discretionary system of pensions, though competition with the civil service often led to *ex gratia* benefits very similar to the civil service ones being granted even when no formal scheme existed.[58] The Bank of England, though still technically a private institution, had one of the longest-standing and most generous pension schemes, with benefits similar to those in the civil service and on a statutory scale, though they were careful to specify that the pensions remained entirely at the discretion of the Bank.[59]

In manufacturing industry, Siemens Brothers had a formal pension scheme as early as 1872, perhaps influenced by the welfare practices of the German firm of which it was an offshoot.[60] British manufacturing firms do not seem to have seen much need to emulate this, preferring to continue with discretionary *ad hoc* pensioning. Some of the very largest firms in the closing years of the nineteenth century – J. & P. Coats, Colmans, and W. D. & H. O. Wills – did pioneer formal schemes.[61] In other sectors, formal pension arrangements were few and far between, though they were occasionally found among the larger employers. The West India Docks started a scheme for clerks as early as 1852, providing pensions of £30 per annum; and the wholesale and retail newsagent chain, W. H. Smith, replaced its provident scheme with a formal pension scheme for both clerks and workmen in 1894–5. No doubt diligent research would reveal further examples, particularly in the larger industrial and commercial organizations created by the revolutionary technical and market transformations in many industries of the late nineteenth century.

This picture of private occupational pension provision in the nineteenth century is inevitably incomplete. *Ex gratia* provision was widespread, but its extent is unknown. Sometimes such provision was so certain and well understood by all parties that *ex gratia* pensioning was difficult to distinguish from the formal schemes. The majority of pensions at the end of the nineteenth century may well have been of this kind, though we know little of the aggregate picture statistically.[62] From what we do know, it is unlikely that the number of employees in the *formally constituted* pension schemes in the private and public sectors combined exceeded a million even as late as 1900: thus perhaps around 5% of the work force were covered.[63] These members accumulating pension rights were probably about equally divided between manual workers and the salaried classes. There was, however, a very clear contrast between the style of provision for the two classes, corresponding to the sharp cultural and social divide represented by the uniquely strong British class structure. Most of the middle class espoused the gospel of self-help: not only were they not members of pension schemes, but they would have considered it rather inconvenient and indeed demeaning to be so.[64] Provision for old age and widowhood was seen as the duty of the individual, and the flexibility and personal control offered by private saving would not be sacrificed lightly. None the less, all established civil servants, almost all railway clerks and managers, and a few similar employees, for example in banking, did have clearly defined pension benefits, the greater part of them enshrined in statutory schemes. The employers in all cases exercised substantial control over the nature of the schemes, particularly where they were non-contributory, though in the railway schemes, which were to form an important model for later pension trusts, the members typically made substantial contributions and their representatives participated in the management of the fund. In the civil service, railways and banks, mandatory retirement at a fixed age was imposed on some clerks, but it was still unusual: pension funds had been (and continued to be) founded without any provisions on retirement other than a minimum age at which full benefits could be paid.

The working-class funds were generally organized on a different basis, sometimes through trade unions, but most commonly as occupation-based friendly societies. With only a few exceptions, coverage for old age was in most occupations patchy. For almost all of the working classes, working life continued until incapacity prevented it. Savings, family, or ultimately the poor law were then the only recourse. Friendly societies were typically concerned with a wide range of insurance needs, including sickness, accident, health, and unemployment provisions; but their members showed little interest in extending this to include specific cover for old age retirement; indeed, this was then less likely than the other eventualities to be experienced by the working classes. Industrial insurance companies, equally, had not yet penetrated the popular market for old age provision.

There were a few occupational friendly societies in the north-east coal mines and the railways which provided a model of what could be achieved by mutual self-help through this medium by relatively well-off workers. The labour movement was, however, by the turn of the century about to commit itself to a very different political approach, which for the rest of the twentieth century was to transform the traditional balance between private and collective provision for old age.

2 Rival pioneers of collectivism: pensions, the state and employers (1899–1927)

> The need of pension provision for employees upon retirement extends as our system of commerce and industry tends to concentration, and men become more and more dependent upon an organization and less and less able to influence their own destiny . . .
>
> John C. Mitchell, Chairman,
> Association of Superannuation and
> Pension Funds, 'Pension schemes for
> office staff' address, February 1935,
> p. 3.

The rising pressure by the local poor law authorities to limit expenditure on the old was paralleled from the 1870s by a growing tide of opinion favouring a national system of pensions to deal more generously and comprehensively with the problem of old age poverty.[1] Opponents of state pensions advocated self-help and pointed to the disincentive effects of state nannying; supporters suggested that a national pension system would be more likely to encourage thrift if pensions were given widely and without the penalties associated with the poor law. There was some division among supporters on whether national pensions should be contributory like Bismarck's scheme in Germany or financed from general taxation. Gradually the supporters of state pensions gained political ground. Middle-class social reformers pointed to the extent of poverty in old age shown by social surveys, and politicians were increasingly conscious of the potential popularity of a more humane system of pensioning among the working classes. The labour movement, initially hesitant about old age pensions, switched to supporting them by the first decade of the twentieth century,[2] and this may have been one factor propelling the Liberal government of 1906 toward a national scheme. In the 1908 budget, Asquith announced a selective, non-contributory scheme to pay old age pensions of five shillings a

15

week from the age of seventy to those of few means. The passage of the pensions bill was relatively uncontroversial: the first pensions were paid from 1909. To satisfy critics, those who had shown an insufficient propensity for self-help and fallen on the poor law were initially excluded, but the absurdity of this disqualification was soon removed; by 1912 60% of the seventy-plus age group were regularly collecting their pensions.[3] The pension was means-tested: those with an annual income above £31.10s. a year received nothing, and those with over £21 a year only qualified for a reduced pension; but most pensioners had incomes below this threshold and received the full five shillings. The distribution of the new pensions through post offices and their clear separation from the poor law authorities made them a highly acceptable substitute for poor relief. Thus began that process (still incomplete) of removing the stigma of welfare provision from the minds of needy beneficiaries. The new pensions were extremely popular.

Although it was a big political step, the 1908 Pensions Act was only a very partial solution to the problem of poverty in old age. The state pension was overwhelmingly important for women, who constituted the majority of beneficiaries, and had a longer life expectancy and typically lower earnings and investment income than men. The new pensions also enabled the poor law authorities to cut their expenditure on the old substantially, and probably reduced the proportion of the old forced into the workhouse and other institutions.[4] As a measure to facilitate secure retirement, however, the 1908 Act had severe limitations. Many employees were worn out and incapable of working well before reaching their seventieth year; and indeed, the majority of adults at this time could not expect to live to seventy. For those who did, five shillings was better than or equivalent to the normal poor law relief, but was below the generally accepted subsistence level in the urban areas where the majority of the old lived.[5] About a fifth of the average wage, it was clearly insufficient to compensate for loss of earnings and, indeed, it was expressly presented as a supplement to support from casual earnings, charities, families, former employers, and the savings or friendly society benefits which the old were still expected to accumulate. If a couple were both over seventy, they both received full pensions (a government proposal to award only seven shillings and sixpence to married couples was defeated in the Commons), but the disparity in ages of husbands and wives and the low life expectancy of men meant that there were few such couples. Even the double pension became clearly inadequate in the severe inflation of the First World War, when Treasury pressure succeeded in keeping pension increases behind the rise in prices, thus cutting pensioners' living standards drastically. It was not until the mid 1920s that the post-war fall in prices clearly made old age pensioners (since 1920 receiving ten shillings a week) as well off as when pensions were first introduced.[6]

By then, the Conservative government, facing a much stronger threat now from the rise of Labour, determined to put the pension on a more realistic basis.[7] In 1908 pensions at age sixty-five had been ruled out on the grounds that they would cost twice as much as the already expensive new proposal.[8] In 1911 a contributory national insurance scheme had to some extent made up for this, in that unemployment and sickness benefits paid under it could in some cases amount to old age pensions for the incapacitated or unemployable under-seventies. There was, however, general agreement that sixty-five was a more realistic age for pensions to be more widely available, though there was no agreement on how this could be financed. Eventually, in 1925, Winston Churchill, having joined the newly elected Conservative government as Chancellor, extended the contributory national insurance principle in the 1925 Pensions Act. The new scheme applied to roughly the same proportion of the population, about two-thirds, as were then qualifying for pensions at seventy, contributions being compulsory for all manual workers and for all others earning less than £250 a year. After further extensions of voluntary coverage in the 1930s, the proportion of the population covered was to reach 84% by the early 1940s.[9] Male employees paid fourpence a week each and their employers an equivalent amount from 1926 (married women benefited mainly through their husbands, but could make lower contributions to qualify in their own right). The Treasury subsidized the scheme initially to permit pensions of ten shillings a week to be paid from 1928 to those reaching age sixty-five, or, in the case of widows, from the death of the breadwinner. For the first time in Britain, most adults among the poorest two-thirds of the population who contributed could realistically expect to draw old age pensions from the state. The new pensions were, moreover, insured benefits to which contributors had a right. There was no means test, and no retirement condition: pensions were paid on attaining age sixty-five, irrespective of other income or employment. And most of those who reached that age did, in fact, still continue working as well as drawing the pension.[10] Even when they reached seventy, and qualified for the earlier non-contributory pension, that pension was no longer means-tested, and a minority even chose to continue at work beyond that age too. The relatively modest level of the pension, even when – as was sometimes the case – it was topped up by a few shillings by the local poor law authorities, continued to make the option of retirement less than compellingly attractive to many of the aged.[11] The central government's involvement in funding old age was, however, clearly growing: old age pensions had cost only 0.3% of GNP in 1910, but had risen to 1.5% by 1930, and the proportion was to reach 2.3% by 1950.[12]

The attitude of businessmen to the growth of state pensions was equivocal. They did, of course, regret the financial consequences: the increased taxation or employers' national insurance contributions, which added to their production costs. Their representatives attempted to persuade the government to postpone both the 1908 and the 1925 legislation because of its anticipated effect on costs.[13] Some employers also expressed the traditional Victorian concern about the effect of state pensions on reducing self-help through private thrift.[14] On the other hand, businessmen like Charles Booth, the shipowner, and Seebohm Rowntree, the chocolate manufacturer, had been in the forefront of the social analysis of poverty and of the political campaigns to introduce old age pensions; and some business pressure groups, like the Birmingham Chamber of Commerce, had strongly pressed for national contributory pensions.[15] Leaders of larger enterprises in the new industries seemed particularly keen on extending state provision. In 1917, for example, H. G. Tetley of the rayon company, Courtaulds, and Sir Herbert Austin, the motor-car manufacturer, were advocating a reduction in the pension age to sixty-five, to be financed by employers matching what the workers were prepared to pay.[16] Their motives were clear and explicit: they saw welfare benefits as an encouragement to workers to show the goodwill essential if the capitalist system were to run smoothly. Many employers saw clearly that social reform and welfare measures would preserve and strengthen the existing political and economic order, rather than weakening it, as the Shavian caricature of business attitudes had it.

Such motives were not just expressed on a national level, but were also increasingly reflected in the labour strategies of employers in their individual businesses. In the first quarter of the twentieth century, a range of employers introduced occupational pension schemes confined to workers in their own firms, often drawing for their models on the experience of railway companies or on actuaries who advised friendly societies.[17] For example, the directors of Colmans, the large, Norwich-based mustard firm, decided at the turn of the century to replace their existing system of *ex gratia* pensions. They proposed to set up a trust fund providing clear rights to the pension benefits on a more generous scale than was being discussed for the state scheme and, at the same time, to encourage private thrift among their employees. Their initiative was given a cordial reception by the men. Under the scheme, formally inaugurated in 1900, the trustees provided pensions of eight shillings a week at age sixty-five, funded entirely by the firm, to any man who saved twopence a week. The men's savings could be higher if they wished, but at twopence a week produced enough to provide an additional pension of two shillings a week for a man with forty-five years' service, making ten shillings a week in all. At the members' request, they were permitted to take a lump sum rather than a pension for their own contributions, though the firm's benefit had to be taken as an annuity. Leavers forfeited the firm's contributions entirely, but received their own savings back; and the widows of employees who died received a substantial sum also.

A novel feature of the Colmans scheme was its use of the private trust as a legal vehicle for pensioning. Trust law had been developed for quite other purposes but, from being virtually unknown in large pension schemes in the nineteenth century, it became the most favoured vehicle in the twentieth. Initially, the concept of a 'trust' had emotional appeal for those who were trying to create more harmonious relations between masters and men; it was especially favoured by liberal employers anxious to share the administration with employees, as had been traditional in most earlier statutory or friendly society schemes. It was soon realized, however, that a pension trust was simply a cheap and effective vehicle for *any* pension scheme. It was cheaper to establish than a statutory fund, and it was agreeably flexible: creative lawyers could draw up a trust deed with virtually any characteristic the employer chose. Those who wished to retain control of the funds themselves found, for example, that they could do so *de facto* by appointing all the trustees themselves, and many schemes of this nature were founded. Often these were non-contributory (i.e. entirely financed by the employer), so that all rights to pensions or refunds were lost by employees who left the firm. Schemes of both the liberal and more tightly employer-controlled types soon proliferated among the large firms in the economy. Pension schemes were established in the first two decades of the twentieth century by firms as diverse as British Electric Traction, Cadburys, J. & P. Coats, Commercial Union, Cunard, Distillers, GEC, Home & Colonial Stores, Marconi, and W. D. & H. O. Wills.

Not all of these adopted the trust form initially, but in 1921 a change took place which decisively favoured the new trusts. In the inflationary conditions of the First World War, many employers who ran pension funds became concerned about the impact of inflation and increased taxation on the value of the pensions which the funds could pay. It was rapidly becoming evident that the benefits would be well below what members had expected in real terms. Most pension funds then paid income tax on that part of their investment income which was not distributed in the form of pensions, though there was a wide variety of practice in different tax offices. There was also some variety in the treatment of employer and employee contributions.[18] The opportunity to benefit the funds by lobbying for a standardization of tax treatment and a reduction of the tax burden was seen by J. C. Mitchell, then Treasurer of the Underground Electric Railway Company of London, and also chairman of its staff superannuation fund founded in 1912. He contacted colleagues in other funds who shared his concerns, and in 1917 eleven funds agreed to form the Conference of Superannuation Funds to lobby for a change in the tax treatment of the funds. Mitchell became chairman, and by 1919 fifty-five funds had joined, representing employers in a wide field, including railways and other public utilities, retailing, shipping, manufacturing, and local authorities. The Conference, together with various occupational pensioners' organizations, lobbied MPs[19] and also gave evidence to the Royal Commission on Income Tax.[20] Central to their case was the argument that 85% of pensioners of the funds had annual incomes below the £130 tax exemption limit, and most of the remaining 15% paid tax only at the standard rate. The Inland Revenue were conscious of the growing lobbying by the funds, and of the administrative complications of the current tax arrangements. Moreover, their representatives suggested to the Royal Commission that reasonable concessions would cost only £100,000 a year in lost revenue.[21] The pension funds' case did, then, meet surprisingly little opposition from the quarter from which it might have been expected. The government did not, however, implement the Royal Commission's favourable recommendation immediately; but in 1921 pressure from a group of backbenchers led by the Conservative MP Sir Leslie Scott finally forced the implementation of the concession.[22] The Finance Act of that year confirmed the usual exemption from income tax of both employers' and employees' contributions to the funds, and also exempted the whole of the investment income of the funds from taxation. Tax was to be paid only on the pensions when they were paid (usually at that time this meant not at all, as most pensions were below the exemption limit). The trust funds had thus gained taxation treatment as favourable as the friendly societies', though, unlike the friendly societies, there was no low statutory limit on the size of pensions they could pay: a decisive advantage for employers and better-paid employees in the years to come.

The members of the Conference of Superannuation Funds were delighted at the result of their lobbying, and they were able to win further concessions from government in subsequent years.[23] They were formally constituted as the Association of Superannuation and Pension Funds in 1923, and launched a campaign to extend the tax concession to widows' benefits as well as occupational pensions, a campaign which was to meet with success in the 1930 Finance Act. Furthermore, when a legal decision in 1924 showed that many pension trusts might be void because they offended against the law on perpetuities, the Association successfully lobbied for the Superannuation and Other Trust Funds (Validation) Act of 1927, which provided one means for the trusts to be revalidated.[24] A few employers still found that a tax-exempt trust fund did not allow them to attain their pension objectives, though this view was increasingly rare by the 1920s.[25] The spate of new pension funds, and the increasing popularity of the approach to them embodied in the activity of the Association, are shown by the rise in membership: from 55 when the proto-association gave evidence to the Royal Commission on Income Tax to 254 by 1930. Although reliable statistical information on total fund numbers or membership is sparse, by the 1920s an increasing number of employers clearly considered pension benefits to be an essential part of the employment contract.

Why, then, was old age saving increasingly rooted in the employment relation? The tax concessions given to the pension trust funds in 1921 partly explain the increasing popularity of trust schemes. Two actuaries, in their contemporary pensions manual, estimated that the investment income concession cut the cost of pensions by 10–30%.[26] This kind of publicity may have influenced employers and employees, though it was a gross exaggeration, since pension funds had rarely paid tax at the full rate earlier. It is evident, moreover, that the majority of members of pension funds did not, in the inter-war years, pay income tax. The value of the clarification of tax exemption for contributions was thus not a major factor for most members or employers.[27] At least until the 1940s, then, tax factors were not the engine driving the pension machine. For a proper understanding of this largely new phenomenon, we have to look to the employment relationship, and evidence on changes in it, first in the nineteenth-century pensioning pioneers like the railways and gas companies, and then more widely in the twentieth century. Both the pattern of spread – the kind of companies which early adopted pension schemes – and the archival records on the inauguration and development of early schemes can provide important clues to the motivation behind their foundation and extension.

The outstanding common characteristic of the Victorian pioneers of pension schemes – the central government, the large municipalities, the railways, and the gas companies – was that they were the largest nineteenth-century employers. As pension schemes spread to other sectors – banking, insurance, manufacturing, retailing and shipping – in the later nineteenth and early twentieth centuries, they were also concentrated on the large firms. There were still many large employers without pension schemes, but the association of early pension schemes with large employers is unmistakable.[28] Even when schemes were more widely established, there remained a tendency for them to be associated with the larger, more bureaucratic employers.[29] Indeed, the change in the size of enterprises was a factor behind the spread of schemes. In all sectors of the economy around the turn of the century, there was a tendency for output to be concentrated in the hands of fewer, larger firms: in manufacturing industry, for example, large multi-firm mergers were created; in retailing, multiples grew rapidly; in banking, the five largest clearing banks had acquired many rivals and dominated the industry by the First World War. In local government, metropolitan authorities especially were growing large as their local responsibilities multiplied. And new technologies, markets, and organizational innovations were promoting increases in the scale of employment in a range of industries as varied as gas production and shipping lines.

Pension schemes were not the only preoccupation of such large employers, though they often appear as part of a package of changes in policy towards labour. They were, for example, often associated with attempts to get away from 'hire and fire' policies; with dissatisfaction with traditional labour market disciplines; with a feeling that the driving foreman was not as efficient in the large-scale undertaking as the driving owner-manager might have been in early Victorian enterprises; and with the desire to create a longer-term identity of interests between employers and employees. In part, this represented a formalization of the practices of the smaller work communities of the earlier industrial era, where the payment of *ex gratia* pensions already betokened a reciprocity between master and servant. Some employers saw their schemes as spreading middle-class standards of thrift to their workers in classical Smilesian terms.

It would be wrong, however, to see pensions and associated personnel policies purely as an outgrowth from earlier paternalistic labour relations; they were, to an important degree, an expression of new requirements. Paternalism took on a novel dimension, particularly in enterprises such as those led by Quaker businessmen like the Cadburys, who had a genuine feeling for the rights of workers, and a real commitment to fair dealing in employment contracts.[30] This level of idealism was, however, not widespread; and more hard-headed reasons also drove employers in the same directions of cooperation and reciprocity rather than arm's-length dealing and conflict with employees. The sense of mutual interest which they were attempting to create was often vague and intangible, but it was of the essence that trust in each other should be based on long-run factors rather than short-run calculation; and there are few things more long-run than a pension scheme. These feelings were manifested in other policies involving a bureaucratization of employment relationships and attempts to create a stronger identity of interest of capital and labour in larger organizations, among them increased on-the-job training, progressive pay scales, promotion procedures based on seniority and formalized assessment, negotiated wage rates, works councils and other consultative discussions, rule-bound rather than discretionary hiring and firing policies, and greater stability of employment. It is true that pension schemes existed in firms with none of these tendencies; furthermore, all of these trends were developing in only rudimentary form.[31] None the less, pensions fitted unmistakably with these modern developments in personnel management, and they did so more and more closely in later decades. In short, pensions appeared as part and parcel of the growth of what modern social scientists have dubbed 'internal labour markets', islands of coordinated labour management separate from the competitive, 'spot', labour markets, within whose larger constraints they operated, and which in the nineteenth century had been more dominant.[32]

The link between the paternalistic and incorporationist rhetoric of pensions, and the very real functions of creating internal labour market institutions, can be clearly seen in the way the employers presented their new pension schemes to their employees, when, as was almost invariably the case, employers took the initiative. The printed flysheet[33] of July 1919 announcing the Distillers Company's scheme, for example, had the following preamble:

IN ORDER TO PROMOTE
1. The well-being and contentment of their workpeople;
2. The length and improvement of service;
3. The removal of friction between Employers and Employed;
4. The encouragement of thrift among their Employees, The Directors of the Distillers Company Limited submit for their workpeople's consideration and acceptance the following proposals . . .

Almost identical wording (together with the obvious fifth objective: provision for old age) was common in many contemporary pension proposals: similar lists, for example, are found in the rules of the Copartnership and Pension Fund of the Exeter Gas Light & Coke Company and the Fine Cotton Spinners' and Doublers' Association schemes. Like sentiments are implicit in the recommendations of managers to their boards: 'We are also satisfied by the adoption of a scheme such as this, the men will feel they have a stake in the company, and they are likely to render better service.'[34] Outside publicists stressed similar benefits: 'There are other investments besides those in stocks and shares, raw material and machinery. There are investments to be made in humanity, bringing in substantial dividends in the form of goodwill, and enthusiasm and steady, loyal behaviour.'[35]

These general incorporationalist sentiments tell us something about the background motivation, but the crux of the role of pensions (rather than pay increases or other welfare measures which might equally well attach labour to the employer) was item (2) in the Distillers' list. The length and quality of working commitment to the firm was uppermost in the rationale of many of the early schemes, and this is most clearly seen in the rules for leavers. Many of the schemes had their origins as work-based thrift institutions,[36] and employees, when discussing the establishment of a scheme, always seem to have tried to entrench the savings element. Thus, it was common for leavers (or, if they died, their widows) to be able to withdraw their *own* contributions, often with interest at around 3% (then the current rate on savings). It was, however, extremely unusual for *employers'* contributions to be returned under such circumstances.[37] Moreover, some actuaries advised employers to pay all the costs of the scheme, in order to get more freedom of manoeuvre and reduce the need to consult staff; and the majority of the one-third of pension scheme members in such 'non-contributory' schemes got nothing at all on leaving.[38] Such rules limiting leavers' rights were not just detail in small print: without them the typical early-twentieth-century schemes would have been quite insolvent. Even in the most stable of employments, such as the banking and railway bureaucracies, only about one in four of those who joined pension schemes at age twenty typically remained at the pension age to draw a pension. Death, and more importantly, withdrawal (on which the employ- ers' contribution reverted to the fund) were central to the actuary's calculations of the necessary rate of funding. Only because most employees in schemes never got the pension benefit was it possible to keep contribution rates down to levels then expected by employers and employees. Typically, in the early decades of the twentieth century, employees paid about $2\frac{1}{2}\%$ of their earnings into the fund, and employers an equivalent amount. However, the employer's contributions forfeited by withdrawing members reverted to the fund and boosted the pensions of those who remained to draw them. The pay structure that was implicit in such pension schemes did, then, reward those who maintained a life-long commitment to the firm with pay, albeit in deferred form, of up to one-tenth more than employees who chose to leave the firm earlier. (For some of the stayers in final salary schemes who received promotion to higher-paying positions towards the end of their career, moreover, the effective bonus for lifetime loyalty implicit in the pension was much greater than one-tenth of lifetime pay.)[39]

What caused the pioneering employers with pension schemes to bias their pay structures in this way? One benefit, which applied particularly to money-handling clerks in banks, railways and gas companies, was that deferring a portion of pay gave the company an effective sanction against fraud: an employee dismissed for fraud at least left a large slice of deferred pay behind (and the longer serving and more senior the defaulter, the more was accumulated). Employees were, moreover, less likely to commit such crimes if they were to lose their pension rights. Fraud against the employer, as any reader of Dickens recalls, was a not uncommon Victorian complaint, and cash-handling bureaucracies spent a good deal of time trying to counteract it.[40] Sometimes a clerk would be asked to deposit a sum of money with the bank – a 'fidelity' bond – or he might be asked to persuade one or two solid citizens to stand as his surety. When the supply of suitable clerical labour was exclusively middle-class, such bonding did not restrict the supply of labour and was arguably efficient. But with the increasing potential of upwardly mobile children benefiting from state education after 1870, and changes in the nature of clerical work, the incentive structure built into pension schemes frequently appeared more compatible with evolving recruitment and employee relations policies, and bonding schemes tended to disappear.

Another special kind of loyalty was required by firms that developed secret processes which employees with technical knowledge could easily convey to competitors. With the increasingly science-based nature of technical development in industry in the late nineteenth century, this problem was increasing, though these developments were somewhat slower in Britain than in the United States or Germany. Advisers on industrial payment systems in Britain did, however, recognize the value of pension funds in these circumstances. Thus, pension funds in which the benefits were reserved for long-serving employees were recommended for firms which required to maintain the loyalty of technical personnel in order to preserve a competitive advantage.[41]

The desire for loyalty in employees was particularly strong in the case of money-handling clerks or key technical personnel, but employers were also more generally interested in inducing workers to behave in the overall interests of the firm. To the employees, initiatives to induce or enforce this could appear heavy-handed: they were often interpreted as unwelcome additional work disciplines which increased effort without commensurate increases in rewards. It is not uncommon for radical historians to see the aim of increased control of capital over labour as a one-sided shift of power, with no countervailing advantage to labour – in economist's parlance, a 'zero-sum game': what the employer won, the employee lost. No doubt changes in the employment relationship, including the deferred pay element in pension schemes, did frequently take this form, particularly where there was a dominant employer in a local labour market who had significant monopoly buying power over labour. (It is noticeable, moreover, that recognition of the employer's equity interest in his employee through a conditionally deferred pension was more widespread than explicit financial recognition of the reciprocal equity interest of an employee in his job by generous severance or redundancy pay agreements where the parting was at the initiative of the employer.) More generally, however, these new initiatives in labour management around the turn of the century had greater significance than a round in the power struggle for shares in a fixed cake between capital and labour: they could also result in cooperative labour–management interactions which created a bigger cake, so that both parties could end up better off, and this could be true even in apparently one-sided situations.

As new technologies and production systems developed in late-nineteenth-century British industry, the prospects of sharing the gains from cooperation were significantly enhanced. The gas industry, for example, was a classic exemplar of capital-intensive, continuous-process technology, and the commitment of workers to the firm was vital if safety and productivity objectives were to be achieved. When growing union power and a strike in 1889–90 caused serious problems for the South Metropolitan Gas Company, the directors' response, after calling in blacklegs to defeat the strike, was to strengthen the pension provisions and introduce a profit-sharing scheme to win over the workers. Their strategy was to create a high-productivity, highly paid work force, amenable to managerial discipline and loyal to the firm rather than the union. It was, moreover, successful: productivity improved and wage costs per unit of output fell despite the extra costs of pensions and other benefits.[42] There were, of course, other strategies available to increase employee work effort, such as offering piece rates, but it is far from clear that in the long run they were as efficient as the assertion of managerial control, legitimated by welfare and other measures to win worker cooperation. British industry experienced a serious productivity crisis in the early decades of the twentieth century, and at least part of this can be traced to the failure to devise methods of management appropriate to the large-scale, complex, integrated production processes on which many of the new industries of the twentieth century were to be built.[43] It may be no accident that some of the exceptions to this story of dismal productivity failure – the gas companies and some of the mass-producers of branded packaged products, like Colmans and Cadburys – were also the pioneers of pension schemes and of other personnel policies associated with the replacement of the spot labour market by longer-term, internal labour incentives, by continuity and security of employment, and by stronger managerial control.

This strategy might have been expected to bring management into conflict with trade unions, but the attitudes of unions were ambivalent. The Trades Union Congress generally opposed pension schemes, initially because they saw them as unnecessary in view of the existence of voluntary friendly societies and trade union superannuation funds,[44] but also because the schemes were plainly inimical to unionism.[45] Their fears were based on very real experiences: in 1912, for example, the Port of London dockers had their pension rights withdrawn for participating in strikes, and in 1926 the glass workers at Pilkingtons who supported the general strike forfeited their pension rights and were only reinstated with one shilling per week reduced benefit.[46] In the engineering and shipbuilding industries, where company pension schemes were quite rare (and piece rates, spot market hiring, labour subcontracting and insecurity common), the employers nonetheless tried to counteract union influence over foremen by founding in 1899 the Foremen's Mutual Benefit Society, whose rules explicitly forbade union membership. Key workers such as foremen were enrolled as members, and a generous level of pension and other benefits was made possible by employer support. Membership increased rapidly, and the Society remained for many decades a key element in the (unsuccessful) strategy of engineering employers to break the grip of trade unionism.[47]

However, not all pension schemes were inimical to, or met with opposition from, trade unions. Few employers went as far as Cadburys in permitting workers who contributed to a trade union superannuation fund to reduce their subscriptions to the company fund by an equivalent amount; but, equally, few schemes had a 'no union membership' rule. Many white-collar unions welcomed the creation of pension schemes, and indeed, some of them, such as the National Association of Local Government Officers, were formed in the heat of battles to establish pension rights for their members.[48] The National Union of Distributive and Allied Workers successfully pressed for pension rights so that by 1932 62% of cooperative society employees were in schemes.[49] Where manual unions were strong, as in local government, they too confidently pressed for the extension of pension rights to their members.[50]

Despite the clearly leading role of employers in the setting up of pension schemes, there was much to be said for their gaining the willing cooperation of workers, and they generally preferred to do so. Although the law was far from clear, and some employers did make employee pension contributions compulsory, the general legal advice was that employers could not compel manual workers to join.[51] They also rarely compelled existing staff to join a scheme, though it was standard practice to make membership a condition of employment for new recruits to the salaried staff. The take-up rates, where employees had the option to join or not, varied considerably, but they were typically about 80%. Most putative members could see that their rights, however limited, were more secure than in *ex gratia* pension arrangements, and they were happy to put their own money into a scheme provided they were sure of getting it back. The early schemes not only returned members' contributions in the event of withdrawal, but often guaranteed the widow the accumulated contributions in the event of death and, even after retirement, guaranteed the payment of the pension for a fixed period (often five years) even if the pensioner died, so that his family could be sure that they would get their 'money's worth'. Early schemes were, then, characterized by the survival of a strong savings element, and a partial negation of the sharing of mortality risks implicit in normal insurance and annuity contracts.

Most employees would, despite these safeguards, probably have preferred an extra shilling in their pay packet to a shilling on their employer's contribution to a pension fund: liquidity and security were powerful attractions of cash in hand which the distant pension right did not offer. Why, then, did not employers (to whom the cost of either shilling was the same) choose the more obvious form of remuneration? If our analysis is correct, it was because the bargain they were making was not part of a zero-sum game, but one in which the structure of lifetime pay implied by pensioning had bigger pay-offs in terms of loyalty and productivity than a straight increase in cash remuneration. In so far as this was true, the alternative to pension rights was not a shilling in the pay packet, but nothing at all. Employers and employees thus had a clear mutual interest in developing this (on the face of it somewhat esoteric) compensation contract. Such a trade-off was rarely explicit, and both managers and employees had a less than perfect understanding of the nature of pensions. Yet the resilience of schemes, the willingness of employers to bail them out when (as was frequently the case) they proved unable to meet their commitments, and the large extent of membership where joining was voluntary, all suggest that all the parties to labour contracts with a pension element were aware of the value of the incorporationist features we have described.

As bureaucratic 'internal labour markets' developed, pension schemes were also valued for reasons which had not played a major part in the foundation of the pioneering schemes.[52] In firms where workers had a reasonable expectation of long-term employment, employers, even without the paternalistic or charitable influences which were common nineteenth-century motivations for *ex gratia* pensioning, would find it almost impossible to sack workers merely because they were no longer as efficient at their job as they had been. Where fixed pay scales existed, either because of union-negotiated rates or because of internal pay scales (as was the case in a number of skilled manual trades or in an increasing number of large bureaucracies), the cost of an ineffective worker could not easily be balanced by reduced pay in old age, as had earlier been the normal result of the free working of labour market forces.[53] The creation of managerial hierarchies in large organizations also made it difficult to taper off pay in old age for senior men for fear of compromising hierarchical disciplines by demoting them as they aged. Increasingly, then, large, bureaucratic companies began to compel the retirement of employees, often at fixed ages, and the existence of a pension fund made such a policy, although unpopular, at least feasible without creating excessive employee bad will. The firms which did impose mandatory retirement were, moreover, the first to recognize the inadequacies of the benefit structures in early pension schemes, and hence the first to modernize and upgrade their schemes. The railway companies, for example, around the turn of the century (when, after forty years, their pension funds were maturing) increasingly retired their clerks at sixty. They found, however, that a pension based on average salary over a period in which salaries had been rising (owing to general economic growth and progressive salary scales) gave many of their personnel pensions which were well under half of final salary, and hence offered only a poor incentive to retire. (Inflation in the First World War was to make average salary pensions even more inadequate.) The increased pensioning caused by compulsory retirement was, moreover, greater than the actuaries had allowed for in determining the initial contribution rate. By the first decade of the twentieth century, a number of railway companies, faced with massive deficits in their pension funds, had to bail them out.[54] Some also chose to move to pension benefits based on final salary, typically the two-thirds of final salary already adopted in the civil service scheme for full-service employees. The railways thus pioneered a cycle of pension quality improvement which was to become familiar in many other firms as the century progressed. As other employers newly establishing schemes became more aware of the problem, they were likely to include generous provision for back service to existing employees in order to permit adequate pensions, and to legitimize a firm approach to enforcing retirement either at a fixed age or when the employee's performance was clearly falling off. Thus, many pension schemes founded in the first half of the twentieth century included substantial payments from employers for back service, typically funded over a period of years to lighten the load on cash flow.[55]

In the opening decades of the twentieth century, then, two parallel systems of pensioning were developing: one organized by the state, covering the poorest two-thirds of the population; and one organized by employers, covering a much smaller and more diverse group of employees of 'core' firms with internal labour markets and bureaucratic employment features. Both pension systems had an important effect on employer costs: by the late 1920s, the contributions of employers alone to pension schemes together with their *ex gratia* pension payments probably exceeded £50 million a year, still only a few percent of total labour costs, but already more than the £42 million a year cost to employers of the national insurance scheme (including the state old age pension provision).[56] The two systems were seen by most contemporaries as complementary rather than competitive, though signs of future conflicts were already visible. For some workers with occupational pension provision and for some of their employers, the additional costs of the state pensions introduced in 1926 were too high, and employers sometimes actually cut or eliminated pensions to take account of state benefits. A few schemes even managed to gain exemption from the national insurance pension contributions, because they were already offering equivalent pensions.[57]

The most serious concern of the occupational pension schemes had been with the means-testing of the state pensions introduced in 1909.[58] This had meant that their members were not getting the full benefit of their saving, but in many cases had their state pension reduced or eliminated. The 1925 Pensions Act was, therefore, welcomed, since it promised the removal of the means test: the new pensions were to be paid on the insurance principle, as of right, to contributors. Employers with pension schemes could adjust their own scheme to pay pensions additional to the ten shillings a week state benefit, which was recognized as inadequate by itself to replace income in retirement for all but the poorest. If they did so, they no longer needed to fear that the central government would reduce its own pension payment correspondingly, thus negating the effect. Employers with either philanthropic motives or a desire for closer labour control and loyalty could, then, work in partnership with the state scheme to provide an adequate level of income in old age to better-off manual employees for whom the state pensions alone offered little incentive to retire. For other employees – mainly the middle classes – who were still excluded from state pensions, there remained a wide-open field for employer provision. For them, the state scheme stood as a stark reminder that others were provided for, while they were not; a powerful fillip to the increasing 'pensions-consciousness' which characterized the subsequent decades of the century.

3 The insurance challenge (1927–56)

Old age provision is no longer a thing which is regarded by the worker
on the one hand as beyond his price, and by the employer on the
other as lying outside his duty. There is no doubt that in this country
the demand for pensions is increasing at a remarkable rate . . .

> Sir Joseph Burn, Foreword to
> Bernard Robertson and H. Samuels,
> *Pension and Superannuation Funds*,
> 1928, p. v.

The friendly societies and trade unions had been reconciled to the insurance
legislation of 1911, which provided protection against unemployment and
sickness, by being designated 'approved societies', authorized to receive and
channel contributions from members to achieve the protection designated
by the Act. They had generally welcomed the earlier non-contributory
pensions as lightening the burden of old age sickness and unemployment
payments they had to make. However, in 1925, when contributory national
insurance was extended to cover old age, the trade unions and friendly
societies did not actively seek a role as a channel, and it was not offered to
them. They had effectively accepted that the provision of a minimum
income in old age was the business of the state. Their members now readily
acquiesced in this, looking to these traditional working-class savings
institutions less and less for basic protection in old age. For many decades,
small numbers of the old continued to retire with benefits from trade unions
and friendly societies,[1] but it was more and more difficult for these
institutions to persuade their members to subscribe for these purposes. The
Leicestershire miners, for example, had been discussing the possibility of
emulating the most successful of nineteenth-century pension schemes, the
Northumberland and Durham Miners' Permanent Relief Society, but when
Asquith announced his state pensions in 1908, their proposals were
dropped.[2]

The Northumberland scheme itself was also gravely weakened by the
availability of state benefits. Schemes run by workmen had always relied

partly on advance funding (sometimes using actuaries to advise on the level required), but they rested also on a kind of solidarity between the generations, on the confidence that the young would pay subscriptions sufficient to pay pensions to the old and that they in turn would be similarly treated by their juniors, if it were necessary.[3] In the Northumberland scheme, the combination of state pensions and the downward pressure on real wages during the coal industry's troubles of the 1920s broke that solidarity between the generations.[4] The numbers seeking superannuation benefits increased, while the active membership declined; deficits emerged, but subscriptions could not be increased without driving even more potential members away. The reduction of the state pension age to sixty-five in 1925 provided some relief to the funds in the short term, but the compulsory insurance contributions which came with the new pensions made even greater demands on the miners' already stretched pay packets. The society's own old age benefits were reduced progressively, and in the 1930s the superannuation benefit was abolished. Thus, within a few decades, the largest pension fund of the early twentieth century had disappeared.

Not all such funds suffered a disastrous decline, but where they did not it was often because of support from an employer. The Great Western Railway Superannuation Society, for example, continued to pay healthy pensions to supplement those from the state. However, when the railways were nationalized, after the Second World War, the new Railway Executive threatened to cease making membership compulsory. The men, fearing this would weaken the scheme, went on strike, forcing management to back down.[5] Other friendly societies were effectively run by employers though, given the legal restrictions to protect members' rights and the low maximum benefit that could be paid (limited to a £300 lump sum or £1 per week pension in the inter-war years), most employers preferred the trust fund as a more flexible vehicle for their pension scheme. There were also some hundreds of provident societies, often having their origins in nineteenth-century firm-based employees' savings associations, which continued to pay lump sum benefits to less well-off retiring workers. These too were increasingly dependent on employers rather than members for their income.[6] Such cases only served to underline the fact that old age saving once organized by the working class had lost its independence; that trade unions saw their main function even more centrally now as negotiators rather than as savings institutions; and that employers had become the major force in pension arrangements supplementing the state scheme.

In the nineteenth century, the other major force in old age saving had been the insurance companies. They proved more resilient than the trade unions and friendly societies as savings institutions in the changed conditions of the twentieth. Consumers' expenditure on life insurance rose from around 2% of their total spending in the late nineteenth century to nearly 4% by the late 1930s. Much of this growth was in sales of endowment policies – principally designed for old age saving – by the 'ordinary' branch which aimed at the middle-class salary-earning market. The number of ordinary life policies in force rose from two million to over six million between 1900 and 1937; and from the 1920s, endowment policies were the dominant form.[7] The 'industrial' insurance companies – selling policies mainly to a working-class market, with weekly premiums paid to a door-to-door collector – also expanded rapidly, and an increasing share of their business was in endowment policies, costing sixpence or more a week, which provided a lump sum in old age, rather than the penny-a-week policies covering burial expenses which had predominated earlier. By the end of the 1930s, estimates of the coverage of industrial insurance companies suggested that between 75% and 90% of working-class families had policies of one kind or another: greater market penetration than the occupational pension movement was ever to achieve.[8] It is clear, moreover, that voluntary savings through insurance exceeded in value the compulsory contributions by employers and employees to the national insurance scheme.[9] Despite the impact of the high level of unemployment in the inter-war depression and the squeeze of living standards in the Second World War, the years from the 1920s to the 1950s overall were years of improving living standards, and this was reflected in continually increasing longevity. Thus, unlike their nineteenth-century counterparts, adult employees could realistically expect to live to sixty-five. In this environment, the market for voluntary savings was a comfortably expanding one in which the insurance companies, with their emphasis on old age savings, were increasing their market share.

There was, however, some concern about new market developments which led insurance companies to review their position and devise new marketing strategies. Political attacks were made at the time of the First World War on life assurance premium relief, which biased the savings behaviour of the wealthier tax-paying class towards endowment policies. The gradual growth of income tax, the introduction of capital taxes in 1889, higher income tax rates on 'unearned' (i.e., investment) income in 1907, and graduated taxes with supertax on very high incomes (above £5,000) in 1909, all removed some of Gladstone's original justifications for life assurance premium relief, yet also increased its value to the taxpayer.[10] At a time when safe investments paid 3%, post-tax yields of up to 10% were available to supertaxpayers from safe endowment policies and a large portion of insurance business was soon being written for the still small, taxpaying and supertaxpaying classes as a form of tax avoidance. In the Finance Acts of 1915 and 1916, the government limited premium relief to one half of the standard rate of income tax, and 7% of the sum assured. The insurance companies could not help but notice, by contrast, that pension schemes were in 1921 granted a concession greater than the one they had themselves just been deprived of, especially as both were competitors in the same market for old age savings.[11] None the less, until its eventual abolition in 1984, life assurance premium relief (even at the restricted rate) remained a valuable selling tool; and, as income tax developed into a more general tax (particularly after 1940), the reliefs increased the appeal of saving through endowment policies. Even for non-taxpayers, moreover, there could be advantages in saving in this way. The insurance companies had in 1915 negotiated a new tax concession by which they could write off general management expenses against their investment income, and this increased their ability to offer attractive savings-orientated policies.[12]

At the other end of the market, the 'industrial' branches of insurance – selling small policies door-to-door to a largely working-class clientele – also met some political challenges.[13] Criticism from the left centred on the very high expenses ratio: the cost of collection and administration alone often amounted to as much as 40% of premiums. Another source of complaint was the high proportion of policies which lapsed: until 1923, when the industrial life companies were forced to guarantee surrender values, policy-holders who found they could not keep up payments sometimes lost all their accumulated savings. The industrial offices did improve their expenses ratios, principally by increasing the volume of business per call, but this remained an expensive way of transacting insurance business by its very nature of personal service in small retail transactions. As the president of the Institute of Actuaries pointed out in 1919, 'it was going to be a strong point of attack by those who were out to do something, which whatever form it might ultimately take, would not be of benefit to industrial assurance companies as they at present existed'.[14] He, and the other insurance men, were by then aware that state provision for widowhood and old age (to follow in 1925) could rightly claim to have lower expenses ratios. One response to the political threat to industrial insurance business was suggested by developments that had already occurred in the United States. American insurance companies had pioneered attempts to reduce the costs of mass insurance in the popular, low income markets by selling insurance through employers rather than door-to-door.[15] They could provide death benefits of around £100, more cheaply than in Britain, for an employer's entire staff by payroll deduction or employer subsidy. The economies came partly through the reduced transaction costs of such wholesale deals. There was a further, underwriting advantage, in that if a whole group were insured, the risks to the insurance company of adverse selection by poor lives were virtually eliminated. By the 1920s, American insurance companies were also writing group *pension* contracts in the same form to gain the same economies of scale and pooled risk, and pass them on to consumers via their employers.

Initially, none of these new developments progressed as far in Britain as in America. This was partly because the poor law, and, from 1925, the widows' provision in the new Pensions Act, provided state-backed life insurance coverage for the majority of male employees and thus reduced the attraction of group insurance. Another factor was the belief in British insurance circles that American-style group contracts were unfair, in that when employees needed the protection most – when they were leaving their employer through sickness – they lost it. However, this objection could be overcome by writing policies with individual continuation rights for leavers, and the several dozen British insurance companies which did begin to write group life contracts in the 1920s usually adopted this form.[16]

By this time, the insurance companies could not help but notice that their traditional niche in the old age savings market was being encroached upon by trust fund pension schemes directly administered by employers. Thus, even if they kept out of group insurance and pension business, they might increasingly find employers organizing it for themselves. There was a burgeoning literature in the 1920s recommending the establishment of self-administered schemes, considerably stimulated by the tax concessions of the 1921 Finance Act.[17] Such schemes did not entirely exclude the insurance companies, for it was perfectly possible – indeed generally thought essential for small employers[18] – to insure the mortality risks in such schemes with an insurance company. Many employers also bought insurance policies – endowment insurances or deferred annuities for the current members of staff and immediate annuities for retiring pensioners – on an individual basis. These did not gain access to the full economies of scale and pooled risk of the fully-fledged group contract, but they might gain some of the advantages. As early as 1881, for example, the Clerical, Medical & General had sold a series of individual policies to Alliance Bank employees through their employer as part of their pension arrangements, without any need for individual medical examinations;[19] and by the 1920s there were dozens of schemes taking advantage of one or other of the economies of employer-based insurance sales.[20]

The catalyst for more fundamental changes in strategy by British insurance companies was the entry in 1927 of the largest United States insurance company, Metropolitan Life of New York, into the British market. Metropolitan offered the full advantages of the American-style economies of group life and pension contracts organized through employers.[21] They initially responded to the needs of their American corporate clients – firms like Kodak, Woolworth, Armor, and General Motors – with United Kingdom subsidiaries, but they were soon also selling group pension policies to British employers. The window displays of their offices at Bush House in the Strand on 'Fear of Old Age', 'Fear of Sickness', and 'Fear of Death' attracted considerable attention. The new group pension contracts, which within a few months were also offered by several British companies responding to the competition, proved significantly cheaper than the existing insurance contracts, as well as more attractive to employers in other ways. The economies in transaction costs and pooling of risks inherent in group schemes were fully exploited, but the method of costing – technically known as the 'single premium' method – also produced savings, especially for young employees.[22] In the 1930s staff in group pension schemes typically paid out about 2–4% of their salaries, and were promised life assurance of about one year's salary together with a pension of 1–2% of average salary for each year of service. Manual workers more commonly had fixed contributions of around one shilling a week in return for a £1 a week pension and perhaps £100 worth of life insurance. The employees' contributions alone were usually sufficient to fund the pension benefits for young employees up to age thirty or more, but the residual cost for older employees were shouldered by the employer. This mimicked the actual cost structure for self-administered schemes. (In these the employer's contribution might be specified as $2\frac{1}{2}$% of pay for all staff, but this was actuarial obfuscation for simplicity of presentation. The real liability of employers was in fact much greater for older than for younger employees, given the longer period of interest accumulation for the younger employees' own contributions.) The marketing strategy which this new costing method inaugurated was commercially extremely successful. It was attractive to employers who wished to minimize the losses (common in endowment-based schemes) on surrender of policies on younger leavers. Moreover, it could be more conveniently structured to reproduce the essence of self-administered employer-based pension schemes with incorporationist motives: forfeits of employer contributions by leavers, from which the employer could reward stayers with better pensions. Finally, the lower initial expense relative to traditionally costed insurance contracts also enabled employers to offer some credit to existing employees for back service, the extra cost of this usually being spread over a period of ten years or so. This significantly increased the value of pensions as a measure accompanying mandatory retirement policies. As actuarial purists were quick to point out, if the labour force was static, the cost of these new group contracts (but not of the more expensive traditional 'level premium' endowment insurance schemes) would rise.[23] But most employers were unaware of this, or (as in self-administered schemes) were happy to bet that continued new recruitment and growth would prevent the average age of their work force from increasing sharply, and thus postpone the problem indefinitely.

Some insurance companies, like the Clerical, Medical & General, continued to try to sell traditional contracts. These generally entrenched the vested rights of employees in the manner that had been achieved in a few of the more liberal insured schemes such as the pre-war Federated Superannuation System for Universities.[24] The business of such companies was stagnant despite their best publicity efforts. There could be no more impressive testimony to the effectiveness of rooting pension provision in the needs of modern, bureaucratic employment practices, rather than marketing it as a means to promote individual savings for old age. By contrast, the insurance companies that successfully emulated the American methods reported rapid growth. The most remarkable of these was the Legal & General, then under the leadership of an unorthodox and imaginative management team headed by W. A. Workman and H. E. Raynes and with a brilliant pensions salesman, T. A. E. Layborn. When in 1930 they sold their first big pension scheme, for 6,000 employees of the Gramophone Company (later EMI), Layborn persuaded his golf partner, then editor of the *Sunday Express*, to run the story 'Killing the Dread of Old Age' as a front page lead.[25] This inaugurated a decade of favourable press comment on such innovative schemes.[26] In another coup, Legal & General in 1933 took over some 150 group pension schemes from Metropolitan Life, when the latter decided to extricate itself from its innovative overseas adventures.[27] The two biggest firms in the British market in effect merged, and Legal & General remained dominant thereafter. Their largest scheme at this time, in 1935, was for 19,000 employees of the United Steel Companies; other major clients were Gallaghers, the Belfast cigarette manufacturers, and Austin, one of the leading car producers.

Competition from self-administered schemes did remain strong, especially for large employers who had the specialist financial and personnel experts needed to run them efficiently. Consulting actuaries and others continued to extol the virtues of self-administered pension trusts,[28] and, especially after the merger wave of the 1920s,[29] many large employers felt able to inaugurate their own schemes, without assistance from insurance companies. The record-keeping and investment functions for a trust fund were relatively simple for a large firm with office management and finance specialists, and the more esoteric function of actuarial investigation to predict future liabilities was easily bought in. A few firms of consulting actuaries had previously specialized in similar work for friendly societies, but by the 1920s major firms like Bacon & Woodrow and Duncan Fraser had developed a widening client base of employer pension funds.[30] They stressed particularly the need to provide for clerical employees (whose higher salaries usually placed them outside the state scheme, which provided basic level benefits for manual workers), and suggested that large employers would do better to gain the tax benefits of a self-administered trust fund rather than entrust their business to an insurance company.

For small- and medium-sized firms, however, the specialist intervention of an insurance company was considered essential;[31] and, even for firms with thousands of employees, the lack of expert knowledge within the firm often led to the decision to use an insurance company. Most of the growth in membership of private sector pension schemes between the early 1930s and the early 1950s thus came in insured schemes. More than half the new members of insurance schemes in the 1930s and 1940s were covered by the Legal & General: as a result this firm (which had ranked only tenth among British life companies when it first entered the pensions field) quickly reached second place. The leading company, the Prudential, soon realized this threat to its dominance, and built up a business half the size of Legal & General's. Other companies such as Eagle Star, Friends' Provident, and Standard Life also performed well in this new and rapidly growing market.[32] By 1934, the five major British life offices selling group pensions had sold schemes covering 120,000 members; ten years later the figure was half a million; while by 1956 (when many more insurance companies had begun to offer group life and pension contracts) there were more than two and a quarter million members of all insured schemes, forming a clear majority of those in private sector pension schemes. Within two decades of entering the field of group occupational pension provision in its new form, the insurance companies were dominant in it.

The apparently consistent growth in occupational pension provision in the period of depression and world war in the 1930s and 1940s is, at first sight, puzzling. Unemployment had been high throughout the 1920s, and in 1933 it peaked at 16% of the work force.[33] In these circumstances, rates of staff turnover declined markedly as employees received few alternative job offers. Employers were, then, temporarily far less concerned about establishing pension schemes in order to retain staff. Yet other motives favouring pensioning were clearly important in these years. The 1930s, in particular, were years of rapidly rising real incomes for those who were in work, so that the demand for old age savings was increasing. Moreover, despite persistent unemployment, the labour force had grown: by 1939 there were more people in employment than ever before; and a further two million were to be drawn into employment by the War. The tendency for jobs to be concentrated in larger, more bureaucratic enterprises which favoured formal pension schemes did, moreover, become ever stronger in the 1920s, particularly in sectors such as manufacturing and retailing.[34] The large groups created by merger and the rapidly growing enterprises in new industries proved fertile ground for consulting actuaries and pension salesmen.

All the imperfect statistical evidence which is available confirms the picture of rapidly rising demand for pensions. Figure 3.1 shows the major long-run statistical series of the growing number of pension schemes. Particular factors distort the pattern shown by these varying indicators. The upper curve – showing funds which had gained tax exemption under the terms of the 1921 Finance Act – is clearly indicative of the sustained growth

Fig. 3.1 The growth of occupational pension schemes, 1927–56

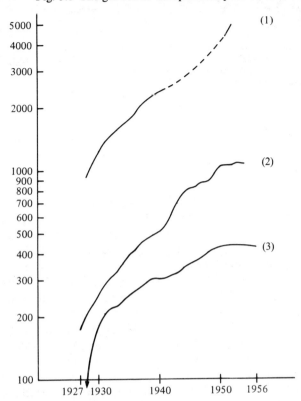

Note: Semilog scale: slopes indicate rates of growth

Key: (1) numbers of pension funds approved under the 1921 Finance Act
(2) numbers of pension funds which were members of the Association of Superannuation
and Pension Funds
(3) numbers of pension funds registered under the 1927 Validation Act

Source: Statistical appendix, Table A.4

in numbers of funds, boosted after the War by the increasing attraction of
the tax concessions. The middle curve shows the rising membership of the
Association of Superannuation and Pension Funds. Smaller schemes
generally did not bother to join, and changes in the fee structure in the 1950s
depressed membership growth, so the flattening of the curve then is
misleading. The registrations under the 1927 Validation Act (the lower
curve) were also depressed in the 1950s by alternative, preferred ways of
getting around the rule of law against perpetuities. Thus neither of the lower
curves in Figure 3.1 does justice to the continuing, strong post-war growth

Table 3.1 *Occupational pension scheme coverage, 1936 and 1956*

	1936	1956
1. Membership of private sector schemes (millions)	1.6	4.3
(of which insured)	(0.3)	(2.3)
2. Membership of public sector schemes (millions)	1.0	3.7
3. Total scheme membership (line 1 + line 2)		
(millions)	2.6	8.0
4. Total work force (excluding unemployed)		
(millions)	20.7	24.5
5. Proportion of work force covered by		
occupational pensions (line 3 ÷ line 4)	13%	33%

Source: see nn. 36 and 37

in pension schemes. The literary evidence on the growth of pensioning in the inter-war and post-war years, and other imperfect statistical data on rising contributions and accumulating assets in the funds, are compatible with the general picture of continuing year-by-year growth suggested by the chart.[35]

We have, moreover, two very full statistical surveys of the coverage of funds. One was carried out by the Ministry of Labour and covered the 6,544 private sector employer schemes known to exist in 1936.[36] A second, sample survey was conducted by the Government Actuary in 1956, and grossed up to cover all private sector schemes (37,500 of which were then thought to exist) as well as the public sector.[37] The overall picture they reveal is shown in Table 3.1. In the first third of the twentieth century the coverage of formally constituted occupational pension schemes rose from perhaps one in twenty to the one in eight (13%) of the labour force shown in the table for 1936. In the two decades between 1936 and 1956, scheme membership in both private and public sectors rose in absolute terms from 2½ million to 8 million, or to nearly one in three of the work force.[38] Some of this rise appears to be due to the growing public sector. Local and central government employment had accounted for only 6% of the British working population at the turn of the century and accounted for only 10% of employment in the 1930s. At this time the state had few employees outside the military, naval and administrative fields, but following the nationalization of a range of public utilities and other services by Attlee's post-war government the state became a major employer in wider fields. By 1950 a quarter of all employed workers were employees of local or central government.[39] The increase in public sector employees with pension rights – up from a million in 1936 to as many as 3.7 million in 1956 – was mainly due, not to the inherently greater pensioning propensity of the public sector, but rather to the transfer of employees with pensions from the private sector, particularly from railway, gas and electricity companies where pensioning was already firmly established before nationalization.[40]

None the less, the public sector had been inherently more prone to pensioning than the private sector in 1936, and in the 1950s this tendency became even more marked. In particular, unions in the nationalized industries were effective in negotiating pension entitlements for manual workers, only a fifth of whom had had pension rights before nationalization. The Labour government was not disposed to bow to this pressure, feeling that flat-rate state pensions should suffice,[41] but in 1951 they reluctantly agreed to a scheme for coal miners. Initially only a minority of the 700,000 eligible miners opted to pay voluntary contributions to the National Coal Board scheme, but most miners had joined by the time membership became compulsory in 1957.[42] In other industries, like electricity supply, the new nationalized boards, under Treasury pressure, merely maintained pre-nationalization schemes but did not establish their own for new entrants. Thus membership of these schemes declined initially. By the mid 1950s, however, the Conservative government had agreed to the establishment of comprehensive (and often compulsory) occupational pension coverage in all the major nationalized corporations. It then became very clearly the exception rather than the rule for public sector employees to be without pension rights.

The Local Government Superannuation Act of 1922 had helped to standardize the pension schemes of local authorities with 5% contributions from employees and the balance from the employer, funding pensions of one-sixtieth of final salary for each year of service. Local pressure from employees had already led to virtually complete coverage for officers by 1936; three years later such coverage became compulsory for all local authorities. A series of acts in the inter-war period also entrenched the pension rights of groups like the police, firemen, and teachers as securely as those in the civil service.[43] Manual workers in both local and central government, as in the nationalized industries, usually acquired rights later. Not all local authorities admitted manual workers to their pension schemes; and the industrial civil service did not acquire 'established' status (and pensions) until 1948, though some *ex gratia* pensions had been paid before that.

The nature of pension schemes in the public sector differed widely, reflecting the variety in their historical origins. The local authority funds and nationalized industry funds were closest to occupational pension funds in the private sector, and, indeed, often had a similar history. They were, for example, typically funded, whereas other public sector schemes relied on pay-as-you-go and state credit rather than advance funding to secure pensions. Pension ages showed wide variations, with the police and firemen generally having younger ages. The generously young civil service retiring age of sixty offered an attractive target for other public sector bargaining groups. The general tendency was for schemes to become more like the civil service scheme over time. Local government pensions, for example, which had usually been based on one-sixtieth of final salary for each year of service, were modified in 1953 to pay pensions based on one-eightieth, the savings going to provide a widow's benefit, on the lines pioneered in the civil service in 1909.[44] A major feature of the development of public sector schemes was the ability of employees to transfer between employment without loss of pension rights. These rights had been established in local authority employment and elsewhere on a piecemeal basis, but an act of 1948 further strengthened the Treasury's powers of sanctioning transfers. In effect, the whole of the public sector then became one employer for the purpose of preserving pensions, though the number of transfers between different branches of the public service remained surprisingly small.[45] Coverage was generally wider in public than private employment, partly because, once a scheme was established for a group of employees, membership was usually automatic, with no discrimination as to sex or age and no qualifying period for entry.

Despite the loss of some of the more pension-intensive industries to the public sector, coverage of occupational pension schemes in the private sector also increased markedly, particularly after the War. Between 1936 and 1956, the number of private sector employees in schemes rose from 1.6 million to 4.4 million, the greater part of the increase coming in insured schemes (which by 1956 accounted for more than half the total private sector membership).[46] By 1936 it was already rare for large companies not to have considered a pension scheme, but only about one in ten private sector employees were in schemes. By 1956 it was rare for large companies not to have a pension scheme, though it was still the case that, in firms with schemes, just less than half of male employees (and only about a quarter of female employees) were likely to be admitted to the scheme. Many small- and medium-sized firms still had no schemes at all, despite the efforts of insurance companies to sell to these firms.

Unions were less influential on pension developments in the private than in the public sector, but here too coverage was being extended to the better-off manual workers. Weekly paid employees probably already formed the majority of pension scheme members in 1936, and coverage increased even more rapidly for them than for monthly salaried employees in the next two decades.[47] Imperial Chemical Industries, for example, one of the leading British manufacturing companies and a consistent pioneer of incorporationist labour strategies for manual workers, initially admitted only foremen to its internally administered pension benefits, with only a voluntary savings scheme and *ex gratia* benefits for others.[48] Other workers were admitted from 1937. After the War, in industry generally there was an increased interest in funds for workers.[49] Even so, in most British firms with pension schemes manual workers were still normally excluded or admitted to schemes with a less generous level of benefits. Only a third of wage-earning employees in these firms were admitted to membership even as late as 1956.

Why were attempts to spread pension fund coverage among the working classes not more effective? One factor was the legal situation: many lawyers advised that to compel manual workers to join pension funds was illegal under the nineteenth-century Truck Acts and other legislation, though a number of employers in fact did so with no obviously adverse consequences.[50] This can, however, have been only a minor contributory factor. The rate of take-up in voluntary schemes was remarkably high: usually above the 80% which insurance companies often insisted on as a condition for inaugurating a scheme, and quite often above 90%.[51] None the less, there was little grassroots pressure for pensions in this period, and unions remained generally hostile to welfare benefits over which they had little control, except in the public sector, where they were already well able to influence pensions through the unions' negotiating machinery. There were also some trade union leaders who saw a constructive role in the private sector for occupational pensions, if they were brought within the sphere of collective bargaining, but their capacity to achieve this was severely limited in the inter-war years. Union membership declined sharply from the peak of 1920 under the pressure of inter-war unemployment, and did not recover the 1920 level until after the Second World War. Trade union leaders found it impossible to persuade the Labour government of 1929–31 to improve state pension benefits and some then turned to direct negotiations with employers to achieve the equivalent benefits in occupational schemes. The foremost exponent of this strategy was Ernest Bevin, of the Transport and General Workers' Union.[52] His greatest success was the scheme negotiated with Legal & General in 1931–2 by the Joint Industrial Council for the flour-milling industry, of which he was chairman. The scheme was unusual in including all firms (except one) in the industry, employing 20,000 men in all. A particularly attractive feature was that entitlement could be transferred between employers, thus reducing the extent to which workers were tied to one firm by pension rights.[53] Most of the other schemes sold for manual workers were, however, for single firms,[54] and Bevin found considerable resistance from both employers and union members to his pension strategy. In 1935, for example, Bevin, together with Arthur Pugh of the Iron and Steel Trades Confederation, persuaded Sir William Firth and other South Wales tinplate producers to start a contributory pension scheme for tinplate workers. Twenty thousand men had contributions of $2\frac{1}{2}$% of their wages deducted to finance pensions of one pound per week from age sixty-five.[55] Rank-and-file members were, however, sceptical of the benefits; they demanded ballots, and eventually a delegate meeting successfully supported the disbandment of the scheme by 316 votes to 303.

One of the factors behind this rejection was a feeling among the men that they would lose means-tested benefits. They feared that they would pay 2½% of their income into the fund over a period but end up no better off than if they had spent their money and relied instead on the state benefits. The framers of the 1925 Pensions Act had hopes that such considerations would have been banished from the minds of potential pension savers, because the new state pensions were insured benefits, given as of right and without means test.[56] In fact, though, by the 1930s the practice was growing more widespread among poor law authorities of paying means-tested supplements to old age pensions.[57] These rising standards of acceptable poverty relief for the aged poor were institutionalized in the Assistance Board from 1940 onwards and the number of beneficiaries rapidly increased. Thus neither the 1925 Act, nor, indeed, any subsequent legislation, succeeded in removing the means test.[58] Bevin deprecated the attitude of the tinplate workers who wanted to rely on poverty relief rather than save for themselves: 'When a large community develops a relief complex of this character it is not good for democracy.'[59] There can, however, be no doubt that some less well-off manual workers rejecting these schemes were rationally pursuing their own self-interest. The pensions being paid from the later 1940s to workers who had saved in pension schemes of the kind negotiated by Bevin were often no more than ten shillings a week.[60] This amounted to a little more than the means-tested state pension supplement which workers who had not saved could typically get from the Assistance Board, but it hardly justified the lower spendable income imposed on workers in contributory schemes in earlier years.

With the improvement in state benefits during and after the Second World War, and the raising of national insurance contributions, many manual workers considered that the state now deducted quite enough from wages and, moreover, provided an adequate basis for old age security. Employment opportunities for the old who were fit also increased with full employment. In this atmosphere, attitudes to occupational schemes seemed for a time to be hardening. Some proposed schemes were again rejected by workers for whose benefit employers were supposedly advocating them.[61] Wartime conscription also disrupted pension scheme development by increasing withdrawal rates, and not all employers continued membership for those serving in the forces, or extended pension benefits to those who replaced them.[62] The Beveridge proposals for extending state pension coverage for all raised high hopes for more adequate comprehensive national insurance coverage, and insurance companies feared that their market for pension sales would cease to expand in the post-war climate.[63]

In fact, however, the coverage of occupational pensions continued to increase. The major factor behind this was the transformation of the tax base during the War, which converted the tax benefits of pensions from a minor assisting force to a leading engine, driving development of the whole pensions institution. The standard rate of income tax rose to 50% during the Second World War, and taxes on companies could be as high as 100%; after the War, tax rates on companies remained higher than on individuals, and the standard rate of income tax for employees never fell below 30%. More importantly, the standard rate (which previously had been paid only by a few million of the relatively affluent) became during the War a general tax on all except the lowest-income earners, and the real income levels at which income tax began to be levied declined even further in the post-war period. There were more than 17.25 million assessments under the newly-introduced 'pay-as-you-earn' tax system for employees in 1945–6, and most workers then expected to pay income tax in addition to the national insurance contribution which they had long been accustomed to see deducted from their pay packet. Insurance salesmen thus increasingly stressed the tax advantages of pensions, pointing out to employers that, if they were paying 100% excess profits tax, a pension could have zero cost. Employees in tax brackets were also increasingly aware of the pension fund as a tax-efficient form of saving for old age.[64] Insured pension schemes were now quite generally written in trust form to gain the advantage of the 1921 Finance Act. However, for low-paid manual workers who did not pay tax, the older form (giving no tax relief on employees' contributions, but also avoiding the problems of the composite tax rate on withdrawal refunds which annoyed such non-taxpayers) remained the norm.[65] 'Top hat' schemes, providing generous pension benefits for senior personnel, also proliferated. In these, a senior employee would typically accept a salary reduction or forgo an increase, the funds being applied by the firm (qualifying for tax relief as an expense of the firm) to buying an endowment policy to provide a lump sum (tax-free) on retirement. Almost all schemes paying pension annuities from an employer now modified their rules to qualify for Inland Revenue approved status, though many had not bothered to do so in earlier decades. By 1956–7, the cost to the Treasury of the relief specified in the 1921 Finance Act had reached £120 million annually, mainly in relief on employers' contributions.[66] There can by then have been few employers whose employees paid income tax and who themselves paid tax who had not encountered an actuary or an insurance salesman who could show that all parties could benefit from an extension of private pensioning at the expense of the Treasury.

4 *The state: partner or competitor? (1940–78)*

The fundamental question is whether we are to regard the State as partner or competitor. For my part I still cling to my original opinion that this package of legislation provided and continues to provide a springboard for new business.

Legal & General manager,
staff *Annual Conference*,
privately printed, 1963,
p. 73

Until the twentieth century was well advanced, British government departments knew very little (and, in general, did not want to know more) about occupational pension schemes. Early proposals to undertake a survey of private sector pension schemes were for nearly three decades shunted from ministry to ministry until finally the Ministry of Labour undertook the first comprehensive survey in 1936. The concerns of the Government Actuary's Department (established in 1919) were mainly confined to national insurance matters and public sector pensions.[1] Pension schemes were, of course, affected by legislation, but its impact for the first four decades of the century had been slight. The 1927 Validation Act,[2] for example, brought several hundred funds into the purview of the Registrar of Friendly Societies, when they wished exemption from the law against perpetuities. Parliament laid down certain minimal conditions for such approval: for example, that registered pension funds could not invest in the employing firm unless the loan were properly secured and the firm had a good dividend record. Most funds did not, however, bother to register, and lawyers devised other, simpler means of avoiding the law against perpetuities, advising that by the time any disadvantages emerged, the law would be changed. (They were right, though only in the long run which law reformers find congenial: pension funds were eventually exempted from the law against perpetuities by the 1973 Social Security Act.[3]) The Pensions Acts of 1908 and 1925 also only marginally affected occupational pension schemes, either directly in their provisions for means testing of state pensions and contracting out, or indirectly by establishing a floor of benefit and contribution levels for many workers. Some employers, for example, reduced the levels of contributions or benefits in their own schemes to take account of the national insurance old age pensions of 1925, particularly for low-paid workers for whom the state scheme represented both a substantial contribution burden and a substantial pension benefit.[4]

This low level of government influence on the development of occupational pension schemes was fundamentally transformed by developments in taxation and state policy from the 1940s onwards. Already, before the War, the Inland Revenue had, usually for quite narrow fiscal motives, influenced the provisions of schemes. Under the 1921 Finance Act, unless the funds could meet the relatively narrow gateways specified, they had to obtain Inland Revenue approval to gain the tax exemptions, and this gave the Revenue considerable discretionary power to affect schemes. Some of their policies appear capricious: they initially discouraged widows' provision, reduced employees' rights to transfer values on leaving schemes, and penalized employers who made provision for back service rights unless they were spread in specific ways. All of these might have been considered to be inimical to rational pensioning objectives, but that was not their purpose: their motivation was to restrict tax evasion and avoidance, not to pursue social or employment objectives. As the tax burden mounted from 1940 onwards and the incentive to avoid tax correspondingly increased, the same motives dominated the Revenue's reactions. For example, during the War, the Revenue began to restrict employee contributions to 15% of total remuneration when approving new schemes. They also pressed for legislation to curb what they felt were abuses of the tax reliefs, particularly in 'top hat' schemes for higher-paid employees. In the 1947 Finance Act, the Labour government plastered over some of the more glaring loopholes. Lump sum payments had not been permitted in 1921 Act schemes, but they were common in insured 'top hat' schemes. These large sums had been classified as capital receipts rather than as income, and thus completely escaped tax; but, from 1947, they were limited to one-quarter of the pension's total value. (This provision backfired somewhat, by giving publicity to the loophole: the insurance companies continued to do a lot of business in 'top hat' schemes, promoted by aggressive, fast-growing firms of insurance brokers like Noble Lowndes.) The 1947 Finance Act also sought to limit tax-privileged pension benefits to levels which could be considered reasonable, defined for the purposes of the Act as being the level provided in public sector schemes.

The 1947 Act was no more than a makeshift patchwork, covering up a fundamentally rotten edifice of conflicting tax privileges for different kinds of pension schemes. Trust funds, exempted under the terms of the 1921 Act, generally gained exemption from all tax on contributions by employers and members and on their investment income. However, withdrawals were partially taxable and all pensions were fully taxable as earned income (with no tax-free lump sums allowed).[5] Insured pension schemes (unless they were written as trusts) gained general exemption on employer contributions, partial exemption on employee contributions (according to the principles of life assurance premium relief as revised in 1916), privileged tax rates and expenses relief on investment income, no tax on withdrawals or certain lump sum benefits, and exceptionally high rates of taxation on annuity benefits.[6] Payments for back service were subject to a variety of different rules, while unfunded or *ex gratia* schemes and provident clubs had their own separate regulations. No one was quite sure which was the most privileged form of treatment: indeed no one could be sure, because it depended partly on unknowns like the future rate of inflation. However, the feeling gained ground from the 1940s (and later experience proved it to be correct) that for most employees at average to modestly affluent earnings levels the 1921 Act privileges were the most advantageous.

Employers and pension interest groups had successfully lobbied to limit the anti-avoidance provisions of the 1947 Finance Act.[7] Nonetheless, many in the pensions industry were shaken by the abuses which had been revealed. Conscious that the tax treatment of pension funds contained inequitable and unsustainable anomalies, four of the interests closely involved – the Life Offices' Association, the Association of Superannuation Funds, the Association of British Chambers of Commerce, and the Federation of British Industries – established a joint committee to examine the issue in greater detail. In February 1948, thanks largely to Mr Frank Bower (formerly a Revenue official and chairman of the ABCC's Taxation Committee), they produced a policy document suggesting major new initiatives. They aimed fundamentally to recast the tax treatment of retirement benefits into a logically coherent, equitable, and defensible form. Their thirty-two page report was the clearest document ever produced on the subject by any British pressure group or government department.[8] The Committee called for a simplification of the law according to recognizable principles, rather than the mere closing of loopholes: suggesting, broadly, that all reasonable contributions to retirement schemes (whether by employer or employee) should be tax deductible, and that benefits (whether lump sums or annuities) should be taxable at the time of receipt at rates which would have been applied if they had been entirely in the form of pension annuities. Most of the group's remaining recommendations could be derived from these central principles. Contributions were to be taxed if they were excessively high in order to shift tax liability to lower post-retirement incomes; almost all lump sums were to be taxed; the investment income of trust funds was to be free of tax (since it was to be taxed in the hands of the ultimate beneficiaries).

Although pension schemes were now proliferating rapidly under the muddled provisions of existing tax law, it took more than two years for the Labour government to respond to this initiative. In 1950, they appointed a committee, under the chairmanship of James Millard Tucker, KC; but that committee then took nearly four more years to report. (The 1952 Income Tax Act thus merely recodified the existing law, adding nothing new to the treatment of pension funds.[9]) Meanwhile, the committee wrestled with Revenue officers to try to understand the complicated and rapidly changing treatment of pension schemes in case law, and took evidence from a wide range of pressure groups. The resulting Millard Tucker report of 1954[10] was far from radical in temper, and eschewed the attempt made by the pensions interests' own Bower Committee to restore logical order and clarity to the field. Instead, the official committee aimed to limit the more glaring anomalies by tinkering, and to standardize the treatment of the various different kinds of schemes, if necessary by extending anomalous provisions to areas where they did not yet exist. They proposed that tax-free lump sums (limited to one-quarter of the total value of benefits) should be extended from insured schemes and public sector schemes to '1921 Act' trust funds. By the same token, schemes run by insurance companies should benefit from the tax reliefs on employee contributions and investment income that were already available to '1921 Act' schemes. The Committee was dominated by self-employed professionals, who found little difficulty in agreeing with the evidence from professional organizations that the Revenue practice of excluding the self-employed from the tax exemptions of the 1921 Act should be discontinued. The Committee thus recommended that these exemptions, together with the proposed new lump sum concessions, should be extended to the self-employed.[11] There were good reasons in equity for some pension concessions to the self-employed. However, the whole package of concessions smacked too much of extending 'top hat' privileges to their own kind for George Woodcock, the trade unionist on the Committee, to accept it.[12] The Royal Commission on Income Tax also understandably took a dim view of the more extreme recommendations of the Committee.[13] Even the Conservative government, generally sympathetic as they were to the interests Millard Tucker's recommendations promoted, swallowed hard when they realized that the proposed concessions would be expensive. It was to take a further two years for them to decide what to do.

The pensions industry believed that reform of taxation was required, but could hardly believe their luck at the extent to which the Millard Tucker Committee's 'reforms' proposed to gild the lily.[14] The Committee had achieved that rare feat of going beyond what political lobbyists felt they had any right to expect! The government had similar feelings, and the 1956 Finance Act only partially implemented the Millard Tucker proposals. The concessions to the self-employed were limited to pension contributions of (initially) the lower of 10% of earnings or £750 p.a., and all pension benefits were to be fully taxed, with no lump sum concessions. Given the already considerable tax advantages available to the self-employed through direct investments in their business and through endowment policies providing retirement lump sums, it is hardly surprising that the take-up of this limited tax concession was initially much lower than forecast.[15] A decade later higher and sustained inflation increased the value of the investment income reliefs on tax-exempt pension plans and capital gains taxes reduced the attractions of the alternatives. Only then did insurance companies manage to create a large market in pensions for the self-employed written under the terms of the 1956 concessions.[16]

Other provisions of the 1956 Finance Act were of more immediate benefit to the insurance companies. A concession they had long wanted – the charging of tax only on the interest element in annuities (rather than on the capital element which had typically already been taxed) – was generally welcomed as equitable. More significant for pension sales was that the tax concessions on employee contributions and fund investment income (which had been offered to pension trusts since 1921) were extended to insured schemes; a concession which enabled Legal & General, the market leader, to cut their premiums for group pensions by nearly a quarter. Neither the insured schemes gaining these privileges nor the original '1921 Act' schemes were, however, allowed to offer tax-free lump sums of the kind permitted in the civil service scheme or in endowment insurance schemes, though the Millard Tucker Committee had recommended this for all schemes.

This somewhat ham-fisted attempt to limit the lump sum concession was, however, ineffective, since there was no provision to prevent both insurance companies and self-administered funds combining tax-privileged fund benefits with separate lump sum benefits. What increasingly happened in subsequent years, then, was that some pension schemes were rewritten as hybrids to provide both '1921 Act' privileges and lump sum benefits up to the maximum allowable one-quarter of total benefit.[17] Thus, at considerable administrative cost,[18] the pensions industry was able to rewrite its schemes so that the Millard Tucker proposals were substantially achieved *de facto* (though some of the build-up of the lump sum was taxed), despite the government's intention of barring lump sums. The next major piece of pensions tax legislation, the 1970 Finance Act, introduced a 'new code' for the approval of pension schemes which regularized the situation, allowing tax-free lump sums equivalent to one and one-half times final annual salary (roughly equivalent to the old limit of one-quarter of benefits) after twenty years' service to all tax-exempt schemes. From then on, lump sums could be paid tax-free from funds which had themselves been accumulated without tax, thus further increasing the tax privileges of pension accruals. This appeared to be the only alternative in equity to the (presumably unthinkable) withdrawal of the civil servants' lump sum privileges which are now accepted as the standard by which the tax status of private schemes should be judged.

Unlike its predecessors, the 1970 Finance Act was retrospective in overriding previous approvals: all new schemes had to conform by 1973 and all old schemes by 1980. This overcame a problem, inherent in previous administrative changes by the Revenue, which had generally respected vested interests and eschewed retrospective change. Some pension schemes, such as the Federated Superannuation System for Universities, had been frozen in undesirable forms because they had been approved under earlier, more liberal administrative rules, and trustees were reluctant to innovate because they feared that a new application for approval would result in more restrictive conditions.[19] The tax authorities had, then, by 1980 achieved a position of reasonable uniformity and equity between different kinds of pension schemes, within the general context of a more generous tax regime for pension funds than had been envisaged by the original framers of either the 1921, the 1947 or the 1956 legislation. This generosity had a profound effect in stimulating the growth of pension schemes. By the 1970s, pension funds alone accounted for as much as a third of the savings of the personal sector of the British economy.[20] This was significantly higher than, for example, in the United States: Britain had clearly become a country in which an unusually high proportion of savings was being channelled through institutional investors such as pension funds, and personal capitalism was correspondingly on the decline. The tax incentives for saving in this form appear to be the major reason for this remarkable development.[21]

Taxation policy not only altered the quantity of pension saving, but also increasingly influenced the nature and quality of pension schemes, through the Revenue's tight control over the granting of tax-exempt status. Generally, tax relief was offered only to schemes which fitted within the traditions of existing public sector schemes and good private sector schemes: typically, this meant paying pensions of no more than two-thirds of final salary or lump sums of no more than one and one-half times final salary. In effect, this froze schemes in a conservative form: the tax concessions provided guidelines and incentives for straitjacketing innovation.[22] By the time of the 1970 Act, however, the focus of government regulation of pensions had already clearly shifted from taxation issues to broader questions of old age poverty relief, employment policy and pensioner rights and expectations.

The newly emerging approach to problems of national policy on pensions arose naturally from the post-war conditions of full employment. The unemployment rate, which had peaked at 16% in the 1930s, remained below 2% for more than two decades after 1940.[23] With so tight a labour market, employers and governments were seriously concerned that the supply of both skilled and unskilled labour would prove to be a brake on economic expansion. The absence of vested pension rights would, it was feared, artificially restrict the mobility of labour considered vital for efficiency. Pension entitlement might also restrict the willingness of older workers to seek employment, at a time they were very much needed. The state scheme was the first target for change. The Labour government modified their national insurance scheme in 1951 to encourage later retirement by relaxing the earnings rule for pensioners, and increasing the pension for those who deferred retirement.[24] Yet private pensions too were seen as erecting artificial barriers to employment. The Ministry of Labour received an increasing number of complaints about discrimination against older workers caused by the operation of pension schemes.[25] It was alleged that older workers were refused employment on the grounds that they were too old to be admitted to the pension scheme; that the cost of their pension entitlements were greater than for younger workers; that the absence of transfer rights prevented older workers taking up new job offers; that mandatory retirement ages forced employees to retire against their will; and that fixed retirement ages or restrictions on improving pensions to levels above two-thirds of final salary prevented older workers from staying on after reaching the normal retirement age. Some of these appeared to derive from employer motives in establishing the schemes, some from Inland Revenue requirements for tax exemption, and some from the insurance companies' terms of business aimed at avoiding bad risks. Further discussion by the Ministry and their advisors with the pensions industry usually showed that there were many misunderstandings by employers or employees which did create rigidities. In most cases, however, there were readily available ways around most of these problems, at least where employers agreed that they were desirable. Increasingly, in the post-war conditions of labour shortage, employers did attempt to attract or retain older workers by removing or suspending the operation of restrictive rules in pension schemes. The junior minister at the Ministry of Labour, Harold Watkinson, harangued employers in professional and public meetings, which played a part in the spread of consciousness about this kind of problem. However, after thus stimulating public discussion, the government eschewed legislation and were content to rely on voluntary reform.[26]

In another major area of government interests in pension funds – the overlap with the national insurance pension scheme – the state inevitably had to take a more direct and active role. Increasingly in the 1950s, politicians were forced into new choices which had a fundamental impact on occupational pension provision. The hopes of the framers of the 1925 Pension Act had been that they were establishing a contributory state pension, paid as of right and without means test for manual workers and other less well-paid employees. This left top-up benefits for those employees (and the entire provision for better-off employees) to occupational pension schemes or other forms of private savings. Yet, despite the hopes of 1925, poor law supplements for the aged had already been increasing the means-tested element in pensions and a new Pensions Act in 1940 further improved old age pensions on a means-tested basis. The latter was, however, seen as a war emergency measure. Sir William Beveridge's famous 1942 blueprint for the post-war welfare state[27] envisaged a more full-blooded reform, attempting again to establish a firm basis of insured state pensions without the means tests. His committee proposed to bring everyone into the national insurance scheme, and to pay more generous pensions, to which no means-tested supplements would be necessary, phasing these higher benefits in over twenty years. Some of the costs would be met by imposing a retirement condition (the 1925 pensions, by contrast, had been payable at sixty-five even if the person continued working);[28] other savings would come from withdrawing widows' pensions from young widows without dependent children; but most of the higher benefits were to be financed by substantially increased national insurance contributions.

Beveridge's package was widely admired and created expectations of post-war betterment which were politically irresistible. The commitment to universality was made almost immediately by the post-war Labour government. Requests from the pensions industry for contracting out where occupational pensions already provided adequate cover had been accepted in 1925 (and were to be accepted in future schemes), but in 1946 they were confidently brushed aside.[29] Labour with equal confidence extended state pension rights to middle-class employees (or, more precisely, to those earning more than £420 p.a.) who had previously been excluded from the national insurance schemes and to those of the less well-paid self-employed who had chosen not to contribute voluntarily. Under the 1946 National Insurance Act, they were to qualify for full pensions in only ten years, on the same basis as manual workers and others who had already in 1946 been contributing for up to twenty years. Thus, many people like civil servants, bank and insurance officials, and others who already had generous occupational pensions, were given a generous subsidy in old age from public funds: a 55-year-old entering the scheme in 1948 could expect to gain pension entitlements worth ten times the contributions he had paid when he retired in 1958.

This transfer of income to the rich was implemented by Labour because the slogan of universality appeared also to imply the end of the hated means test of the 1930s. Yet, while some of the more objectionable elements of means testing were removed, it was already clear that means tests would not be abolished even if the scheme were liberally conceived. Beveridge had proposed that higher national insurance benefits should be phased in over twenty years, but the ten shillings a week old age pension to which most of the aged were then entitled was clearly inadequate. (By 1946, average weekly earnings of male manual workers in manufacturing were nearly 121 shillings.) Following strong back-bench pressure, new retirement pensions at the more realistic level of twenty-six shillings a week for a single person and forty-six shillings a week for a married couple were paid from 1946. They were financed almost entirely by savings on the system of means-tested pension supplements (£61 million), and by increased contributions (£78 million), with virtually nothing (£2 million) from general taxation. Already, however, it was evident that even these new retirement pension levels were inadequate to cover socially acceptable living expenses for the poor, particularly for those with high rents. The National Assistance Board was thus set up in 1948 to pay new supplementary pensions on a means-tested basis from general taxation.[30]

In the 1950s, the new combined system of national insurance and national assistance, intended to cover the major hazards of life from cradle to grave, benefited from the unprecedentedly high post-war employment levels, which reduced expenditure on unemployment benefits and encouraged workers not to retire. However, the proportion of the aged in the population was forecast to rise rapidly, and this eventually increased the financial strains on the system. The number of retirement pensioners had reached 4.2 million by 1950 and was to rise to 5.6 million by 1960. A growing proportion of pensioners also received supplementary means-tested assistance: 0.7 million in 1950 and 1.1 million in 1960. The rise in expenditure on the aged caused a moment of hesitant reflection for the Conservative government in the early 1950s; but the Phillips Committee, to which they referred the question, could not produce any politically acceptable solution.[31] Their badly argued report, suggesting that pension ages (still sixty-five for men, but reduced to sixty for women in 1940) should be raised by three years, was ignored. Nor could pensioners in the long run be allowed to fall behind imperceptibly as the rate of inflation accelerated: the single person's retirement pension (£1.30 when fixed in 1946) had been increased in money terms, but fallen slightly in real value by the time of the Phillips Report in 1953; it rose (in constant 1946 prices) to £1.84 in 1963, and £3.24 in 1979 (with increases in supplementary means-tested pensions also).[32] Beveridge's hope of identifying a sustainable, fixed subsistence minimum was frustrated by rising political and social standards of provision for the elderly in the post-war era of prosperity. The rising pension was not just keeping up with inflation, but provided a continually rising real standard of living for the elderly. Their incomes were rising even faster than the incomes of those in work, and by 1979 the single person's retirement pension (even without the then more generous means-tested supplement) was 26% of the average male manual worker's wage, as compared with only 16% in 1953.[33]

Although the aged were not well organized politically,[34] the very size of their vote and general public sympathy for their cause made them an obvious target for politicians' generosity; and the political system responded appropriately in the long run.

The appointment of the Phillips Committee showed the Conservatives' discontent at the rising cost of financing old age pensions, but in the event they were unwilling to face the political consequences of cutbacks. Labour politicians surveying the post-war affluence were also far from satisfied at the results of their earlier policies, though for different reasons. Their euphoric creation of the welfare state in 1946 had been financed by highly regressive national insurance contributions rather than by progressive taxation, yet the insurance basis of benefits (which Beveridge felt to be so important) was already a sham. Moreover, as the numbers of pensioners increased and the middle classes began to qualify for pensions in the late 1950s, it was evident that the contributions required to pay for the rise in cost would have to be graduated like the income tax, since a flat rate levied on everybody would place politically unacceptable burdens on the lower-paid. It might have been better to recognize the logic of this earlier, and integrate the social security and tax systems, as some insurance company managers had seen at the time.[35] An alternative strategy would have been to concentrate pension rises on the less well-off by increased means-tested benefits financed by taxation. The latter still appeared unacceptable in Labour circles, implying as it did a means test with all its burdensome pre-war connotations, but they recognized the need both to increase pensions and to finance them in a new way. Labour's answer came from a group of Socialist intellectuals gathered around Professor Richard Titmuss at the London School of Economics. Titmuss had already been frustrated by the somewhat inconclusive discussions at the Ministry of Labour on occupational pensions and age discrimination.[36] He was increasingly convinced that the development of pensions in the private sector (particularly the insecurity of rights of transfer and the partial coverage with a bias to the better-off) was a false trail for old age income provision, and that a state take-over of the system was required. He and his colleagues therefore worked to gain acceptance within the Labour Party of a state system of earnings-related benefits. These would be financed by contributions graduated according to income, and in this sense, the scheme was similar to the proposals then being implemented by a right-wing government in Germany. In the Titmuss plan, however, the contributions would not directly determine benefits, but would be partly redistributed. The less well-off would gain pensions on retirement at somewhat higher rates than their contribution record justified, and the better-off would finance this by taking poorer pensions than could have been bought privately for similar contributions.[37]

Titmuss's ideas appealed to a number of strands in Labour Party thinking.[38] The Party's policy-makers had been flirting with the idea of nationalizing insurance and there had been some demand from trade unions for improved transfer rights for leavers and better coverage for workers excluded from existing schemes. The mature proposal of the Titmuss group – accepted as official Labour policy at the Party conference in 1957 – did, moreover, look politically attractive.[39] It promised inflation-proof state provision of one-half of final salary for typical workers when the scheme matured, in return for earnings-related contributions of 3% from employees (supplemented by 5% from employers and 2% from the Exchequer). Occupational pensions by now already covered a third or more of the work force, and many employers were considering introducing, upgrading or expanding schemes. This did, then, probably represent the last practical moment at which a state earnings-related pension scheme could have wiped out the bulk of demand for private provision in Britain. When the Labour scheme was announced, the shares of insurance companies fell sharply. Shareholders were right to be worried: this scheme could kill the bulk of their expanding business in pensions.

The Titmuss plan was ardently backed by Richard Crossman, on the left, and by Hugh Gaitskell, the right-wing party leader, but it did not have an easy passage in the party. The white-collar unions were anxious that their schemes should be allowed to contract out of Labour's earnings-related scheme, and Aneurin Bevan and others on the left were less than enthusiastic about a scheme which appeared to perpetuate inequalities from working life into old age. However, the real opposition came from the pensions interests. The Association of Superannuation and Pension Funds had little influence, being more a discussion forum for its large but varied membership of actuaries, financial advisers, and pension managers than an effective pressure group with clearly defined common interests and objectives. It was the representatives of employers' organizations and, above all, the Life Offices' Association who organized the more effective barrage of opposition to the plan. They argued that the state should not step beyond the provision of a basic retirement pension, and that occupational pension schemes were capable, albeit with improvements to transferability, of meeting needs above that level more effectively without the state becoming involved. They had little difficulty in showing that the Labour Party proposals represented a poor deal for those on average or better incomes compared with what private pensions could offer.[40]

The Life Offices' Association were none the less at this stage not averse to state intervention. Indeed, recognizing the demand for universal coverage and the limits of commercial development, they suggested privately to ministers and MPs that they would welcome legislation to compel all employees to join occupational pension schemes.[41] However, John Boyd-

Carpenter, the Conservative Minister for Pensions and National Insurance, considered this a non-starter, and moreover, he had other, more urgent priorities.[42] He recognized the political need to finance more generous old age pensions, but realized also that quite modest increases would be sufficient to take the heat created by Labour's plan off his party. He did, moreover, believe strongly that the occupational pensions movement in the private sector was better fitted than the government to provide earnings-related pensions; he was thus anxious that any state intervention should leave wide scope for private initiatives. Early in 1958, he therefore increased the flat-rate pension generously (more than compensating for inflation since the last increase), and later in the year he announced a state graduated pension scheme which was to be implemented in the 1959 National Insurance Act. Those earning up to £9 per week would pay flat-rate contributions and secure the increased flat-rate pension, but employees earning between £9 and £15 per week (the latter being around average earnings) would pay higher graduated contributions. Most of the revenue thus raised went into paying flat-rate benefits for all, but there were token graduated benefits (sixpence per week extra pension for men for every £15 of contributions) as a sop to the idea of earnings-related pensions.

Occupational pension schemes were permitted to contract out of the graduated element in the state scheme: a vital condition which Boyd-Carpenter saw as the principal means of encouraging the growth of the private sector. This aspect of the plan met stiff opposition from the Treasury, who (correctly) saw it as a major leakage of government revenue. Even among pension fund interests there was only muted support, with some opposition to the whole principle of depriving scheme members of state benefits. The principle of contracting out was conceded only after an unusually intense Cabinet battle in which Boyd-Carpenter triumphed over the Chancellor. The incentive he offered for pension schemes to contract out was that members then paid reduced national insurance contributions of somewhat less than those required to finance flat-rate state benefits (which they, nevertheless, could still draw); in return, they were required to provide *minimum* occupational pension benefits equal to the *maximum* graduated benefits in the state scheme. This sounded tough, but, since the state scheme provided such low maximum benefits, it was in reality not difficult for pension schemes to meet the contracting-out requirements except for the lowest-paid workers. Contracting-out did not require inflation-proofing of pensions, for the state graduated benefits were not inflation-proofed. Somewhat less logically, contracted-out schemes were not required to provide a widow's benefit, equivalent to half the state graduated pension, from which contracted-in employees would benefit. Seeing this weakness of the scheme, one insurance broker marketed an infamous scheme providing only the minimum benefits necessary for contracting out: thus, in effect, depriving some employees of widows' cover at a small saving in employers' national insurance contributions. The cost of Boyd-Carpenter's graduated pension scheme was trivial compared with Labour's proposals. Moreover, Labour's aim of achieving transferability of pension rights was not achieved above the level of state benefits: contracted-out schemes which did not preserve pensions equivalent to those in the graduated scheme had to make a 'payment-in-lieu' to the National Insurance Fund, but this guaranteed only trivial preservation of rights for leavers up to the low level of benefits in the state scheme. As the insurance world recognized, Boyd-Carpenter's plan was 'a political gimmick, not a pension scheme'.[43] None the less, as it left them a relatively clear field, the main pension interests understandably supported it. For the electorate, too, it appeared to be enough; the 1959 election, at which Labour offered their alternative, produced a victory for the Conservatives, and in 1961 their graduated pension scheme was implemented according to plan.

The Conservative strategy had been to achieve as little for the state scheme as politically possible; and, if the primary measure of success is the consonance of objectives and achievements, their graduated pension scheme must rank as the most successful piece of pension legislation ever. The plan achieved little in the way of earnings-related state pensions, and it did so at considerable cost. National insurance contributions, now graduated according to income, essentially became part of an (increasingly oddly structured) tax-collecting mechanism. Instead of using the existing income tax system to administer it, however, Boyd-Carpenter created a large new group of civil servants administering graduated contributions on a slightly different basis. For the pension industry the decision on whether or not to contract out was in principle difficult, and those who bothered to consider it rationally used professional resources wastefully. As the Institute of Actuaries said, it was impossible on the available information to take an unambiguously correct decision.[44] A minority of employers did contract out, especially for employees earning near the national average wage (the upper bound of the scheme).[45] Only a few schemes for poorly paid workers were actually abandoned in favour of complete reliance on the state scheme. Some of the least generous schemes for manual labour were upgraded to meet the minimal contracting-out requirements. The most sensible position for many employers was to ignore the state scheme completely and carry on regardless. Most employees in pension schemes were not contracted out, neither they nor their employers considering that the contribution or benefit levels in the state graduated scheme much affected their pensioning decisions.[46]

The Labour Party consistently warned that they did not intend to forget their commitment to a more ambitious earnings-related state pension plan. Pension interests were thus well aware that Boyd-Carpenter had given them only a brief respite.[47] The insurance companies stepped up their selling efforts, finding a ready response among employers who were now bound to contribute to the state graduated scheme if they did not start their own contracted-out scheme. Self-administered pension funds also considered extending benefits to a wider range of employees. The upshot was an increase in the coverage of occupational pensions from a third to nearly half the work force in the decade following the Boyd-Carpenter announcement. Richard Crossman, who had won the Labour Party over to the earlier Titmuss proposals, became very aware that any new scheme would have to take note of the now clearly established pensioning institutions, if only because the white-collar unions in the TUC would insist on it. Much to the chagrin of the Titmuss group (who feared too much would be given away to interest groups), Crossman initiated detailed discussions with industry experts. He aimed to produce a scheme which was acceptable to them, yet one which forced them to change in ways which were compatible with his state scheme. While many in the occupational pensions movement deprecated this *rapprochement* with Labour, the more sensible of them recognized the need to achieve some political consensus if pensions were not to be destabilized by the inter-party struggle. They were, moreover, convinced that the state could provide coverage for some workers – casual or part-time workers, frequent job-changers, employees of small firms – better than they could themselves. The majority of the members of the renamed National Association of Pension Funds still stuck to the view (supported in principle then only by the Liberal Party) that the state should confine itself to flat-rate pensions, leaving earnings-related provision to voluntary initiatives. However, broader political considerations led to support for Crossman's scheme from some former opponents of state provision. In the Legal & General, for example, the dominant firm in the insured pension market, the actuary Stewart Lyon was quietly arguing for a new approach. Much as the occupational pension movement had achieved in its breathing space, men such as Lyon could not but be aware of the strong political demand for more generous pensions and the superior achievements in other countries which had taken the state earnings-related route. By the early 1970s, in Germany, for example, the average married worker could expect to retire on 60% of net final earnings. Similar state provision was by then not unusual in other advanced Western nations: even in the traditionally *laissez-faire* United States, the level was 56%. In Britain, by contrast, the average worker could expect to replace only 35% of his pre-retirement earnings from the state scheme.[48]

Richard Crossman unveiled Labour's plans to change this, after considerable discussion and delays, only in 1969.[49] The new scheme was recognizably derivative from Labour's earlier blueprints, and its scale dwarfed the token graduated system of Boyd-Carpenter. It also marked some new departures in party thinking. The idea of a state pension fund, for example, was dropped in favour of the pay-as-you-go principle, and the scheme was planned to mature in twenty years, rather than the forty years which the earlier funded scheme would have required. The proposed contributions and benefits involved some redistribution from the affluent to the less well-off,[50] like both Labour's earlier plans and the 1961 Boyd-Carpenter scheme, though the benefits were generous for all: up to the national average wage (then £630 p.a.) 60% of earnings would be replaced by the pension, but between that level and three times the average wage (£1,900 p.a.) the earnings-related benefit would be only 25%. Pensions were to maintain their value in real terms, widows were to be favourably treated, and pensions were to be preserved for leavers. All of these characteristics were, as Crossman pointed out, difficult for the private sector to match, but he proposed to require equivalent benefits in any scheme contracting out, as well as requiring all occupational schemes to preserve benefits after a member had contributed for five years. The pensions industry knew that they would be strained to meet these standards, but they were now resigned to the general principle of state earnings-related provision. A pressure group, STOP ('Save the Occupational Pension'), was formed to oppose the scheme,[51] but the serious lobbying activity was now reserved for the negotiation of the price of contracting out, rather than opposition to the principle.

These negotiations took a new turn when Labour was defeated in the 1970 election, before the Crossman proposals had been implemented. The Life Offices' Association and other pension interests were seriously worried that this would compromise their strategy of achieving stability by cross-party agreement, and would revive the uncertainty which was already reducing their members' ability to sell occupational pensions. They were particularly worried by radicals within the Conservative Party, notably Sir Keith Joseph and Margaret Thatcher, who had been pressing them to support their own plans for widening property ownership by extending pensions coverage. Thatcher and Joseph were contemptuous of the moderate, diplomatic liberalism of the actuaries and other professionals at the Life Offices' Association, finding more congenial the individual insurance brokers and company chairmen who wanted to take a harder line in promoting the private sector of occupational pensions and blocking the expansion of the state scheme. Pension professionals, by contrast, were concerned that a state-funded reserve scheme, with benefits not guaranteed but depending on investment performance and only maturing in forty years – the kind of scheme which met the ideological predilections of the Conservative radicals – could not satisfy political urges for quicker and more secure earnings-related pensions. None the less, it was such a plan that Sir Keith Joseph, the new Secretary of State for Social Services, announced in 1971 to replace the Crossman scheme.[52]

The Joseph scheme passed into law as the 1973 Social Security Act, but it, too, was to be jettisoned. As employers were hurrying to meet its contracting-out requirements in time for inauguration day (projected for 1975), the Conservatives in their turn were defeated at the polls. The new Labour Secretary of State for Social Services, Barbara Castle, soon made it clear that she would abandon Joseph's legislation in favour of a more generous scheme based on Crossman's original 1969 proposals.[53] Discussions between ministers and pressure groups were thus further prolonged. By then, the positions adopted were increasingly entrenched, and had been evolved in a period of considerable financial difficulty for both employers and pension funds. Special interest groups, ranging from trade unions and women's groups to the pensions industry, had, moreover, had their say on numerous occasions to promote self-interested modifications of the scheme. Consensus was a high political priority. What emerged was, then, a set of compromises which was a monument to political accommodation with special interests concerned with the problems of the 1970s, rather than a logical structure of cooperation exploiting the comparative advantages of occupational and state pensions in the long run. The cost in pension promises was high. Even so, Barbara Castle succeeded in preserving intact the major features of the Crossman scheme, and in pushing it through a Labour Cabinet insistently beset with financial pressures of a more urgent kind.

The Social Security Act of 1975 implemented her plans, and the first serious British state earnings-related pension scheme came into effect in 1978, with pension contributions integrated with those for other national insurance purposes. These national insurance contributions were levied on earnings up to 1.5 times average earnings (initially at 14%, though within a few years the rising cost of pay-as-you-go funding approached 20% and was projected to rise even further). The scheme planned to pay full earnings-related pensions from 1998, with pensions based on earnings during the best twenty years of work. For workers on average full-time male earnings this was likely to double the level of income replacement previously attained by the flat-rate scheme. Women did particularly well out of Barbara Castle's scheme: they obtained the same pensions as men, despite their greater longevity and earlier retiring age of sixty, and they benefited from the best twenty years' provision; widows' benefits were also exceptionally good, and, moreover, could be drawn in addition to any pension a woman qualified for in her own right as a worker. (The Joseph scheme had been far less attractive to women, reflecting the actuarial reality of the higher cost of providing pensions for a gender whose members retired earlier and died later.)

That Labour finally introduced a state earnings-related pension scheme after twenty years of trying, and that Britain thereby finally caught up with what a (conservative) regime in West Germany had introduced twenty years earlier, are perhaps not surprising. That they did this on such generous terms at a time of severe economic stringency following the oil crisis was due to the momentum that had built up over twenty years. None the less, the Conservatives agreed not to overturn the new scheme.[54] After a decade of uncertainty, it seemed that cross-party agreement to take pensions out of party politics had been achieved.

Why was Labour able to achieve this? The earnings-related scheme of 1978 was superimposed on a flat-rate pension system of long standing which for half the work force was already supplemented by occupational pensions. Inevitably, it influenced the scope and nature of the private systems. As part of the strategy of taking pensions out of politics and entrenching her own scheme in the statute book, Barbara Castle had been willing to offer some help to the occupational pensions industry to meet the tough standards which the contracting-out provisions for such a generous scheme required. Many schemes were then in severe financial difficulties, following the oil crisis and the collapse in the value of their investments.[55] The government was thus sympathetic to their difficulties in meeting the standards of inflation-proofing of pensions which were necessary to match those in the state scheme. In effect, Castle offered the occupational pension movement state insurance against some of these risks. Thus, most employers found it both possible and worth while to contract their pension schemes out of her scheme.[56] For these contracted-out schemes, the elaborate requirements to guarantee minimum pensions considerably increased correspondence and record-keeping costs; and some companies, like GEC and Unilever, seriously doubted whether the lobbying for contracting-out had been worthwhile in the longer-run perspective. A minority of employers chose not to contract out, either abandoning their own schemes (particularly for low-paid workers) or remodelling them as a top-up to the state scheme (typically for the better-paid staff only). The latter strategy avoided the administrative complications of contracting-out and gave employees the benefits guaranteed by the state earnings-related scheme, yet left them free to offer additional benefits flexibly with the minimum of constraints imposed by the contracting-out procedures. The hopes of Titmuss and Crossman that contracting out would gradually wither away as the benefits of the state scheme became apparent were, however, still far from being realized. Indeed, by the 1980s the signs were that the state subsidy to contracting-out firms, which was necessary to gain their acquiescence, was now so attractive that some firms which originally contracted out were contracting back in to gain access to it. The price paid by Barbara Castle may not only have produced a poor mix of the relative benefits of state and private provision, but may even have been too high a price to achieve this.[57] The more far-sighted commentators already realized that the scheme was unlikely to survive unchanged.

This is not to say that her scheme has not had profound effects on pensioning. For the half of the work force who were not previously in schemes, the new earnings-related state scheme compelled a significantly higher implicit level of saving and increased their forecast retirement incomes substantially. For those already in occupational schemes, the need to meet the requirements of contracting out began profoundly to affect the rules of schemes: typically, this significantly improved the quality of pension benefits and increased their cost.[58] The state had, then, now made a commitment to establishing standards beyond the basic old age subsistence which had been the focus of welfare initiatives in the austere 1940s. However, the new earnings-related scheme did very little for the poorest, who would probably still be dependent on means-tested benefits in old age. It rather affected provision for the mass of the population above the poverty-line whose old age living standards had previously been a matter for separate negotiations with employers. The state had achieved this partly by becoming a pensions competitor – albeit an extremely powerful one – but also by accepting a role of partnership with the existing occupational pensions movement.

This transformation in state responsibility for old age saving, rather than mere poverty relief, could hardly have failed to have a significant impact on the attitude of governments to the regulation of pension schemes. In allowing contracting out, they were implicitly accepting that the private occupational pension movement would be able to honour its commitments. Yet, as we have seen, government had very little control of or influence on the movement, and the little control they had was directed towards the restriction of tax avoidance and evasion, rather than social or economic ends. The 1961 graduated state pension scheme had required some increased supervision of contracted-out schemes, but the resources necessary for these minimal duties (a pension scheme had to be very bad to fail to meet the requirements) were slim. Despite the new interest in pensions at the Ministry of Pensions and National Insurance and the Ministry of Labour and National Service in the 1950s, the Inland Revenue was still throughout the 1960s the government department which had the most effective contact with, and knowledge of, pension schemes. This was not entirely satisfactory, for it created a policy bias to fiscal rather than social considerations. As one consultant actuary remarked: 'The Inland Revnue cannot logically look upon pension schemes with any more favour than the police force can look upon criminals.'[59] The Controller of the Superannuation Funds Office was clear that his department was not a social service department and in developing its practices he looked chiefly to the interests of the Exchequer, though he admitted an increasing pressure for the Revenue not to stand in the way of socially desirable changes in its single-minded pursuit of tax regulation.[60]

There were a number of suggestions, from government bodies and elsewhere, that a supervisory body with broader terms of reference was required.[61] The catalyst for action was the Social Security Act of 1973, the first legislation to force pension schemes to preserve pensions after five years of contributions. At the same time, the Act established the Occupational Pensions Board, charged with oversight of the preservation requirements and contracting-out provisions of the Joseph scheme, and also with advising the Secretary of State more generally on pension matters. While much of the rest of the Act was jettisoned, the Occupational Pensions Board survived to police the contracting-out provisions of the final Castle scheme, as well as undertaking the new regulatory functions such as policing the requirements of equal access for women introduced in 1978. The Board drew on the expertise of the pensions industry, with fourteen members, some from employers, trade unions, and the lay public, but the most influential drawn from the actuarial profession. Its offices, significantly, were located next to the Superannuation Funds Office of the Inland Revenue, and the 119 civil servants who staffed it by 1979 could share some of the Revenue's information and expertise. As with most regulatory bodies, there were conflicting interests and dangers of capture by the regulated: the government had little choice but to call on the expertise of the industry in this highly specialized field. The long-run implications of the Board's work are not yet clear, but it has already proved its worth as channel of communication between the government and the pensions industry. Some of its more ambitious suggestions have been rejected by governments unwilling to expand its personnel or powers further; but since 1973 the Board's impressive series of reports – on member participation, preservation, disclosure, solvency and other matters – has increasingly set the tone of public discussion.[62] Politicians still have a strong independent line, but they are now, more than ever before, likely to confront the pensions industry in institutionalized form before taking political action. Civil servants are steadily acquiring greater expertise on pension issues, while the pension interests themselves have developed a more structured and representative umbrella organization, uniting the efforts of the traditionally effective Life Offices' Association, the newly revitalized National Association of Pension Funds and other interested professional bodies. As the pensions industry has become a power in the land, it has rather belatedly taken a position also in the structure of sponsorship and control with which Whitehall traditionally interacts with the major interests in the British economy.

5 Competition and professionalization: the maturing of the pension market (1956–79)

what the market really wants is not the traditional guarantees of an insurance contract so much as a combination of technical advice, efficient investment of pension funds and a good administrative service . . .

Ron Peet, Legal & General
manager, staff *Annual
Conference*, privately
printed, 1971, p. 15

Government policy has, understandably, been a major preoccupation of the pensions interests in the post-war decades. Both the tax regime and contracting-out provisions for the earnings-related state pensions had profound effects on the coverage and shape of occupational pension schemes in that period. But the pensions institutions and the market for old age savings also had a dynamic of their own. Changes in the employment relationship, with further growth of large-scale, bureaucratic organizations and labour shortages under full employment conditions, increased the demand for pensions from both employers and employees. In the 1960s and 1970s more than a million employees were transferred from the private to the public sector, where employees were more likely to demand and get pension coverage. In private industry, too, a wave of mergers created substantially larger organizations, and this usually resulted in the adoption of pensioning in parts of the organization where it had not existed before. As the size of the pensions market expanded, other financial institutions joined the insurance companies, competing for what was becoming a rapidly growing sector of the market for personal savings. With these developments, the approach to pension fund management became more specialized and professional, advisors and consultants proliferated, and the quantity and quality of the information on which employers could make pensioning decisions greatly widened their horizons of decision-making. Since the mid 1950s, the occupational pensions industry in Britain has come of age, and in the process its complexity has considerably increased.

However, as Figure 5.1 shows, the coverage of the employed work force did not expand as rapidly after 1956 as before.[1] The annual rate of growth in the number of employees in pension schemes (which had averaged nearly 6% per annum in the two decades before 1956) fell to under 4% per annum in the next decade. Even so, the success of Boyd-Carpenter in delaying the birth of a serious rival state earnings-related scheme, and the enhanced tax concessions of 1956 did mean that the buoyant private sector of the economy in the late 1950s and early 1960s maintained its earlier hectic rate of growth in pensions coverage: three million workers were brought into schemes in that period. This, together with a smaller but steady increase in public sector scheme membership, boosted the total number of occupational scheme members from 8.0 million in 1956 (about one-third of the work force) to 12.2 million in 1967 (almost one-half of the work force). Yet this appeared to mark the high-water mark for the occupational pension movement. It was very similar to the peak level of coverage obtained in the United States, though it was somewhat below that in a few European countries such as the Netherlands. In the latter country there was a more sensibly structured partnership of occupational schemes with state provision (the former guaranteeing transferability for leavers, the latter confining itself to flat-rate pensions), and coverage of occupational schemes was as high as 85% of the work force.[2] Coverage in Britain, by contrast, stabilized at below half the work force, with a drop in membership in the later 1960s and early 1970s, when government pensions policy and economic stringency created an atmosphere of uncertainty.[3] The loss in membership was only partially recovered in later years to leave a membership of 11.8 million employees (still below the 1967 level) in 1979. There were also about 400,000 of the self-employed contributing to pension schemes at the latter date, but even if they were included pension fund coverage remained at just under half of the work force.

Some pointers to the reasons for this limited spread of occupational pension schemes can be gleaned from a closer examination of the pattern of spread and of the areas where the recent declines in membership have been concentrated. The spread of pension fund membership and its resilience in the face of the economic difficulties of the 1970s were most marked in the public sector, where trade unions made pension rights a major part of their bargaining strategy. By 1979, there was virtually complete pensions coverage in the civil service, armed forces and nationalized industries, though coverage was less in local government and the health services. The main excluded groups were part-time workers: nearly 1.5 million part-timers in the public sector, mainly women, were not in pension schemes.

Fig. 5.1 Occupational pension scheme coverage, 1936–79

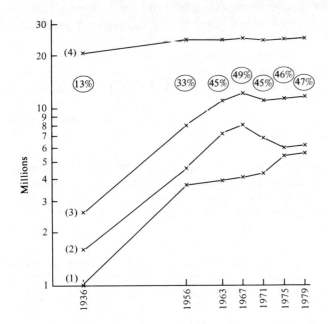

Key: (1) members of public sector schemes
     (2) members of private sector schemes
     (3) total scheme membership ((1)+(2))
     (4) total work force
     (13%) percentage coverage of occupational schemes ((3)÷(4))

Source: Statistical appendix and see n. 1 to this chapter.
Notes 1. Some of the rise in public sector membership (particularly in 1936–56) is due to
transfers of pensionable employees from the private sector. The private sector rate of
growth in the 1930s and 1940s is thus understated.
2. 'Total work force' includes all employees, the self-employed and HM Forces but
excludes the unemployed. 'Total scheme membership' excludes the personal pensions of
the self-employed developed under the terms of the 1956 Finance Act: these numbered 0.4
million by 1979 and their inclusion raises coverage from the indicated 47% to 49% of the
work force.
3. Semilog scale: slopes indicate rates of growth.

However, 90% of male employees in the public sector, and a similar
proportion of full-time women, were by 1979 members of pension schemes,
with a total public sector membership of 5.6 million.

In the private sector, by contrast, though aggregate membership was
larger at 6.2 million, the percentage coverage was more limited: only 50% of
men and 25% of women belonged to occupational pension schemes in 1979.
This was partly because the majority of firms in the private sector,
employing 4.2 million, simply had no pension scheme. While virtually all

employers of 1,000 or more had a scheme, only a third of employers with between 10 and 99 ran one. Some of the small firms which once had schemes appear to have jettisoned them when they saw the tough contracting-out requirements of the Castle earnings-related scheme.[4] We do not know much about the pensioning practices of such firms, but it seems likely that the majority of them were content to rely on the state scheme, perhaps supplemented in some cases by the granting of *ex gratia* pensions to favoured employees. Certainly substantial resources were still devoted to such pensions in the 1960s; and other traditional forms of pensioning, such as the retirement lump sum for manual workers, also survived.[5] By the 1970s, however, with increased social security contributions and the prospect of a long-run increase in earnings-related pensioning by the state, it seems likely that such policies will have come increasingly under review.

Even in the private sector firms which *did* have formal pension schemes, only a bare majority of employees were scheme members. The proportion of those covered generally increased with the size of the firm: from around a third in firms employing 10 to 99 to nearly two-thirds in those employing 10,000 or more.[6] As in the public sector, part-time workers were generally excluded from pension schemes, and much of recent employment growth has been in part-time jobs. None the less, these accounted for only one-eighth of the 5.3 million employees of private sector firms with pension schemes who were not scheme members in 1979. Most of the excluded employees can be conceived of as belonging to the 'periphery' of the company work force, and the pension scheme explicitly excluded these from the benefits reserved for 'core' employees. Such employees did, of course, have to join the state earnings-related pension scheme from 1978, and for some of them (with, for example, a casual or part-time employment pattern) that scheme would almost certainly serve their long-run pensioning needs better than one employer's scheme. The employer also benefited from excluding workers who were likely to have a short or irregular employment record, since such workers increased the costs of administering funds. In the private sector, therefore, it was common to limit membership to long-term employees through devices such as excluding those under a certain age (typically twenty-one) or insisting on a minimum period of service (typically one or two years) before allowing membership of the scheme. There were also some employees whose employers did not compel membership (or who only compelled it for staff over, say, twenty-five or thirty-five) and who voluntarily chose not to join. Formerly, it was also common practice for employers explicitly to exclude women or to specify tighter conditions for their entry, though since 1978 such explicit discrimination has been outlawed by social security legislation.[7]

It was, however, still possible to exclude certain classes of employees, and those typically excluded (notably part-time workers) included disproportionate numbers of women, who have made up an increasing proportion of the post-war work force. More generally, it remained quite legal to exclude categories of employees on grounds other than gender, and even quite large firms often excluded manual workers. Indeed, manual workers (and particularly unskilled workers) accounted for the majority of employees of firms with schemes who were not members of those schemes.[8] This discriminatory tendency had historical roots in the greater need for employers pursuing an 'incorporationist' strategy to gain the loyalty of clerical and managerial employees than that of manual workers. More recently, such discriminatory motives have been strengthened by the prospect of state earnings-related pensions. Manual workers themselves are probably now less resistant than they were in earlier years to joining occupational pension schemes, since the compulsion to join the state scheme has removed from them the option of choosing not to save in any scheme, relying instead on means-tested assistance in old age.[9] But, for the employer, the cost of the quality improvements required for contracting out of the state scheme was typically greater for manual workers than for the staff. Thus, whatever the views of the workers, more employers preferred to delegate their pensioning problems, at least for lower-paid workers, to the state. In 1956 a majority of pension fund members had been weekly paid manual workers (though then, as now, the proportionate coverage for manual workers was less than for salaried staff), but by the 1970s they were clearly outnumbered by salaried staff.[10] Paradoxically, then, the state scheme has strengthened the tendencies, already criticized by Titmuss in advocating the scheme,[11] for there to be 'two nations' in the matter of pension rights.

Even where manual workers were members of pension schemes, they were more commonly in the post-war period admitted to schemes separate from the salaried staff schemes, and such schemes were usually characterized by a lower level of both contributions and benefits.[12] This was partly because of the earlier flat-rate state pension scheme, which provided a higher proportion of retirement income replacement for manual workers than for better-paid staff. However, other factors were also involved. Initially, tax regulations had encouraged the setting up of separate schemes for manual workers,[13] in marked contrast to the USA, where tax regulations encouraged equality of access as a condition of the tax exemption of schemes. A number of employers also found that manual workers were more attracted by higher pay than by higher pension benefits, particularly as social security contributions took a bigger slice of their pay packet.[14] The deep-rooted British class structure made the distinction between 'works' and 'staff' a natural one in the minds of both employers and employees, and this heritage remained imprinted on pension scheme practice. From the beginnings of railway and local authority funds (with, almost invariably, separate schemes for 'officers' and 'servants') to the post-war period of separate 'works' schemes, the distinction was less commonly seen as abnormal than might have been the case in a less class-ridden society.

There were, moreover, reasons why the workers themselves would oppose closer integration with staff schemes. Workers died earlier, and usually had a less progressive lifetime earnings ladder than 'staff' employees, so they could often obtain better benefits for any given level of contributions in separate 'works' schemes.[15] None the less, the labour market needs of full employment and general incorporationist motives were by the 1960s leading an increasing number of employers to attempt to break down class barriers, offering 'staff status' to manual workers, with the same conditions on holidays, hours, sickness and pensions as were offered to office workers. There was a distinct, but slow tendency to extend 'internal labour market' institutions – ranging from incremental pay scales, modern job evaluation techniques and more secure employment through the replacement of piece rates by measured day work to membership of pension schemes – to those manual workers.[16] The transition was not always easy: Unilever, for example, took ten years before they finally succeeded in merging their staff and works superannuation funds in 1972, mainly because of employee resistance to the integration. There were similar problems in parts of the public sector: the British Steel Corporation achieved similar integration in 1982, reducing staff contributions and increasing manual workers' benefits in order to bring the two groups into line. Such cases were, however, rare: many employers continued to think of pension benefits as mainly a perk for their administrative, technical, clerical and managerial staff which it was not necessary or desirable to extend to manual workers.

Even for non-manual staff, there was a considerable decline in pension fund membership in the private sector during the 1970s. Employers found the rising cost of pensioning, caused by the need to meet the standards of the state scheme or simply by staff pressure, a heavy burden on their operational costs. In competitive industries, especially, staff associations and white-collar unions found it extremely difficult to persuade employers to commit themselves to higher pension costs.[17] Moreover, while the costs were thus rising, the pay-offs to the employer, in terms of tying the staff to their jobs, were declining. With rising unemployment, voluntary turnover declined, and employers were less concerned to provide this incentive for their key staff to remain loyal to the firm. Even firms with schemes were now constrained from using them to the maximum effect for inducing staff to stay: the 1973 Social Security Act required the preservation of pension rights for leavers with a five-year contribution record. There were still some pay-offs in employee goodwill for the access to tax-privileged savings which the schemes offered. Also, some disincentive effect to leavers remained, for they were often still treated with as little generosity as possible within the limits permitted by the law.[18] Yet inevitably the changes which entrenched leavers' rights made employers more hesitant about extending the coverage of pension schemes.

The initial slowing down of the *quantitative* extension of pension coverage in the 1960s, followed by an actual decline in the 1970s, did not, however, preclude very substantial *qualitative* improvements to the schemes that existed. Indeed, paradoxically, many of the factors which made employers hesitant about extending coverage also compelled them to improve benefits for those to whom they did offer pensions. (In that sense, in a way quite unintended by its formulators, the state scheme may have reinforced inequality.) The preservation requirements of 1973 compelled employers to protect the pensions of leavers, thus increasing the cost of funding the pensions for those who stayed. Also, the contracting-out requirements of the state earnings-related pension scheme normally required two major improvements to schemes, namely a move to a final salary basis and a substantial improvement in widows' benefits.[19] Even before the state scheme came into operation, there were other pressures favouring the improvement of schemes. Earlier legislation helped put pension improvements on the agenda of corporate management. In 1956 the insurance companies, able to offer cheaper pension policies as a result of the new tax concessions,[20] persuaded many employers to use the gains to upgrade scheme benefits. Contracting out of the Boyd-Carpenter scheme in 1961[21] also initiated further reviews of scheme benefits. Meanwhile, post-war changes in the structure of the economy were favourable to pensioning. The scale of business organization continued to increase, bringing more employees into large, bureaucratic firms with internal labour market institutions. In the 1960s there was an intense merger wave greatly accentuating these tendencies to larger scale. Such mergers inevitably raised the question of harmonizing pension benefits between the constituent firms; and that question was quite likely to be answered by upgrading to the highest common factor rather than downgrading to the lowest common denominator. With rising living standards (in the 1950s and 1960s the rate of improvement was faster than any other time in the twentieth century), staff were also willing to devote a larger proportion of their income to savings. The high contemporary rates of taxation made them even more receptive to tax-efficient ways of doing so, and if employers did not point this out to them, the large army of insurance brokers and other salesmen would. Most employers could see that the benefits they were getting in 'top hat' pension schemes were only slightly less valuable in pension schemes for their lower-paid, taxpaying colleagues, and for similar reasons: firms which wanted to bid for labour aggressively often found tax-efficient fringe benefits more effective than improved salary offers. In consequence, more and more savings were channelled through pension funds. Between 1936 and 1972 occupational pension rights grew from only 4% of total personal wealth in Britain to 12%.[22]

Inflation, gently accelerating and beginning to cause alarm in the 1950s, becoming a major policy issue in the 1960s and causing real anxiety in the 1970s, was also a major factor affecting the thinking of pension fund managers. In the public sector, this led to adequate protection of pensioners against price rises, but in the private sector the main response was a move to final salary schemes (already well established in the public sector), which accorded with the employers' need to retain the correct incentives for retirement.[23] Average salary schemes and 'money purchase' schemes simply did not produce pensions sufficient to permit people to retire on a decent proportion of their former income, but final salary schemes (effectively compensating for inflation during working life) were much more expensive to fund. Nevertheless, by the end of the 1970s the great bulk of private sector pension fund members could look forward to a pension related to their final salary.[24] These quality improvements were costly. By 1979 the average annual contributions per member (from both member and employer together) in private sector occupational pension schemes were around £750, representing a considerable addition to labour costs (the average earnings of these employees at the time was just over £5,000 a year).[25]

This level of funding of schemes was very much higher (in real as well as money terms) than had been common in earlier schemes.[26] Private sector pension schemes at the turn of the century had typically required contributions of only 2.5% of salary from the member and 2.5% from the employer. In the first four decades of the twentieth century, it became more common for each side to contribute 5% in the better staff schemes (with rather lower rates in schemes for manual workers). After the Second World War, it was unusual for member contributions to rise much above the 5% level, but employer contributions continued inexorably to rise. By the later 1970s the employer had to add a further 7% of earnings in the average scheme but as much as 12% to fund a generous contracted-out scheme with final salary pension, some inflation-proofing and partial preservation of leavers' rights.[27] Between 1956 and 1979, total contributions to pension schemes rose from nearly £500 million a year to more than £9,000 million a year (increasing by more than three times, even when corrected for price inflation). By the latter date employers' contributions were clearly dominant: they accounted for more than three times as much as members' contributions in the funding of schemes.[28]

The constantly rising income of the pension schemes created a rapidly expanding market for the financial institutions which competed to manage their assets, and a greatly increased demand for the services of pensions professionals. As we have seen, insurance companies had first realized the potential for servicing these needs.[29] By the early 1950s they had built up a commanding market lead, and insured schemes accounted for the majority of private sector occupational pension scheme membership. From then on, they met increasingly tough competition, which forced them to review their ways of doing business. They had, of course, already had to meet competition from consulting actuaries, who, since the 1920s, had been expanding their business beyond the friendly societies in which they had previously specialized to include advice on actuarial risks and investment policy for self-administered pension schemes.[30] Typically, consulting actuaries advised their clients to set up self-administered trust funds rather than subcontracting their business to an insurance company. The consultants' claim to professional neutrality in this respect was, however, hotly disputed by the insurance companies, who pointed out that actuaries cut themselves out of potential business if they recommended an insured contract, since the insurance company would then handle the actuarial work.[31] Even so, the consulting actuaries represented a very welcome source of expert professional advice on a subject which both personnel and finance managers found esoteric. Their expert knowledge, not just of the arcane mathematics of their mystery, but also of the everyday practices of the Inland Revenue, of contracting-out provisions, and of the legal niceties of running a fund, could offer a reassuring lifeline to employers who chose to organize their scheme without the help of an insurance company.[32] Larger employers also developed their own pension staffs, recruiting those with a background in general administration, law, accountancy, secretarial or personnel management or occasionally, by the later 1940s, with finance or actuarial experience. By the 1960s the growth of this specialist pension profession was evident in, for example, the more than a thousand scheme administrators and other professionals who attended the National Association of Pension Funds' conferences.

A major new area in which expertise was demanded, either inside the company pension department or from outside advisers, was investment management. Prior to the Second World War the investment strategies of almost all pension funds had been based on fixed-interest securities. The big railway companies and municipalities had often invested their pension funds in their own (extremely safe) securities; but both their and other funds' trustees recognized the benefit of keeping the funds' risks separate and the norm became to invest funds in outside securities. In the first fifty years of this century, this typically meant fixed-interest securities issued by British and overseas governments and by public utilities. Returns on these investments were expected to, and did, go up or down in conformity with the general trends of interest rates in the economy. Typically, actuaries assumed a valuation rate of interest (which allowed them to calculate the level of contributions needed to fund the specified level of benefits) of around 3% or 4% per annum; and investment returns did not fluctuate far around this, being a little higher, for example, in the 1920s, but a little lower in the cheap money conditions of the 1930s and 1940s.[33]

Only a few pension funds and insurance companies departed from this conventional wisdom and adopted a more aggressive strategy of investing in equities to achieve higher rates of return. At Rowntrees, for example, Sam Clayton (who became head of pensions in 1923 and later a director of the company) invested in the equities of investment trusts, banks, insurance companies and industrial enterprises, consistently achieving rates of return above 5% (nearly double the going rate on fixed-interest stocks) in the 1930s and 1940s. Many pension funds were, however, prohibited by their trust deeds from investing so adventurously; in others actuaries and financial advisers were content to accept the conventional wisdom that the money liabilities of the funds were best matched by the fixed and predictable money returns of gilt-edged and similar fixed-interest stocks rather than by 'risky' equity investments.[34]

This attitude had already caused some problems for the funds in the First World War, but it was possible to view that inflationary period as an exception to the general rule. However, in the prolonged economic boom of the 1950s and 1960s, with inflation continually gathering pace, this whole approach to the investment and benefit structure of pension funds began to disintegrate. The most articulate and consistent (though by no means the first) of the advocates of the new approach was George Ross Goobey, an actuary who had learned his craft in the insurance world but in 1949 had been appointed as the first investment manager of the Imperial Tobacco pension fund.[35] He was faced with the need to meet the liabilities of a generous final salary scheme set up in 1929, and saw clearly that the fixed-interest securities in which the fund was heavily invested would not produce an adequate return. He persuaded his trustees to invest more of their funds in equities, and by 1953 had produced a healthy surplus. Funds which, like the Imperial Tobacco fund, did invest heavily in equities in the 1950s and 1960s did extremely well. After allowing for inflation, the *real* return on equities averaged 12.6% per annum in the 1950s and 5.4% per annum in the 1960s (whereas over the same two decades government stocks showed a negative or barely positive real return).[36] By the 1960s, property investments (again with a potential for equity appreciation rather than merely a fixed-interest *rentier* return) were also a major feature of the investment strategy of some pension funds. The National Coal Board pension fund had been directly involved in property development from the 1950s; while among the insurance companies Legal & General was by the early 1960s directing a quarter of its funds to buying commercial, industrial, and other properties. Many funds entered into partnership with major property developers who were then transforming the urban landscape of Britain. In 1960, for example, ICI reached agreement on a joint development company with the property tycoon Jack Cotton, and similar ventures soon followed for the Unilever and Imperial Tobacco funds.[37]

The investment managers of the self-administered pension funds of such major corporations developed investment expertise as they wrestled with these new problems; and they could afford to do so. By the later 1970s, for example, there were thirteen pension funds (owning two-fifths of all self-administered funds' assets) each with portfolios worth more than £500 million.[38] These included seven nationalized industries (the joint pension trusts of the Post Office and British Telecom alone accounted for 7% of all funds' portfolios) and, in the private sector, Barclays and National Westminster Banks, British Petroleum, ICI, the Imperial Group (formerly Imperial Tobacco) and Shell. These companies recruited teams of investment advisers from insurance companies, stockbrokers, and banks, and handled most of their investments directly; but most funds of more modest size relied on outside advice. Already in the 1930s clearing bank trust departments had undertaken some pension trust investment work, and by the late 1950s they were promoting their services more vigorously. Other financial institutions had then also realized the potential of this rapidly expanding new market. In 1957, Edgar Palamountain's M & G unit trust group launched the first tax-exempt unit trust designed for pension funds, and produced spectacular rates of return in the early years, winning a good deal of new business.[39] In later years unit trust groups were innovative in developing specialist funds for clients who lacked particular expertise. Thus, there were tax-exempt unit trusts, designed principally for the pensions market, specializing in property, small companies, new technology, venture capital or overseas investment. Stockbroking firms (with Phillips & Drew as the leader) also marketed their services vigorously, and were retained by many pension funds to advise on investments. Smaller-scale new entrants to the financial services industry (known, somewhat derisively, as 'pension boutiques') also made their appearance in the later 1950s, offering a range of actuarial and administrative as well as investment services.[40] Both actuarial firms and insurance brokers (who were already heavily involved in advising funds in their respective fields of expertise) also occasionally offered investment advice. However, the most glamorous advisers, whose prestige and contacts soon won them the lion's share of the market for advice to self-administered pension funds, were the merchant banks. In the later 1960s they began to take a large amount of business from insured pension schemes, and in some cases they acquired insurance brokers specializing in pension business to facilitate their entry, much to the annoyance of the insurance companies, which had traditionally depended on these brokers for business. Among the merchant banks, Warburgs & Schroders did particularly well as competitors in the new field.[41] Faced with this plethora of advice, some pension fund managers began to divide up their funds: sharing the portfolios between several advisers and rewarding the more successful with a greater share of the portfolio management.[42]

In this growing and increasingly competitive market, the original market leaders, the insurance companies, were forced fundamentally to change the product strategy which had made them so dominant in the field of occupational pension provision by the early 1950s.[43] Already, by then, they were realizing the difficulties in marketing traditional guaranteed contracts with firmly defined contributions and benefits. The Labour government's cheap money policy was creating losses on old policies, but if it failed (as eventually it did) there would be large windfall gains to the companies on contracts predicated on low interest rates. Led by the Prudential in 1950, they introduced 'with profit' options in group pensions contracts, which allowed their clients to share in any increased returns. The Prudential's move (copied within several years by the other major insurance companies) weakened the 'Inner Circle' of life offices which had previously fixed the prices of pension contracts. Increased competition raised selling costs, and insurance brokers firmly resisted attempts to curtail their commissions. None the less, the cost of insured pension contracts declined rapidly in the 1950s, as competition increased and the high profits made by the innovators in this business were squeezed to normal levels. The new tax privileges of the 1956 Finance Act also enabled them to reduce the cost of pension contracts substantially or to offer a better benefit package for the same price. The development of 'with profit' policies meant that there was some uncertainty about future bonus levels, and this naturally led to more flexible funding arrangements. The cost of the pension in such 'controlled funding' plans was not firmly established in the initial contract, but, as in self-administered schemes, was reassessed from time to time in light of mortality experience and investment returns. This did, however, make advance contractual quotations meaningless, so that it was increasingly hard for clients to judge the value of competing offers. In effect, what an employer client now had to do was guess which life office would be the best investor in the future, for on that would depend the extent to which the employer was or was not required to make good any future deficiency in the pensions that the 'with-profit' bonuses produced.

Until the mid 1960s, these changes in product strategy were sufficient to permit conventional insured contracts to maintain their share of the market.[44] There was, however, a distinct shift in customer base. Large firms steadily deserted the insurance companies in favour of self-administered schemes, often managed by merchant banks; while the group pensions business of the life offices grew most rapidly among small- and medium-sized clients. Such firms did not typically have a bureaucratic structure and only a limited number had initially been interested in formal pension schemes. With the post-war growth of interest in tax-privileged pension savings, however, many more small firms showed an interest in these benefits for their employees. For these firms, an insurance company offered the cheapest, most convenient, and most risk-free solution to pension problems.[45] By this stage, several insurance companies had already realized that their group pension contracts offered a package of services which was fine for this market, but which did not entirely suit larger employers. The traditional core of insurance contracts – managing the risks of death (widows' benefits) or of longevity (retirement pensions) – were very valuable to small clients with up to a hundred or so employees; but medium-sized and larger employers could afford to shoulder these risks just as well as the insurance companies, since they too had the benefits of the law of large numbers on their side. Actuarial services were required by most clients, and the administrative support of an insurance company was helpful in matters such as maintaining contribution records and paying pensions. Investment advice was a fourth specialist service bundled into the typical group pension package, and was increasingly important with competition for the best 'with-profit' performance, though such services were also now offered separately by merchant banks and stockbrokers. The logical step was to split the services offered and compete more directly where competition was the strongest. From the 1950s a few insurance companies were offering what were in effect tax-exempt unit trusts to self-administered pension funds.

In 1971 the market leader, Legal & General, introduced their own 'managed fund'. Their new managed fund contracts showed clearly the 'unbundling' of services which competition was forcing on the industry quite generally.[46] Larger clients could choose just to invest the assets of their funds, deciding themselves the mix of equity, fixed-interest and property. Additionally, if they wished, they could buy further services on a fee-for-service basis, including advice on the investment mix, actuarial assessments, and administrative or advisory services. Significantly, insurance was *not* a part of these pension contracts: nothing more clearly showed that the insurance companies were not now primarily in pensions as risk managers, but rather as producers of administrative services and invest-ment advice. With this product mix, Legal & General were able to stem the loss of business to competing financial institutions and maintain their market leadership, so that by the end of the 1970s they had more pension money under management (in managed funds and traditionally bundled insurance contracts combined) than their nearest merchant bank competi-tor. The insurance companies collectively also were able to build up and maintain their share of private sector fund management in the increasingly competitive post-war conditions: in the early 1950s their share had been just over a quarter, but by 1979 was nearly a half. Sixteen billion pounds of the total of £36 billion in private sector funds was under their management,[47] the remaining £20 billion being divided among the pension funds' own managers and financial institutions such as merchant banks.

There was considerable optimism among pension managers when the benefits of these market changes were working through in the 1960s.[48] The costs of insured contracts had fallen rapidly. For self-administered pension schemes, the high returns on the equity investments (in which they had invested an increasing proportion of their portfolios) also contributed to the increasing optimism. The major problem, aside from the impending legislation on state earnings-related pensions, was the impact of inflation on the real value of pension benefits. Most of the private sector schemes in existence in 1956, when national concerns about inflation were already showing, had benefits related to the average salary (in money terms) during working life, or were fixed directly in money terms: as X pounds of pension for Y pounds of contributions. Inflation devalued these benefits and made it far easier for pension funds to meet their promises. Thus, contrary to pension fund lore, inflation proved a positive boon to the finances of funds in these circumstances.[49] Only the minority of scheme members who had pensions related to their final salary achieved, in effect, the inflation-proofing of their benefits until the time of their retirement; though even they then suffered when inflation continued to erode the (usually fixed) money level of their pension after retirement. Increasingly, however, pension trustees came to the view that they could afford to use the increased rates of return on their investments to finance improvements in benefits, and there was a gradual but sustained move to final salary schemes and other forms of compensation for inflation.[50]

These changes were costly, but they appeared justifiable in a period of improving investment returns. Actuaries had been used to interest rates in the 3–4% range, with divergences from this being temporary, and they had also been used to thinking of benefits as predictable in money terms. They were therefore at first confused when returns seemed to be rising permanently above those levels, and they resisted the attempts of some pension managers to take credit for capital gains as well as income (though the two were interchangeable in practical terms for pension funds which paid tax on neither).[51] As the surpluses accumulated in the 1960s, however, actuaries usually did increase the valuation rate of interest, sometimes making a compensating allowance for the effect of inflation on the required level of benefits. There was, however, much that was hit-or-miss in this, and actuaries were generally reluctant to think about the long-term *real* rate of interest and a *real* level of benefits, which was what in fact determined the relationship between their clients' real pensioning needs and current contributions. By the later 1960s, their confusions were being overridden by the trustees and managers of funds with clearly high rates of return which they felt could fund much higher levels of benefits, and some actuaries reluctantly accepted this. Unfortunately, in some cases they overcompensated for earlier reluctance to raise the valuation rate, and real rates of interest as high as 5% or more were implicit in some calculations of required funding rates.[52] This was higher than had been achieved over very long periods except in the recent past, and did not sufficiently discount for the one-off nature of equity appreciation in the equity boom of the 1950s and 1960s. Insurance companies, faced with competition from self-administered funds, were also tempted into declaring unrealistic bonuses on their 'with-profit' pension business in order to match the high rates of 'return' being assumed by actuaries, but they did generally act as a conservative, restraining force.[53]

The bubble burst with the oil crisis and the stock market crash of 1973–4, when it became evident to everyone that real growth in investment values was very far from likely to occur at the rate being predicted earlier. In the investment revolution of the 1950s and 1960s, equities had come to be regarded as, in effect, index-linked stock: yielding real returns in an inflationary era. However, as the conservatives in the investment world had emphasized in the 1950s, when (wrongly) advocating traditional fixed-interest stock as less risky, equities did have another characteristic: they carried the residual risks of the company sector. In the major downturn of 1973, profits fell and equities collapsed too, quite unable to sustain their apparent role as an inflation hedge. Equities appeared to have failed, moreover, at the very time when an inflation hedge was most needed. In 1974 the average return on assets was − 31%, yet wage inflation (which partly determined the level of benefits) was + 29%. Not surprisingly, there were fears that this would spell the end of funded occupational pension schemes, as similar experiences with inflation in France had done three decades earlier. Substantial improvements had been made in the level of benefits being promised to prospective pensioners, yet most employers were anxious to preserve good staff relations by meeting these commitments, which were often now expressed in final salary (and hence, virtually, in real rather than money) terms. With many funds making substantial short-term losses, actuarial valuations became more conservative, particularly in their assumptions of the long-run rate of interest, and required funding rates increased accordingly. Funds being valued in the mid 1970s showed substantial deficits and, despite the contemporary profit squeeze, major employers usually made these up at their own expense to restore the funds' long-run finances.[54]

In the long run this strategy of bailing the funds out proved sustainable, for the stock market did recover, and by the later 1970s and early 1980s respectable positive real rates of return were again being achieved. The Institute of Actuaries in London (and the independent Scottish-based Faculty of Actuaries which collaborated with it) continued to insist that actuaries must come to their own personal judgements on valuation practices, and refused to provide standard guidelines on central matters of this kind. This was frustrating to employer clients and fund members alike (it meant that no two actuarial reports were drawn up on a clearly comparable basis), but it reflected a genuine puzzlement about the real problem of predicting the future, on which their work was essentially based but which was (equally essentially) impossible. The high rates of return being assumed in the 1960s *might* have been sustainable if Britain had achieved rates of economic growth comparable with those of her continental European competitors; on the other hand, there was, contrary to common assumption, no logical reason why capitalism could not survive with negative real returns persisting indefinitely.[55] None the less, real rates of return had over long periods been around 3%, and most actuaries were by the later 1970s willing to assume conservatively that they were not in the long run going to fall more than a percentage point below that level.[56] Investment managers, moreover, seemed to agree with this prognosis, for when the government issued index-linked gilts in 1981 (giving, for the first time, a government guarantee that positive real rates would be permanently sustainable for the period of the issue) the market appeared to value them on optimistic assumptions about long-run real rates of return on other securities. The initial real yield of index-linked gilts was just above 2%, and they were soon yielding even more as fears of inflation receded. Pension fund managers may, then, be presumed from the fact that they did not bid up the price of these securities to have been confident that they could gain higher returns than this from their alternative investments.[57] Paradoxically, despite all the earlier suggestions to the contrary, real rates of return had proved easier to predict than money rates of return in a period of substantial economic uncertainty and fluctuating inflation rates. Despite all the turmoil of the investment world, the actuary who had decided a hundred years ago to forgo all concern with money interest rates and to base all his calculations on a real interest rate of 3% (as obtained at the beginning of the century) and on real benefit levels would not, in fact, have gone far wrong. However, he would, at least until recent years when the fall in the value of money benefits became a real concern to employers, quite possibly have found himself without any clients.

Part II *The shaping of the modern pensions institution*

6 Accident and design in the evolution of pensions

The process should be one of continual experiment, with those innovations that prove most generally acceptable and fitted to employees' needs, gaining ground at the expense of less satisfactory systems. It is in its capacity for continual adaptation to changing circumstances that the strength of the occupational pension movement is most evident . . .

National Association of Pension Funds,
*The Future Relationship of State and
Occupational Pension Funds*, 1968,
p. 24

The narrative of the growth of occupational pensions in the previous five chapters has shown the twentieth-century development of the system to be driven by three powerful forces: the desire for old age saving, becoming more insistent with increased longevity and greatly reinforced in recent decades by the tax advantages of pension saving; the political drive for adequate pensioning, defined originally in terms of poverty relief but ending with comprehensive income replacement objectives; and the evolving nature of the employment relationship in large bureaucratic enterprises. The latter was a major factor in the early growth of pension schemes, but the tax benefits of pension saving and the conditions for contracting out of the state pension scheme have more recently made the advantages of schemes less exclusive to large employers (and in some respects less attractive to any employer) than they were in earlier decades. The focus of the first part of this book has been on the interplay of these three forces and their impact on the growing coverage of occupational pension schemes, particularly in the private sector. I now turn to the way in which the pattern of historical evolution has shaped modern practices of pensioning and retirement: in particular, how the security of pension rights has improved, particularly for leavers; how pension benefits have been structured; and how the choice of retirement age by both employees and employers has been determined.

A Victorian employer (or his actuary) surveying the pensions institution as it exists today would find many aspects of it familiar, but many strange; he would no doubt admire some of the changes, but show a marked reserve about others. The spread of the basic idea of regular saving for old age, for example, might seem to our hypothetical Victorian to be part of the natural progress of society to which he had looked forward; the generous level of benefits provided would appear a virtuous reward for a thrifty society. Other things which puzzle us – such as why women retire at sixty but men only at sixty-five in many schemes – might seem to his male protectionism perfectly understandable, especially if he were unaware of the muddled politics from which it emerged. Other aspects of pensioning would, however, frankly amaze him. He would be surprised at the extent of compulsory retirement at a fixed chronological age, a device which, he would be convinced, was not only an affront to the old and fit, but also grossly wasteful of potentially useful labour. He would also perhaps find some difficulty in squaring the modern development of the earnings-related state pensions and final salary-related pensions with other features of our society which seem to mark it out from his own. The state scheme would appear to go well beyond poverty relief in extending the inequalities of working life into old age, and he would be surprised that such an apparently inegalitarian state measure should have been pressed, in particular by the Labour Party. Final salary schemes he would recall being opposed in his own day on the grounds that they redistributed income from the poor to the rich, yet a devotion to that end would not strike him as being one of the characteristics of modern society. He would be mystified on being told that trade unions had actually pressed for final salary pensions in recent years. He might welcome the increased preservation of leavers' rights, though he would be incredulous that employers were still willing to run schemes with this characteristic, and amazed that people appeared to accept that whether it was really preserved or not should not be known at the time of leaving but rather depend on the unknown, future rate of inflation. That we have built such a puzzling system can only be understood if the historical process by which it has arisen is understood. It is the purpose of this and the next three chapters to examine some of these issues of pension scheme design in greater detail.

Most of the members of occupational pension schemes today would be astonished to hear the view expressed (as in the opening quotation to this chapter or, more generally, by the free market advocates of private pensioning[1]) that they have a choice in the matter of pensions. Most members of modern pension schemes are compelled to join as a condition of employment; moreover, the degree of member involvement in the running of schemes has been quite low.[2] In spite of this, collective social choices have been made in the past which have profoundly influenced our present pensioning practices, and adjustments have continually been and still are regularly made to schemes at the margin. Moreover, some people do have the choice of moving from a job with a pension to the many without, and if they do they can enjoy generous tax reliefs on any pension arrangements they make privately. More important in practice, any employer who feels his pension scheme is not yielding adequate benefit to the firm can reduce or abandon his commitment to it: it is quite possible that his employees would prefer a pound in their pocket to a pound paid into the highly illiquid pension trust. This option is even more attractive in the post-1956 environment, when tax relief on savings for private pensions has been available for employees who wish to save in this form as well as for employer-organized schemes. Even before that, there was no reason why any employer who wished to give his employees the possibility of investing their money in this way should not institute a purely voluntary scheme. Indeed, many did so, and compulsory membership, particularly for manual workers, has only gradually spread to become a basic feature of modern old age saving.

It is tempting when writing of the evolution of rules and conditions in pension schemes to view the decision-making as a deliberate process in which objectives are clearly spelled out and decisively pursued by employers and employees acting to maximize their benefits from the scheme and minimize their costs. The real world of pensions has rarely been like that. The level of information available to any of the contracting parties has typically been low, for reasons which may vary from the psychological fear of finding out too much about old age (until it is too late) to the simpler but no less powerful inhibition caused by the obfuscation of much actuarial jargon which has surrounded the development of schemes. The incentives to find out more about pensions are enormous, for both employer and employees have a large financial stake in pension schemes. Yet it appears that most employees are willing to leave it to others and trust to things working out well in the end. Indeed, the feeling that things are being looked after collectively and that one will be in no worse a position than one's peers may itself be one of the reasons why the workplace – which often defines one's peer group – is a natural unit of organization for old age saving. Furthermore, the fact that scheme membership is now virtually always compulsory in a particular employment has substantially reduced the incentive for employees to acquire information, since even after they have acquired it their only means of using it is by the drastic measure of changing jobs or careers. This may explain why the level of member participation and the sophistication of member knowledge appears to be lower in a typical modern pension scheme that it was in the case of the pioneering railway pension schemes of the nineteenth century.[3]

Whatever the reasons, surveys have shown clearly that members have a very poor level of information about schemes,[4] and this is confirmed by casual observation. (In no subject of study have I discovered so quickly how little I knew before taking it up, or been so surprised afterwards about how little otherwise sane and rational colleagues knew about their own rights and pension assets.) Moreover, employers and managers appear to be no better informed. It was not uncommon, for example, for actuaries to be asked by businessmen to produce an actuarial report on the deficits or surpluses in 'money purchase' schemes (which, by their nature, cannot have such a deficit or surplus): the explanation presumably being that they had met an acquaintance whose firm (which no doubt had a different kind of scheme) had had an actuarial report, and they felt they should too![5] Lord Sinclair, the chairman of Imperial Tobacco, happily expounded on the virtues of transferability in occupational pension schemes in his maiden speech to the Lords, blissfully unaware that his own company did not provide such transferability, and considerably embarrassing his pension managers in the process.[6] In such circumstances, insurance brokers and consulting actuaries found a very ready market for their services as middlemen; where ignorance prevailed, information was sought, however lacking in impartiality it might be on crucial issues of pension policy. Equally, providers of services found it profitable to buy control of these sources of information: thus merchant banks entering the pensions market in the 1960s bought insurance brokers and consulting actuaries. Experts did, however, recognize that pensions involved wider issues than their own expertise covered. Actuaries, for example, were aware that, compared with their more certain touch in the field of insurance risks, they were acting in only a subsidiary, advisory role when they entered the field of pensions.[7]

Of course, not everyone was acting blindly in making pension decisions, and actors often had a shrewd idea of where their interest lay. Manual workers often rejected schemes that would improve their old age income only a little above the levels of means-tested benefits, and youthful workers cannily saw that the supposed generous levels of contributions being credited to them by employers were in fact worth very little to young workers.[8] But such cases arise as much from gut feelings as from adequate information; and misinformation has commonly led to the rejection of perfectly good schemes.

Another factor limiting the quality of information on which schemes are based is the unusually long-term nature of the pension commitment. A scheme will typically take sixty years to mature: that is, the younger entrants will first draw their pensions forty years after the scheme starts and may continue to draw them for several decades thereafter. It is hardly surprising, then, that most schemes have a considerable historical legacy which limits their freedom of manoeuvre. Equally, historical hazard might explain why the costs and benefits of retirement decisions are somewhat arbitrarily and unhelpfully reflected in pension levels when old age approaches, though the rules might have been fine when they were written. Few firms have stable employment conditions or constant pensioning problems over half a century or more! In the field of pensions, the constraints on action are unusual; motives are exceptionally mixed; and outcomes are not always related to objectives.

Yet the evolutionary process of market selection in competitive capitalism, tempered by state intervention, may produce results which are not wholly dissimilar to a more deliberate process of decision-making, even if the actors involved are only imperfectly aware of the issues. Such an evolutionary model of economic change[9] may be the most accurate description of the process by which our modern pension institution has arrived at its present state. The normal mechanism of selection in such an evolutionary process is the decline and bankruptcy of institutional forms which prove inappropriate, and, as we have seen, some once-dominant pension institutions, such as friendly societies, have been subject to such competitive elimination.[10] However, British pension funds in general, in contrast to those of, for example, France and the USA, have not shown much tendency to liquidation or bankruptcy; and such a market selection mechanism is therefore an unlikely candidate.[11] The most powerful evolutionary mechanism appears rather to be a positive one: that is, the perception by employers in the long run of real benefits from schemes, however confused or possibly irrelevant the motives that led to their adoption might originally have been.

Occupational pension schemes organized by the employer seem to have been no better conceived and no better managed than other forms of old age saving which proved less resilient. Motives for setting up pension schemes, as with all questions of motivation in historical study, are among the most difficult to pin down. Attempts to spread habits of thrift to employees or paternalistic concern for their poverty in old age may be powerful triggers for the establishment of schemes in many firms, rather than the more calculating logic of internal labour markets aimed at tying the employee to the firm. Yet even schemes which start out with an altruistic or paternalistic impulse have often been recognized later as having favourable effects from a personnel management viewpoint: a point made in the opening decades of this century by the few businessmen who then had long-running experience of the usefulness of pensions in labour management.[12] The *ex post* reasons for retaining a scheme may be more important in explaining their survival and shape than the initial motivation for setting them up. Employer-based old age savings were subject to the same actuarial risks as other forms of long-run savings, such as those once organized by friendly societies or trade unions. The actuaries who advised pension funds got their predictions wrong as frequently for employer-based funds as for others. Yet, crucially, employers' schemes have been distinguished by the ability and willingness of their employer sponsors to bail them out when they have proved inadequate or have shown deficits.[13] Repeatedly, employers faced with the threat of emerging deficits in underfunded schemes have chosen to raise their contributions rather than to abandon the schemes: thus, whereas in the nineteenth-century schemes were typically based on equal contributions from employers and members, by the 1970s employers' contributions had reached three times the level of members' contributions.[14] Competition both in the labour market and in the product market prevents such decisions in the long run from being capricious: at least, unless other competitors make the same mistakes. It is to a process of this kind, based on an evolving recognition of the advantages of supporting pension schemes for particular purposes at particular times, rather than on rational deliberation with perfect foresight, that we must look in determining why the pensions institution as it now exists has developed the form that it has.

7 *Pensions in peril? Security, solvency and vesting*

Whether a scheme is successful or not is only partly a question of
where it is now: that is to say, its current degree of solvency. The
main driving force is the ability of the employer to fulfil his
obligations and to increase his contributions wherever necessary.
Solvency is therefore often inextricably bound up with the resources of
the employer.

F. M. Redington (Prudential),
Presidential Address, *Journal
of the Institute of Actuaries*,
LXXXV, 1959, 6

There are several tests by which one might judge a system of pensioning for
old age. A *sine qua non* is that it should be affordable by the employer and/or
employee. Equally fundamental from the point of view of the employee is
that the lifetime savings implicit in a pension scheme should lead to secure
build-up of entitlements sufficient to support old age retirement. The
private occupational pensions movement, at least until recently, has quite
failed to meet this test. In the twentieth-century decades taken as a whole,
neither the majority of those who have been members of occupational
schemes nor the majority of their dependants have ever drawn a pension of
any kind.[1] In the early days this was quite often because death intervened,
and widows' benefits were not initially well developed.[2] Even in schemes
designed in the days before the First World War for middle-class employees
(with their greater longevity), it was usually expected that, of those who
joined at age twenty and stayed with an employer throughout their working
life, more than four in ten would be dead before they reached the normal
retirement age of between sixty and sixty-five.[3] Increased longevity in the
course of the twentieth century has greatly improved the prospect of
pension fund members' surviving to pension age. In the first decade of the
present century a twenty-year-old male could expect to live until sixty-three,

and a woman to sixty-six; by the late 1970s twenty-year-olds would expect to survive much longer: to seventy-two for men and seventy-eight for women.[4]

The risk of early death has declined, but scheme members confiding their old age savings to the newly emerging institutions which service their pension needs have been subject to a changing and uncertain exposure to different collective risks. In many countries, these risks have materialized in catastrophic form, with the collapse of the pension system transforming the nature of pensioning. In France, for example, a well-developed system of collective, earnings-related, funded, employer-based pensions was in place by the 1930s, and in some respects was better developed than the British system. Yet in the turmoil of wartime occupation and subsequent inflation it failed, and had to be replaced by a more comprehensive system of levies on the working population to rescue the old whose savings had disappeared.[5] In the United States, an occupational pension system similar to Britain's (indeed, one which had originally drawn its inspiration from British railway schemes) was put under severe strain by the Great Depression of the 1930s. The consequent collapses and reorganizations of schemes were one of the factors behind the introduction in 1935 of federal earnings-related pensions for aged Americans.[6] More recently, bankruptcies of pension funds in the United States brought home the continuing risks to pensioners, and in 1975 led to a greater degree of government regulation of pension institutions in America under the Employee Retirement Income Security Act (ERISA).[7]

In Britain there have been cases of insolvency leading to the loss of pension entitlements, and these too were usually in periods of 'general social dislocation';[8] but such cases appear to have been rare and temporary phenomena.[9] When a shipping company, the Anchor Line, went into liquidation in 1935, it was found that the trustees had not regularly collected and invested company contributions and the pension fund could not cover three-quarters of its accrued liabilities. There followed a prolonged and bitter dispute between pensioners (whose pensions were cut) and current contributors (who lost not only their jobs but all pension entitlements) in which only the lawyers could win.[10] More recently also some small funds have been unable to meet their liabilities following the financial collapse of the sponsoring employer, and members have lost their entitlements.[11] In general, however, insolvency has not been a problem for British pension funds.

The reasons for this are worth considering. In part, they arise simply from the fact that British funds have not had to meet as serious external threats as American or French funds: the depression in Britain in the 1930s was far less serious than that in the USA; inflation in Britain in the 1940s was far less serious than that in France. However, the crucial factor in all cases of external threat has been the ability and willingness of the employer, or some agent acting in his stead, to stand behind the pension scheme. In this respect, the fact that pension entitlements were more common in public utilities and the government sector in Britain (which were larger than in many other countries in the crucial period of pension fund expansion) has been a major strength of the system. The state has in the case of many pension schemes for its employees simply operated on a pay-as-you-go basis, but since the secure credit of the state has stood behind such unfunded pension schemes, the claims have been honoured. Where there has been a funded pension scheme in the state sector, specifically accumulated funds have often proved inadequate to meet the pension promises made, but the taxpayers have usually bailed out the staff and rescued their pension entitlements. In the case of nationalized industries, captive consumers performed the same function. For instance, the Post Office Corporation established a badly funded pension scheme in 1969 which soon became the biggest in Britain. Massive deficits then emerged, but the prices of postal services and telecommunications over which the Corporation had a monopoly were raised to correct the problem, so that pensions remained secure.[12]

In the private sector, the bulk of pension rights in the period of rapid growth from the 1930s through the 1950s were accrued in insured contracts, so that security depended principally not on the solvency of the employer but on that of the insurance company. From the end of the nineteenth century, the life companies had an extremely good solvency record; and the industry, through the British Insurance Association and the Life Offices' Association, was able to develop an impressive system of self-regulation to maintain its reputation by avoiding losses to policy-holders.[13] Pension business was arguably the longest-term and actuarially the most difficult they had to deal with, but the offices transacting it were among the most secure and well managed of the insurance companies. Particularly for small employers in relatively unstable industries, the financial strength of the insurance companies was a valuable tool in winning the confidence of the staff in the long-run security of a planned scheme. Their financial security was also a major instrument in the efforts of insurance companies to sell to employers who had been worried about actuarial deficits in their own self-administered funds, or had heard of such problems in other firms.

Besides public sector pensions and insured pensions, there were, as we have seen, many self-administered pensions schemes with no such ultimate guarantor. In these the rights were secured under a variety of legal forms, including balance-sheet reserves, statutory funds, friendly societies, and unfunded and *ex gratia* arrangements; but overwhelmingly the most important legal form for new pension schemes in the private sector from the 1920s was the separately constituted trust fund. This provided a significant degree of protection for prospective pensioners. Funding in principle forced the employer to face up to the cost implications of his pension policy at the time the liabilities were accruing. The trust form further meant that once the employer had paid over his contributions to the trustees, he (or his creditors) could not usually lay hands on the funds again.[14] Thus, if the employing firm went bankrupt or changed ownership, the trustees were still able to pay current pensioners and to buy deferred annuities for current contributing members. Many of the cases of pension expectations being frustrated were in unfunded schemes, without this protection. In the celebrated *Daily News* case of 1960, for example, a shareholder prevented an employer from compensating employees for the loss of pension rights in a merger.[15] With the trust fund form, however, at least to the extent that liabilities were fully funded and the assets were well invested, there was a strong possibility that the members of a pension fund would not suffer if the employer met adverse circumstances. Even in once-substantial firms which suffered severe competitive setbacks, pension liabilities initially accrued up to forty or more years before have typically been honoured. Indeed, in many such cases, the pension fund of a company may well be worth more than the ailing company itself.[16]

This protection can, however, be compromised by a number of practices quite legally adopted by pension fund trustees and by employers who may be (and indeed often are) the same people. There is, for example, no prohibition in trust law of the investment of fund assets in the employing firm. Initially this was a common choice of trustees, especially in the case of extremely safe public utilities such as railways or other leading employers, who in the nineteenth century were frequently as secure as (indeed, sometimes more secure than) local banks and insurance companies. Many employers did, however, prefer not to expose their employees to the double jeopardy of losing their jobs *and* their pension rights in a bankruptcy, and most trust funds appear to have aimed at a wider spread of investment. Indeed, if firms did not wish to reduce the investment risk in this way, they could just as easily fund a pension scheme through the balance-sheet reserve method, which also exposed the funds to claims by creditors and hence the employees to double jeopardy. Thus, it was natural that the pioneering Colman's trust deed of 1900 explicitly banned investment in the employing firm to protect employees. None the less, many other major companies at that time, such as Lever Brothers, still deposited their pension funds directly with the company or invested in its preference shares. A large minority of funds like Lever Brothers' remained invested in parent firms, either as a matter of policy or for a variety of special reasons: a desire by employer trustees to forestall take-over bids, a gift of shares on the death of the owner, in order to enable an owner to reduce his shareholding while retaining effective control, or as part of a strategy to minimize the company's tax bill.[17]

The potential conflicts of interest which arose when trustees, often nominated by an employer, were legally bound to pursue the interests of the beneficiaries, but also had the employer's interests at heart, are obvious. Cases have occasionally surfaced in the courts. In 1976, for example, Mr Robert Evans, a pensioner of the London Co-operative Society, successfully sued his fund's trustees for breach of trust following their loan to the employing society at damagingly low rates of interest.[18] A tinge of unrespectability also adhered to the practice of self-investment as a result of increasing state regulation of funds. In 1927 the Superannuation and Other Trust Funds (Validation) Act limited self-investment (in the minority of registered funds to which it applied) to secured loans to companies with a good dividend record. More recently, the Occupational Pensions Board has defined 10% self-investment as normally the maximum acceptable limit for funds contracting out of the state earnings-related pension scheme (now including most funds). The modern tendency has been to regard the practice of self-investment with increasing suspicion, though the 'incorporationist' origins of schemes and the advantage of unifying the interests of employer and employee in common risks are still sometimes claimed as advantages of self-investment, and the practice survives.[19] It is, however, now rare for a very large proportion of the fund to be invested in one employing firm.

Even when a widely invested trust fund was created, it was by no means obvious that the trustees would in the long run be able to meet all the claims upon the fund. These claims had to be predicted for forty or fifty or more years ahead, and the accuracy of the predictions depended on a variety of factors. The motto of the Institute of Actuaries – 'certum ex incertis' – represented their idealized objective, but actuarial 'science' was in fact far from precise, involving as it did the systematic use of past experience to guess at the future. Even on issues like the mortality of employees and pensioners, there was a surprising divergence from the experience tables of life company annuitants on which the actuaries initially based their work for pension schemes. Much of this was because of different forms of selection in the case of special employment groups: death in service was typically less common than they predicted, for example, because employees who were chronically sick tended to leave through ill-health before they died, and thus exit from the population at risk.[20] In many schemes, also, the longevity of pensioners was underestimated initially, perhaps because of the improved effectiveness of antibiotics in controlling broncho-pneumonic diseases.[21] Another possibility is that scheme members and pensioners are themselves a select group of lives: perhaps because of the superior conditions of employees in internal labour markets, or because pensioning itself improves the longevity of pensioners by sweetening the pre-terminal stage of life.[22] The decades of experience tables built up by both insurance companies and consulting actuaries were, however, by the 1950s such that they could speak of the forecasting of the mortality of members and pensioners as no longer a serious problem.[23] Soon afterwards, moreover, as widows' pensions became more common in the better schemes, any change in mortality compromised the schemes' predictions far less than was typical earlier, for in part the two kinds of pensions were mutually balancing when mortality experience changed.[24]

The real actuarial difficulty for the pensioning institutions was not in handling mortality risks but in predicting the rate of return on investment. In principle, it had initially seemed that they only needed to predict the money rate of return, and, as we have seen, this is the basis on which they generally operated until the 1960s.[25] The money liabilities could be matched against money contributions: in many schemes X pounds of contributions bought Y pounds of benefits and the problem was simply to find fixed-interest investments of the appropriate maturity date to be sure that Y pounds in benefits could be paid. Inflation made the fulfilment of such contractual promises trivially easy, but the resulting pension levels failed to meet the real concerns of employers and employees for adequate pensioning to facilitate retirement. In the severe inflation of 1914–20, these problems first became familiar to pension scheme administrators.[26] By the 1930s, however, they were facing the opposite problem of falling prices. This raised the real value of the money pensions they were contracted to pay, but money rates of return on the investments available to them were falling, and many pension funds were thus soon showing deficits.[27] Exceptionally, the reaction of some funds was to cut back benefits. In Lloyds Bank for example, the pension age was raised, while Joseph Lucas Ltd cut back the level of pension benefits. Other firms met the stresses of falling prices and investment returns by raising contributions from employees, or, more typically, by boosting the employer subsidy to maintain scheme solvency. From 1940 onwards, price inflation again came to the rescue. Falling money values devalued in real terms the pension liabilities of most funds, while contributing also to the substantial increases in money investment returns, especially for those funds investing in equities.[28] Actuaries, I have noted, found some difficulty in predicting (or even, given the confusions between income and capital gains, in tracking) the real changes implied. Their actuarial reports, typically carried out at three- or five-year intervals,[29] came up with widely differing recommendations on the desirable level of funding for pension schemes, depending on the underlying assumptions adopted. The wider adoption of final salary schemes, which made pension liabilities inherently less predictable, also increased uncertainties about desirable funding levels, and reduced the financial discipline of the funding requirement. It is perhaps surprising, in view of these factors, that more pension funds did not become insolvent. In general, however, the effect of unforeseen changes in the twentieth century was to benefit rather than compromise the solvency of the funds: inflation has been more common than deflation. Given that the bulk of pension promises, until recently, were denominated in money terms, this meant that pension funds were able to meet their money obligations, while, in effect, welshing on their promises in real terms. Many schemes used the unexpected surpluses created by the combination of this with higher money investment returns to upgrade the benefits. They were not, however, obliged to do so, and, as we shall see, employers skewed these improvements to serve their own objectives. It is somewhat surprising in these circumstances that pension managers were frequently heard to complain of inflation as the bane of their lives. In fact, nothing could be further from the truth: inflation enabled many pension funds to achieve overall solvency and a flexibility in changing real benefits which would not otherwise have been possible, and which, indeed, seemed to many beneficiaries undesirable.[30]

Adjustments to contributions and/or to benefits were more natural in pension schemes than in straight insurance contracts, because pensions, by their very nature, were subject to a wider range of variation in actuarial experience as a result of decisions by the contracting parties. Employers could influence the liabilities of the scheme by encouraging early or deferred retirement or by adopting mandatory retirement. Their policies on these issues varied over time (according, for example, to general labour market conditions or distinct company needs), and they varied in a way actuaries could not reasonably be expected to predict. Equally, employees could unilaterally increase or decrease the real liabilities of a scheme by voluntarily leaving (greatly reducing liabilities under the rules of most schemes); and quit rates did in fact vary greatly between different decades.[31]

The work of actuaries in these conditions can be seen not as a precise measurement of known contingencies, but as a kind of radar tracking system, focused on where the fund is at one point in time, but very much concerned also with where it will be in the future.[32] The idea that a pension fund should always be 'solvent' – in the sense that long-term liabilities should exactly equal current plus future assets – was impossible to realize, for long-term liabilities and assets were not perfectly foreseeable. Instead, actuaries attempted to give signals as they saw that fundamental assumptions that had once generally been considered reasonable needed modifying in the light of experience. In the 1930s, for example, this meant signalling lower valuation rates of interest and lower withdrawal rates; in 1974 it meant greater conservatism about real rates of return; by the 1980s greater optimism on investment returns could be signalled. Employers and employees could, however, accept or reject the suggestions in an actuarial report, and the general tendency until quite recently was to accept a level of funding which actuaries considered inadequate. Most pension schemes (other than insured schemes in which the insurance company had an obvious interest in enforcing realism, and which in consequence promised lower but more realistic benefits) in fact ran with a substantial excess of liabilities over assets.[33] The payment of pensions at the level envisaged thus often depended ultimately on the continuing goodwill of the employer in standing behind the fund and making up deficits.[34]

Legally, in early trust deeds the employer frequently could not change the level of benefit: he could only opt out of a scheme in the future while maintaining any accrued benefits intact. Tightly drawn trust deeds appeared initially to offer a valuable guarantee of employee rights. Yet, as experience developed, it became evident that the real guarantee of rights was continuing employer support, and that tightly drawn trust deeds would in fact discourage such support in a rapidly changing environment. Schemes had to be changed to harmonize benefits with those of the evolving state scheme; to gain new tax advantages; to meet emerging employment and redundancy situations; or to improve benefits or increase funding levels. Modifications were, then, explicitly provided for in later trust deeds,[35] though the trustees' freedom of manoeuvre was sometimes restricted, by, for example, a requirement that 90% of the members should approve any change. Occasionally such changes involved the reduction of benefits and/or an increase in member contributions. However, in the post-war period, when deficits have emerged or benefits have been improved, the bulk of the cost has fallen increasingly on employers. The collective risk of pension funds has, then, been minimized not by the work of lawyers or actuaries (though both have played a small part) but by the continuing usefulness of pension schemes to the personnel management or labour recruitment objectives of employers. Even when unexpected changes enabled employers to get out of their liabilities, they frequently chose not to do so in order to maintain employee goodwill. The improved national insurance pensions of 1946 would have allowed some employers to cease paying occupational pensions under scheme rules, many of which by then allowed adjustments to take account of state pensions. In fact, many chose not to make any reductions at all.[36]

Occupational pension schemes run by employers have been as prone to develop actuarial deficits as nineteenth-century worker-controlled union or friendly society funds. The latter fell into desuetude as state benefits took over their functions and as the younger members simply refused to adhere to the solidarity between generations on which they fundamentally rested.[37] But, in the case of employer-run schemes, the willingness of employers to fund their deficits has led to their continuing growth and healthy survival. More recently, schemes have tended to be more fully funded,[38] partly because of increased pressure from trade unions and employees to entrench their rights, and partly because government regulation has increased the power of actuarial reports in persuading employers to make up deficits. Following the crash of the stock market and of property values in 1974, for example, major firms spent large sums in making up actuarial deficits on their pension funds, and it was relatively rare for benefits to be cut back seriously as they had been in many firms in the 1930s.[39] From 1978, contracting out of the state earnings-related pension scheme has required Occupational Pensions Board (OPB) approval for funding of guaranteed minimum pensions (GMPs), though currently the levels of GMPs are not sufficient for this test to constitute a severe standard. There have recently been calls for more full-blooded regulation of pension funds, and clarification of trustee duties,[40] but the government has preferred to maintain arm's-length regulation through the OPB, together with the degree of self-regulation within the framework of trust law which the industry readily accepts. This so far appears to have served it as least as well in avoiding widespread insolvency as the more interventionist policies common in other countries.

The pension scheme in a firm pursuing incorporationist personnel strategies is an important part of internal labour market mechanisms. The collective nature of the risks may be seen as one of the advantages of such a scheme, reinforcing mutual dependencies and compelling cooperative behaviour. The most serious limitation on the value of pensions has, however, not been exposure to collective risk, but rather the very individual question of forfeit of pension rights on leaving the job, a characteristic no less central to the original purpose of many schemes. Much ink has been spilt on whether it is correct to speak in this context of 'rights', 'entitlements', or even 'expectations', for the rules of schemes are usually quite explicit in denying any such 'rights' to leavers. But the popular usage represents a central and very real fact: in the past, many people who had pension rights in employment could no longer expect any pension when they were dismissed,[41] or when they voluntarily changed employment. In recent decades, several million people every decade – a large proportion of members of pension schemes – lost all or most of their accrued pension rights on leaving their employer, and had to start afresh accruing rights with a new employer. Only for a favoured few, usually senior managerial staff, was it possible to negotiate compensation for lost rights as part of the remuneration package from the new employer.

The most difficult cases, and the ones most sympathetically treated by employers on a voluntary basis, were redundant employees. Early retirement pensions were frequently offered to soften the blow when technical change or declines in market position compelled a reduction in the labour force, with older workers being offered the most generous terms to quit. In the rules of many early schemes employees were more favourably treated if they were dismissed on account of redundancy than if they voluntarily withdrew. Moreover, employers often topped up the benefits specified in the rules in order to facilitate redundancy. Pensions were already being used in this way in the 1930s: in the flour-milling industry to facilitate rationalization and in the Bank of England to retire clerks who were replaced by their mechanization programme. In the current recession also, firms wishing to cut back employment severely have commonly found pensioning off older workers an efficient means of doing so. This practice preserves the goodwill of a young and effective work force, though in many cases the substantial benefits offered are still *ex gratia* rather than a formal right of pension scheme members.

The most serious failing of the occupational pension movement as a vehicle for old age saving remained in its treatment of those who, voluntarily or otherwise, changed jobs. Before 1950, the question of preserving rights received very little attention. The more liberal actuaries and pension scheme administrators occasionally accepted the desirability of facilitating transfers between schemes.[42] Their pious remarks did, however, fly in the face of the main purpose of pension funds as originally conceived by many employers, which was to encourage employees to remain with the firm. The loss of rights by leavers was fundamental to this purpose, though in most contributory schemes leavers did at least gain a refund of their own contributions, sometimes with an accrued interest payment.[43] The latter provision was usually a *sine qua non* of staff acceptance of a contributory scheme and was the norm in insured schemes. In non-contributory schemes leavers typically got nothing, and employers who wished to create a particularly strong incentive for stayers thus often chose this route to pensioning. Such provisions were, moreover, fundamental to the financial viability of many schemes. The forfeits of employers' contributions by leavers were in most schemes essential to the continued financial health of the funds; without such forfeits, pensions simply could not have been paid to other staff at the level envisaged.[44]

This quite fundamental characteristic disqualified the occupational pension movement as it existed in the 1950s from taking its place at the centre of old age saving provisions. Criticisms on this account were, as we have seen, a major plank in Labour's plans for a state earnings-related pension scheme and a major embarrassment for the defenders of occupational pensions.[45] The typical employee in Britain has at least five employers in the course of his working life, and many are even more mobile.[46] This inevitably limits the time over which pension rights are accrued, and those retiring have typically had much less than a full working life of accrued rights from their last employment alone.[47] Of course, given the nature of the internal labour markets of which pensions are a part, members of pension schemes are less mobile than the labour force as a whole. Modern econometric studies using cross-section data on large samples of employees have shown that the pensionless are significantly more likely to engage in job search and/or to change jobs than those with pension rights.[48] Despite retrospective complaints from job leavers about loss of rights, survey evidence also confirms quite wide knowledge among those affected of the implications for pension rights of resigning.[49] Even so, pension schemes are and always have been unable permanently to tie the majority of employees by their 'golden chains';[50] and outside labour market opportunities can still provide a powerful countervailing attraction. Before the First World War, actuaries expected most employees, even in the conventionally steady jobs in railways and banks which typically offered pensions, to leave schemes before they qualified for a pension. In the 1920s, and even more in the 1930s, high unemployment rates reduced job mobility, and actuaries modified schemes to assume much lower quit rates, and hence lower gains from forfeit of employer contributions. Since the War, however, there has been a substantial increase in mobility among pension fund members, and there were windfall gains to many funds in the late 1940s and early 1950s from unexpectedly high forfeits of employers' contributions by leavers. More recent surveys have measured an increasing tendency of labour turnover among members of pension funds: 7% of occupational pension scheme members in the private sector left their jobs in 1963, by 1971 the figure was 10%, and by 1979 12%. (In the public sector, by contrast, there was only a small increase, from 7% to 8%.)[51]

Whether this increased mobility is optimal from a broader, national point of view is problematical. Policy-makers in the 1950s and 1960s frequently stressed that increased job mobility was a prerequisite for faster economic growth. Yet there is also reason to believe that loyalty, stability, and continuity of employment can advance economic efficiency; indeed, internal labour markets are created by firms which believe precisely that. As political criticism of the forfeits by leavers gathered pace in the 1950s, therefore, employers attempted to maintain a low public profile, but privately did all they could to impress upon opinion-formers and government that action to enforce the preservation of pension rights would be ill-advised.[52] They pointed to the economic benefits of reducing labour turnover; to the greatly increased cost of pensions for stayers if preservation were enforced; and to the unfairness of restricting employers who did pay pensions when other employers were quite free to pay no pension at all. Despite substantial pressure from MPs and publicity campaigns by aggrieved job changers, which won some public sympathy,[53] the employers were generally successful in heading off criticism. In 1966, for example, the joint advisory body of employers and unions at the Ministry of Labour produced an inconclusive report favouring preservation, but failing to agree on any really practical steps to achieve it.[54] Meanwhile, voluntary moves towards increased transferability on the part of individual funds made progress at only a token pace.[55] Such moves were obviously designed to head off criticism, rather than tackling the problem seriously. Government was, moreover, not in a strong position to argue the moral case for more liberal transfers, for even its own employees (while granted excellent terms for transfers within the public sector) were usually deprived of their pension rights if they moved to the private sector.[56]

By this time, pension rights were for many people a significant proportion of old age savings, and the enhanced value of tax concessions in the post-war period had led many to accept pensions as a tax-efficient savings vehicle.[57] It was, then, increasingly unrealistic to take the view advanced by employers. Yet they were abetted in perpetuating the penalties for leavers by the views of older and more settled employees. These were often precisely the ones who became employee trustees or otherwise influenced company pensions policy; and they were, in a sense, the beneficiaries of the policy of penalizing leavers. Even among the leavers themselves, criticism of employer policy was muted by a feature of many schemes which these employees found extremely attractive. While pension rights were not transferable, most pension scheme members on leaving were offered a refund of their own contributions.[58] The popularity of this is attested by the evidence from the relatively few liberal employers who did offer to preserve leavers' pensions.[59] Even in such cases, the majority of leavers chose to take only a refund of their own contributions rather than a deferred pension based on those contributions *and* their employers' accrued contributions. It is not obvious that this choice was a perverse one: the refunds were taxed at an absurdly low rate,[60] and for young leavers were frequently as valuable as deferred pensions.[61] Moreover, for most employees, quite realistic expectations of inflation reducing the value of deferred pensions (which were typically fixed in money terms) made a pound in the hand worth rather more than two pounds in the pension fund.[62] Others preferred to spend the money while they could enjoy it and rely on state means-tested pension supplementation in old age: again, not necessarily foolish for those with low incomes and high costs of borrowing for current consumption.

Defenders of the occupational pension movement, who knew that the absence of preservation for leavers was its Achilles' heel, suggested the withdrawal of tax relief for funds which did not permit it.[63] Insurance company managers recognized that they would get nowhere with their clients if they attempted to promote purely voluntary agreements on vesting rights, and felt that legal compulsion would be required for any progress to be made.[64] Both options were discussed in government circles throughout the 1950s and 1960s, with legal compulsion eventually becoming the favoured choice. However, the Boyd-Carpenter state graduated pension scheme in 1961 side-stepped the issue by limiting the necessary preservation requirement for contracted-out schemes to the minuscule sums which the state graduated pension provided. In the 1970s, opinion advanced more clearly toward state intervention; both the Conservative and Labour Parties were convinced that legislative compulsion to preserve pensions in all schemes should go ahead. The clause in the 1973 Social Security Act which required occupational pension schemes to preserve the pension rights of leavers who were at least twenty-six years of age and had five or more years' service did, then, survive the inter-party wrangling in which Barbara Castle overturned the Joseph scheme. This new compulsory vesting requirement was effective from 1975 for newly approved schemes and from 1980 for all schemes. Thereafter, employees who left a firm after accumulating pension rights were sure of retaining something, and the option of taking contribution refunds for post-1975 service was now only available to those under twenty-six years old or with less than five years post-1975 service. The 1973 Act became fully effective in the 1980s, when it made a striking difference to the number of leavers taking preserved benefits. In Unilever, for example, which had had liberal transfer provisions from several decades earlier, only around 10% of the leavers had opted for preservation, but by the 1980s the majority of leavers were retaining preserved pensions.

The level of compulsory vested rights of leavers depended on the complex rules devised for the different kinds of scheme,[65] but, crucially in the period in which it was implemented, it depended also on the rate of inflation, for there was no requirement that 'preserved' pensions should be inflation-proofed. Since by the late 1970s inflation was rapidly accelerating, a large part of the potential benefit of preservation was lost. Indeed, many of those who supposedly benefited from the new legal requirements, were, in fact, worse off than if they had merely received the return of their own contributions, since preserved pensions fixed in money terms were more than halved in real value. There was, moreover, an expectation that continuing, more moderate rates of inflation in the 1980s would further ineluctably erode their value. The Castle earnings-related scheme did something to counteract this, for it required contracted-out schemes to preserve a 'guaranteed minimum pension' (GMP), equivalent to the state inflation-proofed, earnings-related pensions for leavers (of whatever age) with five years' service. The state pensions which had to be matched were indexed to national average earnings, and schemes which felt they could not guarantee this could, effectively, get state aid to guarantee it. The Act came into force in 1978, taking full effect (under the five-year vesting rule) from 1983. The 1973 and 1975 Acts together greatly increased the take-up of preserved pensions. They also made preservation more attractive, particularly for lower-paid workers, for whom the guarantee of revaluation up to the level of state earnings-related pensions represented more or less complete inflation-proofing. The benefits were for a time limited by the practice of 'franking': that is, schemes were permitted to use money benefits accrued from earlier years to offset the GMP indexing requirements, so that the net change in the value of preserved pensions could for many years be nil. This, together with the effect of rising inflation, meant that public disquiet at the effective loss of pension rights for leavers remained.[66] In 1985 the government responded to this disquiet by abolishing franking and also extended the existing preservation provision to require inflation-proofing of all pensions by the rate of inflation or 5% per annum, whichever was the lesser. The latter requirement was suggested by the Occupational Pensions Board as a compromise affordable to the schemes. However, as members of the Board themselves recognized, it effectively meant that leavers simply did not know whether their pensions were preserved or not: that no longer depended on pension law or the employment contract, but on the unknown future rate of inflation.[67] Equally, employers could not clearly establish in advance what the cost of the preservation requirements would be in real terms. It seems unlikely that such a badly designed compromise can survive and quiet public or employer doubts which have been raised in this debate, but which are still not resolved. Yet camels ('horses designed by a committee') do have a habit of succeeding in the right climate, and this absurd and unsatisfactory compromise may perhaps be expected to survive if inflation remains in single figures.

Have the pension rights of leavers became more secure in consequence of the package of legislative changes of the 1970s and 1980s? One might imagine that a clear answer to the question would be possible, if the reforms had achieved their objectives. Unfortunately this is not the case. Certainly it is now the norm for scheme members who leave their employer either to transfer their pension entitlements (within the public sector) or to receive a deferred pension (as is normal in the private sector). Those leaving after less than five years' service in a contracted-out scheme receive the guaranteed minimum pension required by the state earnings-related scheme. For the remainder of their pension entitlement, the situation remains as it was before: they are normally permitted to take a refund of their own contributions (which are still taxed at a low rate) and are usually not encouraged to take the small deferred pensions they have accrued. For those leaving a company pension scheme after more than five years, the scheme is now obliged to offer a transfer or a deferred pension: first up to the level of the state guaranteed minimum pension, and, after that level, inflation-proofed up to a maximum of 5% per annum. If inflation is at the higher levels experienced in the last ten years, then that guarantee will leave many deferred pensioners in the 1980s and 1990s as badly off in real income terms as before. Only if inflation is held below 5% will pension funds have been effectively obliged to honour their promises in real terms to all fund members, and to abandon the long-standing practice of penalizing leavers which was once a major *raison d'être* of the schemes.

8 *Designing the benefit structure*

---

the only pension fund really worth considering is a final salary
scheme, and I would like to go further than that and say that the
scheme whereby pensions automatically increase after retirement
according to the cost of living, if you can afford it, is an ideal
scheme . . .

G. Ross Goobey (Imperial Tobacco
Pension Funds) in Association of
Superannuation and Pension Funds,
Autumn Conference 1960, p. 41

Pension schemes, when they were inaugurated, usually promised a level of
retirement benefits in an apparently firm formula, which was felt, at the
time, to suit the needs of employer and members alike. When retirement
came – forty years later for young members of newly inaugurated schemes –
it was rare for the original benefit structure to have been retained. The
twentieth-century experience so far thus suggests that pension promises are
not firm, but are subject to quite frequent alteration. As we saw in the
previous chapter, alterations are subject to certain legal safeguards, but are
principally determined by the needs of the employment contract and the
financial well-being of the fund. These factors might be expected to produce
a rich variety in pension benefit formulae, and in the past they have done so.
More recently, however, there has been a remarkable convergence of
pension schemes on what appears to be a standard design. By 1979, there
was surprising uniformity in the basic formulas by which pensions were
determined.[1] Ninety-two percent of occupational pension scheme members
could look forward to a pension related to earnings in the last year or years
of employment: the 'final salary' formula. There were variations only in
detail around this formula: sometimes it was the best three out of the last ten
years, giving a better pension for some individuals than merely the last year
of earnings; sometimes commission and overtime were excluded. Typically,
schemes offered a fixed proportion of final salary for each year of service:
the 'salary–service' principle. An accrual rate of one-sixtieth of final salary,

giving a pension of two-thirds ($40 \times \frac{1}{60}$) of final salary for those with forty years' service, was overwhelmingly the most common in the private sector. For manual workers, for whom state pensions provide a higher proportion of retirement income replacement, one-eightieths were also common. In the public sector, one-eightieths were the norm, but, in addition, a lump sum equivalent to three years' pension (one and a half years' salary) was usually paid, as had been the case in the civil service since the beginning of the century.

The one-eightieths annuity and one-and-a-half times final salary lump sum formula was roughly equivalent to a pension of one-sixtieths without lump sum. The option of commuting part of the pension for a tax-free lump sum has recently been offered quite generally in private sector schemes also: only 8% of members of private sector schemes did not have this option by 1979. Another very common feature of modern pension formulas is provision for widows: only 6% of male scheme members by 1979 had no provision of this kind. Commonly, widows by then could expect half of the husband's pension, though a few schemes did offer only the guaranteed minimum pension required by the state scheme.

This uniformity in benefit formulas is something quite new in pension schemes. It would have surprised an observer of the industry a mere twenty years ago, when a much richer diversity of practice among different employers was common. Variety and flexibility were, indeed, claimed as two of the great advantages of private occupational pension provision over the uniformity imposed by state schemes.[2] The new uniformity has emerged partly as a result of standard incentives provided by the strict contracting-out provisions of the state scheme. But, as we shall see, it also arises from tax incentives and from the reaction of pension funds to the central post-war challenge of inflation, as well as from incentives generated by the spread of rules enforcing retirement at a fixed age. There are still some areas where there is little uniformity, notably in the field of inflation-indexing of pensions being paid, a point on which, however, the earlier advocates of variety in provision would surely find it embarrassing to plead the merits of their case. The design of pension formulas is, moreover, one of the paradoxical areas of pension policy-making in which short-run pressures and limited perceptions have created a system which may not have desirable long-run characteristics. However, as we shall see, some aspects of modern pension design are intimatley rooted in the needs of employers and, as such, may prove enduring, given the importance of employer support to the survival of schemes.

The dominance of final salary formulas is a recent development, though some final salary pensions in the civil service and banking date back to the nineteenth century. Indeed, when pensioning was largely *ex gratia*, and hence typically determined at the time of retirement, some kind of relation to what the employee was already being paid was natural, and was carried over into many schemes in banks and elsewhere when they were formalized. With the development of contributory funds with a large savings element, however, alternative formulas developed more legitimacy. Hence, in the first six decades of this century, it became common for salary–service pensions to be based on average salary throughout the whole of service rather than on final salary, and there was also a wide range of other formulas. 'Money-purchase' schemes were common: in these, the contribution level was defined, and the pension was related to it in various ways. In many early, self-administered schemes there was a fixed, annual interest rate (typically 3%) on all contributions, so that younger employees accrued a higher pension entitlement per unit of contribution than older employees, to reflect the longer period over which they could earn interest before drawing the pension. In the insured schemes being introduced in the 1930s, a defined unit of member contribution produced a defined unit of pension, the employer making up any extra cost, particularly for older employees. Other benefit formulas commonly used in the first half of the present century were a fixed sum per year of service (common in *ex gratia* pensioning), and a lump sum (common in the less generous provident schemes for manual employees).

By the 1950s, as insured schemes were turned over to a with-profit basis,[3] the contributions were defined, but the benefits sometimes depended on the performance of the underlying investments. However, as competition between companies for the pension contracts of employers increased, the with-profit bonuses were usually handed over to the employer rather than being used to increase pensions, making the contracts cheaper, but the pensions inadequate. Actuaries continued to devise money-purchase schemes for small employers or others who wished to have a clear idea of the cost of the scheme defined at the outset: these schemes were characterized by a definition of the contribution level, whereas the costs of defined benefit schemes (such as those on the salary–service principle) were uncertain, depending on changing rates of return, inflation and salary structures. None the less, in most employments salary–service schemes provided more certain knowledge of benefits available at retirement, and they were increasingly popular among employers and employees where they could be afforded. With-profits, money-purchase schemes increasingly became the preserve of the self-employed, for whom such contracts were natural, there being no employer to make up the uncertain costs of salary–service schemes.

Although employee representatives now tend to view these older formulas as inferior, money-purchase formulas were popular when they were first introduced, and employees welcomed them as giving fair value for individual savings.[4] The pension was proportional to the amount contributed by each individual (and/or by the employer on his behalf), whereas schemes related to average or final salary typically benefited higher-paid employees more than those on average or lower earnings. The Federated Superannuation System for Universities, introduced in 1913, was widely admired, not only because of its entrenched rights for leavers, but also for its money-purchase formula in which the individual could choose between many different insurance policies and gain the benefits appropriate to his circumstances, while maximizing his return on lifetime pension savings. Some early schemes for manual workers, growing out of works provident and savings schemes, also adopted a money-purchase formula.

By the first decade of the twentieth century, the average salary formula (already generally adopted by railways in the later decades of the nineteenth century) was becoming more widespread, particularly for clerical employees. It was, however, resisted by the mass of employees, because older staff benefited more than young and the higher-paid staff benefited more than the lower-paid staff. This was mainly because higher pay came in the later years of fund membership when the implicit interest on the member's 'savings' was insufficient to pay for the higher pension which the averaging formula entitled him to. Contributions of £100 a year invested at 3% interest, for example, would amount to a capital sum of £2,700 over twenty years, but as much as £7,500 after forty years. In a money-purchase scheme based on accumulating interest on savings, the 65-year-old retiree would thus get much more pension for his service at twenty-five than for that at forty-five, but in an average salary scheme, he would get the same pension accruals if his salary were the same. In effect, the *less* time the members placed their money in an average salary scheme, the *higher* the implicit rate of interest they were paid: the structure of returns on investment was skewed to benefit the old. The inequity to the young and, particularly, to the less well-paid, was greater if promotion occurred in the later years. In one model scheme in the first decade of this century, for example, the actuary calculated that low-paid staff would typically receive pension annuities of 18 to 19% of their accumulated contributions, while the higher paid would receive as much as 26 to 28%.[5]

In the more extreme case of final salary schemes, this inequity was greater still, for those who obtained promotion to higher salary levels gained higher pensions in respect of their whole period of service while paying higher contributions for only a part of it. An employee in a final salary scheme based on 5% employee contributions and a one-sixtieth accrual rate who gained a £5,000 increase in his fortieth year would get an extra pension of £3,333 in every year of retirement in return for only one contribution of £250. The massive extra cost was, of course, paid by the fund: that is, effectively by the other employees who were not so promoted. Understandably, there was widespread resistance to this feature of final salary schemes from employees in the early decades of pension development; and many early commentators took the view that it was unfair of an employer to impose such a system on staff, unless he shouldered a large part of the cost himself and explicitly intended to bias benefits towards the higher-paid.[6] Some firms tried to overcome the objections by setting up separate rules for low-paid workers (for example, many firms ran separate schemes for their manual employees). Others, like Cadburys from 1906, had a unified scheme, but charged a higher contribution rate on higher salaries to moderate the inequity. A few firms attempted to overcome staff objections by paying large additional sums into the fund to cover the extra cost of individual final salary pensions when an employee was promoted. This was an entirely fair reflection of the true cost incidence, but the Inland Revenue resisted the practice, feeling it could be abused as a tax avoidance measure.[7]

Despite the general opposition from staff, some employers in the industries which pioneered pension schemes were, by the early decades of the twentieth century, already pressing hard for a move from money-purchase or average salary to final salary schemes. By the 1930s, many clerical and administrative employees could look forward to final salary pensions.[8] Why did some employers move at this early stage to final salary schemes? There was one powerful personal incentive for senior managers: they benefited more from such schemes than their less well-paid subordinates, and actuaries sometimes suspected that this was a factor in their decisions.[9] No doubt it was, but a more general cause lies in the advantages of final salary schemes to employers implementing mandatory retirement policies. Money-purchase or even average salary schemes produced pensions which, particularly for senior people who had been promoted later in life, were quite insufficient to induce voluntary retirement. Over the typical forty-year working life, the salary levels of most employees had nearly doubled in real terms because of economic growth. Thus, even generously based, average salary pensions with accrual rates of one-sixtieth for each year of service were producing pensions well below half of retiring salary for all staff and at less than a quarter of retiring salary for many senior staff. Employers trying to enforce retirement at a fixed age (as, for example, the railway companies generally were by the first decade of this century) found this much easier if they were willing to pay pensions of one-half or two-thirds of retiring salary. The simplest formula to achieve this was the direct one: the final salary formula which provided a salary related to the required inducement to retire rather than to the previously accumulated pension 'savings' of the individuals involved. The resulting deficits in the railway funds were sometimes made up from increased contributions by members, but agitation against this led to most railway companies making up the deficits themselves.[10] This move to final salary pensions did, then, increase the cost of pensioning very considerably.

The extra cost was a major reason why this style of pensioning did not spread more rapidly. Even in self-administered schemes, employers were reluctant to take on the uncertain future costs of final salary schemes. In the insured schemes on which so much of the expansion of occupational pensions coverage was based between the 1930s and 1960s, final salary schemes were initially almost impossible, though by the 1950s new costing and funding methods permitted them even in insured schemes.[11] By then, moreover, a new factor – the gradual but persistent inflation which had been experienced since the later 1930s – was making the old formulas less and less suited to employers' pensioning objectives. Inflation meant that pensions based on past contributions (or on average money salaries throughout working life) were even more inadequate relative to retiring salaries than they had been earlier on the same formulas. A real salary increase through economic growth of 3% a year together with inflation of 2% a year (both reasonable expectations for the 1950s) would, over a forty-year working life, even without any promotion, raise an individual's salary from £1,000 to £7,000 a year. Thus, any pension based on an average salary formula with a one-sixtieth accrual rate would produce accruals of only one four-hundred-and-twentieth of the salary near retirement in respect of each of the early years of membership of the pension fund. As inflation rates rose, moreover, entitlements accrued from earlier working years became ever more completely trivial. Even where they had not made advance provision, then, many employers began to pay *ex gratia* supplements to pensions at retirement in order to soften the blow to employees who had once had quite reasonable expectations of receiving better pensions on retirement.[12] In effect, members of pension schemes who had thought they had secure pension rights had lost them through inflation. In compensation, they became participants in what amounted to a pension unit trust and, moreover, one which was not even explicitly obliged to share the rewards of its investment performance with its members, but which chose from time to time to do so.

Employers had not wanted a system with these characteristics, though they welcomed the increased but unanticipated discretion it gave them over the level of benefits. For them, the extent to which their employees were forced to share the investment risks of the funds was also an unexpected bonus of inflation. Employers had gained all the *ex ante* advantages of a formal pension scheme, while their fund trustees retained *ex gratia* control over a large element of pension entitlements. Neither employers nor their employees could feel entirely happy with this inequitable and unintended shift. Employee resentment focused on the poor level of pensions at the time of retirement. Trade union and employee pressure led to demands for pensions which were more realistically related to final salary and hence to their retirement income needs. Paradoxically, then, inflation led employee representatives to press for a pension formula which had earlier been seen as inegalitarian and favoured principally by management. Employers were equally concerned that pensions at retirement should be adequate, particularly where they had mandatory retirement rules for which generous pensions were a necessary sweetener. Final salary pensions also increased the scope for employers to skew scheme benefits to stayers rather than leavers at a time when legislation to protect leavers' rights was threatening to reduce the loyalty incentive of pension schemes.[13] The pressure from employees for final salary pensions thus encountered little resistance, and many schemes were converted to a final salary basis in the 1960s.

By 1971, nearly two-thirds of private sector occupational pension scheme members already had final salary pension entitlements. Then, when the contracting-out requirement for the state earnings-related pension scheme (which favoured the final salary basis) became clear in the mid 1970s, the majority of remaining members were converted to that type of scheme.[14] Inflation also encouraged a shortening of the averaging period over which final salary schemes were calculated: previously, the typical period had been five years, but by the end of the 1970s one year or three years were almost universal. At the same time, accrual rates became more generous. Though contracting-out of the state earnings-related scheme only required an accrual rate of one-eightieths, one-sixtieths became more common, and schemes with one-eightieths declined.[15] For those with a full forty years' service in one occupational pension scheme, then, the benefit formulas seemed far more likely by the 1970s to provide pensions as of right at the level of two-thirds of retiring salary whereas this had been true for no more than the privileged few in the better schemes of early decades. The earlier objections to final salary schemes (and particularly their tendency to redistribute income from the poor to the rich) have not been entirely forgotten;[16] but they have been quite generally overridden by the stampede of employees to gain the effective protection against inflation during their working lives which final salary schemes seemed to promise.

It is significant that, while progress has been almost complete in providing this form of protection against inflation, developments in protecting pensions from the erosion of value by inflation *after* retirement have been far more hesitantly pursued. For individuals embarking on retirement with a pension fixed by the now-standard formulas, inflation rates of the kind experienced recently are, of course, catastrophic. Someone retiring on two-thirds pension in 1975 would, for example, have found his pension reduced to half of the original value in real terms within five years, with a prospect, if inflation continued, of ending his days on a real income very much less than had originally seemed in prospect. A man retiring at 65 can expect (if he dies at the average expected age for such retirees of 77), from a mere 5% per annum inflation, that in his last year his pension will be worth under half what it was first worth, while, if inflation persists at 20% per annum, it will be reduced to a mere tenth of its initial value in real terms;

for those living longer than average, such inflation rates can wipe pensions out entirely. In the state scheme, the collective voting power of the old and the general social standards of income maintenance which society was willing to grant ensured that pensions at least kept their value in real terms. Most proposals for state earnings-related pensions from the 1950s onwards (including the scheme actually implemented from 1978) also offered full protection against inflation for state pensions.[17] The state scheme also had an important indirect effect on the inflation-proofing of occupational pensions. Pensioners in contracted-out schemes received a guarantee of an inflation-proofed pension roughly equivalent to the state earnings-related pension for rights accrued from 1978 onwards, but until these rights accrued over a long period, such protection would be small.[18]

Although this state intervention is new, the problem of inflation eroding the value of occupational pensions in payment is a long-standing one. In the years 1914 to 1920, pensions in payment were reduced by inflation to one-third of their former value, but pressure groups of occupational pensioners asking for compensating increases often failed to make any headway. The Great Western Railway Company Pension Society Committee, for example, were met by a 'blank refusal to entertain any part of our programme' in 1917,[19] though some private and public sector employers did later grant *ex gratia* increases to relieve the more serious hardship among their former employees.[20] This problem was considered an exceptional consequence of wartime, and indeed it was: a decade later, schemes faced the opposite problem of deflation leading to excessive pensions. Anyone lucky enough to retire in 1929 on two-thirds of final salary was, four years later, receiving a pension which, though fixed in money terms, was worth nearly half as much again, because of the steep fall in consumer prices in the intervening period. Furthermore, this was, given the widespread salary cuts of 1931–2, likely to be more than those currently performing the job from which he retired were earning in salary. From the later 1940s, however, inflation has been persistent and accelerating; and the tendency initially was for larger employers in the public and private sectors to offer *ad hoc* compensation, usually of rather less than the rise of the cost of living, to their retired employees, though many pensioners received no compensation at all.[21] In insured schemes, liberal employers paid *ad hoc* supplements to some employees, though by the 1960s, life companies were offering policies with regular increases of $2\frac{1}{2}$–3% per annum, designed to compensate for expected inflation. In self-administered schemes, 'bonuses' to pensions were declared from time to time in some schemes to reflect the rising investment returns of the 1950s.[22] Schemes were able to afford this because inflation over the decades was effectively devaluing their real pension liabilities, while their assets benefited from the higher investment returns: in effect they chose to share some of these windfall gains with pensioners. Like member-contributors before final salary schemes were securely established, pensioners became shareholders in a unit trust whose rules for distribution were not known until the trustees decided them. This development was, of course, quite unanticipated by the designers of schemes. Indeed, the reduction in such *ex gratia* flexibility by employers and its replacement by clearly defined benefits had been one of the arguments for the establishment of trust schemes. Like many contractual promises, its meaning had been undermined by inflation.

Employees were, then, understandably keen to win back some of this ground by entrenching their entitlements to pensions in the real terms which really mattered. The unions were most successful in the public sector, initially in negotiating *ad hoc* increases, and then in establishing complete index-linking of public sector pensions under Edward Heath's Conservative government in the early 1970s. This has proved an enduring right, despite investigations initiated by critical Labour and Conservative governments, both of them anxious to reduce public spending by curtailing these extremely expensive concessions.[23] In the private sector, by contrast, employers have agreed to counteract inflation only by adopting final salary formulas, and have been more reluctant to extend the post-retirement protection of pensions in payment. By 1979, there were still almost no schemes in the private sector which offered complete index-linking as of right on the public sector model, but about 20% of pensioners enjoyed guaranteed increases around the 3% per annum level which in earlier decades had been (quite inadequately) estimated as necessary to compensate for gradual inflation.[24] In practice, however, many more funds declared increases for existing pensioners on a more generous scale than this, though extremely few were as generous as the public sector. In 1979, half of occupational pension scheme members and pensioners in the private sector were in schemes which offered no increases or trivial ones, while the remainder typically could expect compensation for only half or two-thirds of the inflation rate.[25] Since these were increases which they had not been promised, most pensioners gratefully accepted them, but the increases typically remained *ex gratia* rather than a right of pensioners.

Why was there not greater progress towards paying pension benefits in the real terms which are, after all, the terms in which pensioning needs are naturally and rationally expressed? The basic problems were costs and employers' objectives. The generous inflation-proofing offered in the public sector could be worth one-third of the whole pension entitlement,[26] and increases in cost of that magnitude cannot be borne by most private schemes. It is, of course, true that pension funds would have been obliged to pay pensions in real terms in the absence of inflation; but it may, of course, have turned out that they would not have been able to do so, or would have been less generous in improving benefit formulas to a final salary basis, if inflation (and higher money investment returns) had not occurred. Also, many of the increases paid had not, in fact, been funded, but were paid by employers out of their own current profits. Uncertainty about the cost, and the employer's ability to fund such benefits, was also a factor limiting inflation compensation, though since the issue of index-linked bonds by the government in 1981, enabling employers to cover such risks, this has been a less serious problem.

Even so, the Occupational Pensions Board in 1982 decided that it would be unwise to recommend to the government that they should enforce even the minimum standard of inflation-proofing which the Board were recommending for leavers' preserved pensions.[27] They recognized the public disquiet at the erosion of pension values, and the difficulties of relying for remedy on unfunded *ex gratia* increases, but equally they were aware of the difficulty for employers of funding the cost in a time of severe profits squeeze. They preferred, then, to leave the matter to voluntary initiative; and, indeed, voluntary initiative had already progressed much further on this than on the preservation and inflation-proofing of leavers' pensions.[28] A few firms such as Rank[29] have recently offered full inflation-proofing following the public sector model, but it remains an unpopular option among employers on the shopping list of pension improvements. One costless option has from time to time been canvassed: that of reducing the pensions initially paid at retirement in return for index-linking them subsequently, thus permitting pensioners to smooth out their real income over their retired lifetime. This has, however, not been widely adopted, mainly, it seems, because of those very factors which made final salary schemes so acceptable as a response to inflation: the pension at retirement is the most potent factor in inducing and sweetening the retirement decision or in smoothing the path of mandatory retirement enforcement. Employers have a clear interest in providing the most attractive package immediately *on* retirement. This, together with the myopia of prospective pensioners about the long-term future,[30] have conspired to limit progress on inflation-proofing of pension entitlements to the period of working life which is achieved by changing to the final salary formula. Thereafter, in the period of retirement itself, index-linking is, as we have seen, less ubiquitous.

A minor obstacle to progress on inflation compensation was the Superannuation Funds Office of the Inland Revenue. They at first resisted change except on an *ex gratia* basis, and then permitted it only if there was full index-linking or an arbitrary low limit (for many years $2\frac{1}{2}\%$–3% per annum), rather than permitting anything in between.[31] However, a more direct influence of the Inland Revenue on modern pensioning formulas was in providing an incentive for pension annuities to be partly replaced by lump sum payments on retirement. There was, of course, no technical reason why a pension fund should be other than neutral on the decision to take benefits on retirement as a lump sum or as an annuity continuing until death. The fund had to build up a lump sum sufficient to cover its liabilities by the time of retirement; but it was largely immaterial whether that sum was paid over or used to provide a regular pension annuity.[32] Some early pension schemes paid over lump sums,[33] and some still pay only lump sums, though these now have only about 30,000 members.[34] Many schemes which normally paid annuities did, moreover, commute very small pensions for single lump sum payments; and, from the early days of pensioning, some funds offered benefits partly as an annuity and partly as a lump sum. Before the First World War, for example, the London and North Western Railway paid workers with twenty or more years' service £50 on retirement in addition to ten shillings a week pension.

The advocates of lump sums pointed to a number of advantages. Prior to 1956, there were tax advantages to carrying one's own risks of longevity, because both the capital and interest elements in annuities purchased through an insurance company were taxed, while lump sum pension benefits were (until 1947) completely free of tax. A lump sum also had practical advantages. It might enable the pensioner more easily to adjust to a lower retirement standard of living, for example, by easing the transition to new housing arrangements; or it might enable a retiree to set up a small business or purchase a house to rent out. Against this was the ever-present fear than an employee would squander a lump sum, whereas an annuity paid in regular instalments imposed a stronger discipline. As the Ridley Commission on the Civil Service said in 1888:

The payment . . . of a lump sum is open to the obvious objection that in the event of improvidence or misfortune in the use of it, the retired public servant may be reduced to circumstances which might lead to his being an applicant for public or private charity.[35]

By the time the nascent Association of Superannuation and Pension Funds was lobbying for tax-exempt status in the First World War, the payment of pension annuities rather than lump sums was clearly the norm among member firms.[36] The Association was quite satisfied that lump sums were not allowed by the Revenue in tax-exempt (1921 Act) funds.

In recent years, however, the payment as a lump sum of about a quarter of the value of the pension (typically one-and-a-half times final salary: the maximum now allowed by the Inland Revenue in tax-exempt funds) has become quite normal. The proportion of members of private sector funds entitled to commute part of their annuity for a lump sum rose from only a third in 1971 (when restrictions on lump sums had just been liberalized) to more than 90% in 1979; and almost all public sector employees also benefited from partial lump sums.[37] The chapter of accidents which led in absurd progression to this situation, which was initially desired by no one, began in the early years of this century.[38] At that time, civil servants enjoyed the finest pension arrangements available, but one feature disturbed them. They saw that, in railway pension schemes, when the member died before retirement, all his own contributions (sometimes with interest and sometimes with the employer's contributions as well) went to the widow: in effect, the railway funds paid a lump sum to the widow because they no longer needed to maintain a reserve for his pension. The Treasury, by contrast, did not fund its non-contributory civil servants' pensions, and thus paid no such widow's benefit. Following grassroots employee agitation, the 'Deferred Pay Movement' was established to argue the case for similar death benefits to be provided for civil servants. The staff agitation and reluctant Treasury response produced tortuous and complex negotiations. Discussions between the Courtney Commission (which investigated the issue in 1902–3) and their actuary, H. W. Manly, resulted in the solution of notionally separating a lump sum (ultimately fixed at one-and-a-half years' salary, and equivalent to the difference between an accrual rate of one-sixtieth and a lower one of one-eightieth). In return for this lower accrual rate, which reduced the pensions paid on retirement, the lump sum was to be given to the widow on death in service or to the employee if he survived to retirement. The provision of a lump sum, even if the employee survived, was quite unnecessary, and no one seems positively to have asked for it. By the time this was pointed out, however, the momentum of discussions was carrying this solution inexorably forward, and a plebiscite of civil servants had shown that three-quarters favoured the change. The Treasury conceded the scheme from 1909. The Inland Revenue (whose officers were themselves beneficiaries of the new arrangements) were asked whether the lump sum payments would be taxable, and they replied in the negative, giving no reasons, though presumably on the argument that lump sums were capital payments, not income.

As in other areas, the tax exemption was not very significant at the time it was granted, but, after 1940, when tax rates were raised and taxpaying became quite general, the increase in payments of lump sum benefits to people other than themselves became an acute issue for the Revenue.[39] They had been permitting insured schemes to pay tax-free lump sums in whole or in part, because their build-up of funds was partly taxed already. During the War, schemes clearly designed as tax avoidance measures for higher-paid employees proliferated and, as we have seen, the 1947 Finance Act attempted to clamp down on such schemes by permitting only those with reasonable tax-free, lump sum benefits. The definition of 'reasonable' which naturally occurred to the drafters of this legislation was their own generous benefit level; since then, public sector schemes have provided the standard by which the acceptability of schemes for tax exemption has been determined. In the case of lump sums, this has meant a maximum of one-quarter of the total pension benefit, more recently redefined as one-and-a-half years' salary: as was accepted in the civil service in 1909. Meanwhile, tax-exempt 1921 Act trust fund schemes, unlike endowment policy or statutory schemes, had not been permitted by the Revenue to pay any lump sums, and in 1956, the government did not implement the recommendations of the Millard Tucker Committee that the concession should be extended to them.[40] Initially, many personnel managers, pension fund administrators and actuaries seemed to agree that this was wise, and that any artificial encouragement of a move to lump sum pensions (and the consequent reduction of pension annuities) would be a retrograde step.[41] There was, however, increasing pressure from staff for partial payment of pensions as lump sums, and a general inclination to concede them because of the tax advantages they offered. Until the 1970s, this required somewhat complex adjustments, creating a taxed section in the otherwise tax-exempt fund to pay lump sums, or a supplementary endowment insurance scheme. After 1970, with all types of schemes explicitly permitted to pay tax-free lump sums from untaxed funds under the new code of approval, the inclusion of lump sum benefits (usually as an option for the employee to commute part of his pension at retirement for a lump sum of up to the maximum permitted one-and-a-half years' salary) became cheaper and hence quite general in pension scheme rules. By 1979, one-quarter of all private sector pension fund expenditure on benefits at retirement was on lump sums, a figure much higher than in earlier years. Many employees still remain unaware of the availability of lump sum commutation, but those who do take it up often find themselves handling the largest capital sum they have ever had to cope with in their lives when they retire.[42] The attraction is no doubt partly the flexibility of a capital sum, and partly a myopia about the future value of the reduced pension annuity, but it lies crucially in the logically difficult-to-justify tax relief on lump sums. Indeed, most of those who do take lump sums invest them to produce an income, suggesting that the tax relief rather than an aversion to regular income is the primary motivation.[43]

A somewhat happier case of the influence of state intervention on pension design is in the modern spread of widows' pensions. Women in twentieth-century Britain have generally been financially dependent on men. This dependency not only reflected the gender divisions of the labour of child rearing and housewifery but also was itself reflected in employment contracts, where marriage was until recent decades, in many occupations, sufficient grounds for dismissal of female employees, or at least grounds for exclusion from the pension scheme. Schemes which did admit women often repaid their contributions as a 'dowry' on their marriage; this followed from the assumption, quite generally made, that married women should rely on their husbands, not on their employers, for support in old age. Until the earnings-related state pension scheme of 1978, married women were also permitted to (and on a large scale did) opt out of national insurance pension contributions and benefits, relying solely on entitlement through their husbands. As late as 1966, an official inquiry by industrialists and trade unionists could take the view that preservation of women's occupational pension rights on marriage was unnecessary and would be resented by women themselves.[44] This set of attitudes encapsulated a cruel social lie. Poverty in old age was pre-eminently a problem for women, and most husbands were either unable or unwilling (other than through the compulsory state scheme) to make financial provision for their wives after their death. For the typical married woman, this was not a trivial matter. With a life expectancy three or four years longer than a man's, and with a husband typically three or four years older than herself, the chances were that a woman would significantly outlive her husband. Not surprisingly, then, women have substantially outnumbered men as beneficiaries of the various forms of state old age income maintenance (the poor law, state old age pensions, and supplementary means-tested benefits) throughout the twentieth century. Not surprisingly also, the state has proved to be the major catalyst for the improvement of widows' benefits after decades of failure by occupational pension schemes to provide adequate benefits.

When employers and employees in the nineteenth century looked to the hazards of life, widowhood through the husband's death in service bulked much larger than it does today. Indeed, widows' funds predate pension funds in some employments such as banking, where employers sought to regularize their provision for the inevitable charitable appeals from destitute widows of men who had once worked for them by ensuring that the employees themselves (usually with some help) made proper provision in advance. Originally, such schemes were either voluntary or confined to married men, but gradually the practice spread of making them compulsory for all male employees. In the inter-war years, widows' provision still occasionally preceded pension provision, though pension schemes dominated, and some schemes included provision for widows as an integral part of the benefits. In the 1920s, there were probably ten times as many pension funds as widows' funds,[45] and, when tax relief was extended to widows' funds in 1930, it became increasingly common to amalgamate widows' provision into a unified pension scheme.[46]

The nature of widows' provision, up to this time, owed rather more to the origins and nature of pension schemes (and particularly their origins as 'savings' institutions) than it did to the real needs of widows. Usually, all widows received for death in service was a return of the employee's contributions or, in generous schemes, the employer's contributions also, sometimes with interest. As we have seen, it was the concession of similar benefits in the (non-contributory) civil service scheme that had led to the introduction of lump sums into that scheme in 1909. Death after retirement required different treatment in these early schemes. A typical provision in the private sector was that, if the husband had not received a pension for a significant period (commonly five years or a sum equivalent to the contributions he had paid), then the pension would continue to be paid for that period. Such rules derive from the view that it would be inequitable if an employee did not at least 'get his money back' from the 'savings' scheme, rather than from any principle of shared risk in common provision against life contingencies. Where the latter did enter into consideration, provision was usually a lump sum on death in service (often in addition to the withdrawal benefit): commonly one year's salary, and sometimes more for those with longer service. Insured schemes typically included a group insurance option, offering one year's salary for death in service in the 1930s, though two years' salary was becoming more common in the 1950s. From the point of view of the widows, these benefits were badly designed. The young widow with children got very little, compared with the older one without dependants, from the death-in-service benefits. Meanwhile, the death-in-retirement benefit in forms such as five-year guarantees left some widows with too much, and many with nothing: a smaller pension over a longer period was more commensurate with needs.

There was a tendency for more generous treatment for widows to develop, often in the more need-orientated and collective risk-sharing form of explicit widows' annuities for life, rather than merely lump sums, or contribution refunds or guaranteed pension periods. Improved longevity reduced the cost of death-in-service benefits and focused attention on the greater needs of younger widows with children, who are few in number but obviously require greater support. Legal & General were the first insurance company to offer group family income benefit schemes, providing annuities to dependants for death in service on an adequate basis from 1937, and met a rather limited but steady demand for those to replace or supplement lump sum schemes. In self-administered schemes, pension annuities for widows (typically one-third to one-half of the pension for the employee on retirement) were also occasionally introduced. None the less, progress was slow: as late as 1971 only a third of private sector pension scheme members had this kind of benefit for death in service.

For death in retirement, a generous solution was more costly, and was initially rarely attempted. By the 1950s, however, with an increasing number of schemes maturing, there was concern among the about-to-be-pensioned about provision additional to the original five-year and similar guarantees. Employers usually responded by offering an option (available from an early stage in some far-seeing schemes) for a male employee drawing a pension to take a lower pension in return for a right for his widow, should he predecease her, to continue to draw a pension of an agreed amount: usually one-third or one-half that being paid to the retired couple. A trade-off could easily be calculated by an actuary, varying according to the relative ages of the spouses. By 1956, three-quarters of retiring scheme members were offered this method of financing their and their wives' retirement.[47] However, very few eligible members did actually take up this option on retirement.[48] Clearly, the low level of pensions being paid by the schemes maturing in the 1950s, particularly those offering benefits on a money-purchase or average salary basis, is a major explanation. The option of lowering the small pensions even further by providing for a surviving widow was not attractive to many men forced to retire, or perhaps even to those wives inclined to be optimistic about their husbands' longevity. Moreover, the actuarially calculated exchange factors were typically harsh: itself a sober, mathematical reflection of how wrong such optimism was, for, given the typical age differential and longevity differential, there was a very high chance of many years of widowhood. Most better-off men appear to have preferred to trust to luck, or perhaps made provision for their wives by private annuities, savings or in other ways. However, for the lower-income groups, who were even less likely to take the widow's option than middle-class employees, there was a real benefit in refusing the post-retirement widow's option. The means-tested state pension supplements were not paid to those with retirement benefits above a certain level. This caused some resentment among working-class people in pension schemes, who found themselves deprived of state benefits which their neighbours could get, merely because they drew a pension which they felt they had earned. It was a simple matter for employees with quite small occupational pensions to work out that, if they enjoyed a higher joint pension while the husband lived, but the surviving widow had no pension and thus qualified for means-tested supplementation (giving her an income perhaps fully equal to the half-pension in the widow's option), they might maximize their joint lifetime income by *not* taking the widow's option.

The failure of the widow's option path of development for death and retirement benefits simply underlined the fundamental blockage in any generous provision for widows: it would cost a great deal, whether in sacrifice of existing benefits or increased contributions by employers or employees. Typically, full provision for widows of half of the pension the husband was entitled to on retirement, whether his death occurred in service or after retirement, increased pensioning costs by a third or more.[49] Few employers were willing to contemplate the 5% increase in labour costs which this implied. Yet, surprisingly, it was at a time of severe economic stringency, following the oil crisis of 1973, that most employers did steel themselves to make the change. The catalyst proved to be the requirements for contracting out of the state earnings-related pension scheme. What had been an annual trickle of improvements to widows' pensions became a flood. In 1971, only 39% of male employees in private sector schemes had provision for widows' annuities on death in service; by 1979, the proportion was 89%. Many widows of deceased employees also benefited from a tax-free lump sum of around two years' salary. Similar improvements, from 35% to 89% between 1971 and 1979, were also made in the coverage of widows following their husbands' death in retirement.[50] Moreover, many schemes improved the widows' annuity benefits beyond the minimum levels for contracting out of the state scheme, which required an accrual rate of one-hundred-and-sixtieths. It became the norm for good employers to offer widows' pensions at about half the level of the men's pension (often implying an accrual rate as high as one-hundred-and-twentieths); and the older forms of provision, such as widow's lump sums, often survived alongside the new, though widow's options virtually disappeared in the 1970s.

Paradoxically, the improved accruals for widows which will bear fruit in larger pensions over the coming decades are not responding to the needs of those decades, but to the inadequacies of the past – as has so often been the case in pension scheme design. To the extent that married women now work and accrue occupational benefits of their own, and to the extent that state earnings-related pensions provide unusually generous benefits for women and widows, they will be less dependent on men in their old age than at any time in the past. Many women will thus continue to draw state and private pensions in their own right, in addition to those they derive as widows of their husbands. Pension schemes have not been tailored to changing long-run social realities; indeed, it is not easy to achieve this when patterns of gender dependency have been changing. The shorter working lives and lower earnings of women will restrict the extent to which this generous formal provision will lead to general over-provision for women. None the less, if this aspect of modern pension design survives, and if the current trend to conceding widowers' pensions as a sop to formal egalitarianism does not also gather pace, women may approach equality in retirement long before they achieve equality in employment.

9 Retirement: age discrimination or the fruits of prosperity?

society has really no right to deny any man, or woman, who wishes to continue working the sense of fulfilment and the sense of usefulness that work can give. Compulsory retirement is an inhuman practice . . .

Arthur Seldon, *Pensions in a Free Society* (Institute of Economic Affairs, 1957), p. 3

The idea of retirement has a long and venerable history; but the twentieth century has fundamentally transformed its nature. Modern retirement practice has a number of distinct characteristics. First, it is a general rite of passage which almost all adult employees can now expect to undergo. Second, it is more likely to be compelled at a fixed chronological age, rather than to be initiated by failing physical or mental powers. And third, the financial status of the retired has greatly improved, so that this form of retreat from the world of work is less commonly seen in negative terms than was once the case. These diverse elements have given rise to a rich variety of interpretations of the reasons for the modern growth of retirement. Radicals on the libertarian right and the socialist left alike have interpreted it as the product of unjustifiable discrimination against the old. Others, by contrast, have seen it as the virtuous consequence of the greater choices provided by increased wealth, greatly augmented by the modern spread of pensioning. This ambivalence in the image of retirement is, moreover, reflected in the mixed trauma and relief of those undergoing the retirement experience. There is a fear of loss of status and of psychological strains in retirement; yet at the same time many welcome the release from the burdens of working life, particularly those to whom generous pensions are paid.[1]

The steady, long-run trend to increased retirement is unmistakable. Figure 9.1 shows the declining proportion of males of sixty-five and over who continued at work.[2] In 1881, nearly three-quarters were still at work; this fell to less than half in the 1920s; and by the 1980s only one in ten males of

122

Fig. 9.1 The proportion of UK males of sixty-five and over still
working, 1881–1981

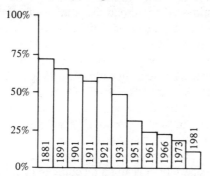

Source: 1881–1973: Charles H. Feinstein, R. C. O. Matthews and J. C. Odling-
Smee, *British Economic Growth 1856–1973*, Oxford, 1982, pp. 57, 560–4; 1981:
preliminary estimate from 1981 Census (England and Wales only)

sixty-five and over were still working. Working women showed a similarly
increased tendency to retire in the twentieth century.[3] Remarkably, these
trends have occurred despite improvements in the overall health and
capacity of the aged population. It is true that many sickly workers who
formerly died before reaching sixty-five now survive to advanced ages, and
they are likely to be relatively unfit. Thus, sickness and incapacity, now as in
earlier decades, still account for a large number of individual decisions to
retire.[4] Moreover, the expectation of life for men aged sixty has risen much
less than the chances of surviving to that age: from thirteen-and-a-half years
in the first decade of the century to seventeen years in 1978–80.[5] None the
less, the average health standards of the old have, as these figures suggest,
probably on balance improved. Better medical care and effective drug
treatments of disabling diseases such as tuberculosis, improved safety and
welfare conditions at work, rising nutritional and sanitary standards, and
less physical and mental stress in homes with better facilities and smaller
families: all these changes in twentieth-century Britain have probably
enhanced the average capacity to work of the older members of the labour
force. Certainly the casual testimony of informed opinion, based on pension
fund experience and other contacts with the old, suggests that 65-year-olds
in the modern era are distinctly healthier and fitter than their predecessors
of generations ago.[6]

Why then, have the old showed such a pronounced tendency to cease
working? Some have suggested that the medical profession can be blamed
for fomenting a modern gerontophobia and for concealing the objective
improvements in the capacity of the elderly for their own purposes; but this
is implausible. It is true that some prominent members of the medical

profession have pioneered the public slandering of the old. Sir William Osler, for example, on the eve of his appointment to a distinguished chair at Oxford in 1905, eulogized the creativity and productivity of the young, quoting with approval the society described in Trollope's (now justifiably forgotten) satirical novel, *The Fixed Period*,[7] in which the old were generally eliminated at the age of sixty-eight.[8] Osler soon came to regret his whimsical remark, as it had been taken to be in bad taste, though he never retracted his views on the incompetence of the aged. There were, however, an equal number of medical professionals who sprang to the defence of the aged or to the assertion of their continued employability. Evidence was produced of the continuing capacity of the aged;[9] and one distinguished doctor, apparently with a considerable private practice as a consultant to employers, took pleasure in devising a machine to electrocute malingering older workers whom he suspected of quite widespread exaggeration of their disabilities.[10] Doctors, in fact, reflected the dotty prejudices of their age in all their splendid variety. They may be blamed for doing so, but we should not mistake the social symptom for the medical cause.

It is possible that, while the capacity of the old to work has been increasing, the demands of the modern workplace have intensified to make their participation less feasible. Technical change, it is sometimes argued, leads to discrimination by employers against older workers, because jobs have become more physically or mentally demanding. Yet many technical changes and more efficient methods have actually lightened the work load and made fewer demands on workers in the course of the twentieth century. It is, moreover, plausible that improved working conditions, better health standards, increased holidays, and massively reduced hours have done much to counteract any tendency towards the intensification of work inherent in modern technological processes. It is, then, far from obvious that men of sixty-five on average now find it physically or mentally more difficult to work in their present jobs than their predecessors of a hundred years ago found it to function in the arduous work conditions of their age.[11] Indeed, such technologically enforced retirement may be less common now than in earlier decades, when there were large numbers of aged workers in casual jobs as gardeners or watchmen: jobs which were then specifically reserved for those no longer capable of working at more demanding occupations.[12]

What, then, is the explanation for the greatly increased extent to which the elderly now withdraw from the work force? The increased capacity to finance retirement and the reduced dependence of the old on income from employment appears to be a central factor. Voluntary retirement is, in a sense, a luxury good whose incidence would be expected to grow in a hundred year period in which general living standards have perhaps tripled. Cross-section studies in all periods have shown that wealthier people tend to

Table 9.1 *The pensioning of the old, 1900–79*

Year	(1) Number of people aged sixty-five and over (millions)	(2) Number of state pensions paid (millions)	(3) Number of occupational pensions paid (millions)
1900	2.0	0.0	0.1
1936	3.9	2.5	0.2
1956	5.8	4./	1.1
1963	6.3	6.1	1.8
1967	6.8	6.9	2.3
1971	7.3	7.7	2.9
1975	7.8	8.3	3.4
1979	8.2	8.9	3.7

Note: The columns cannot be directly compared to show the proportion of the elderly receiving pensions or retired. Occupational pensions (and from the 1940s women's state pensions) were often paid below the age of sixty-five. Moreover, state pensions and occupational pensions were sometimes paid to those who had not retired from all employments. A survey of income tax returns in 1963–4 shows that there were 880,000 occupational pensions payable to people receiving state retirement pensions and 590,000 to those not receiving such pensions, most of the latter being aged under sixty-five: see Ministry of Pensions and National Insurance, *Financial and Other Circumstances of Retired Pensioners*, 1966, p. 14.

Sources: col. (1): C. H. Feinstein, *National Income, Expenditure and Output of the United Kingdom, 1855–1965*, Cambridge, 1972, pp. T123–4; *Eurostat*.
col. (2): For 1936, *Eighteenth Annual Report of the Ministry of Health*, Cmd the United Kingdom, 1855–1965, Cambridge, 1972, pp. T123–4; *Eurostat*. 5516, 1937 (BPP, X, 1936–7), Appendix XXIX. For 1956–79, *Annual Abstract of Statistics, passim*. All statistics relate to contributory pensions only (non-contributory, national assistance, supplementary benefit and poor law pensions are excluded).
col. (3): Government Actuary, *Occupational Pension Schemes: 1979: Sixth Survey*, 1981, p. 12. All figures include widows' and dependants' pensions. The 1900 figure is the author's estimate.

save a higher proportion of their income.[13] As the population as a whole grew wealthier over time, so their aggregate savings increased. The bulk of the resulting investment income goes to those who have saved most, and these are disproportionately concentrated among the elderly households. The pattern of savings suggested by the life-cycle model has been confirmed by empirical research: savings peak at about age sixty-five and are run down thereafter. Yet this private saving for old age is largely confined to upper-income groups, and the majority of the aged still own relatively few assets, other than owner-occupied housing, directly.[14]

The major sources of the incomes of the elderly have not been investment income from directly-held assets, but rather the growing entitlements to state and occupational pensions as shown in Table 9.1. The growth in pension entitlements was particularly marked after the Second World War as many earlier schemes matured and as new schemes were inaugurated, often with generous provisions for the back service of older employees. By the 1970s, as we have seen, nearly half of the employed population were in occupational pension schemes. The proportion of full-time, male employees over twenty-five with pension rights was even higher. They, their dependants, and prospective pensioners in general, could look forward to a standard of living in old age significantly better than their predecessors of a generation earlier. The old not only had higher real incomes, but also increased their standard of living relative to that enjoyed by the working population. In 1951, the average disposable income of those over state pension age (including all income from occupational pensions, interest, etc., as well as the state pension and other social security benefits) was little more than two-fifths of the average non-pensioner's, but thirty years later the average pensioner enjoyed as much as two-thirds of the average non-pensioner's income.[15] The generations retiring in the 1960s and 1970s enjoyed a lifetime experience of continually improving standards in which their retirement was truly a golden age. Having grown up in years of war, low growth, unemployment and depression, their expectations were low; yet their retirement incomes were substantially greater than their earlier experience would have led them to expect. Many owed this good fortune to the occupational pension that they received on retirement. Despite the general absence of vested rights for leavers, the number of those drawing occupational pensions rose from around 0.2 million in 1936 to 3.7 million in 1979. The number receiving state contributory old age pensions increased less sharply, but from a higher initial level: from 2.5 million in 1936 to 8.9 million in 1979.

By the later 1970s, well over a third of these state pensioners already had occupational pensions, and, if wives were included (and many of them can now expect to continue to draw a widow's pension from the occupational scheme if the husband dies), the proportion of the elderly benefiting would be even greater. Nearly half of those without an occupational pension were sufficiently poor to qualify for means-tested supplementary benefits in addition to the basic state pension; by contrast, only a small proportion of those with occupational pensions found this supplementation necessary. Occupational pensions were, then, enabling many people to live significantly above the basic subsistence level determined by the Supplementary Benefits Commission. On average, occupational pensioners drew annuities equivalent to the value of the state pension: in 1979, when the state retirement pension for a single person was £19.50 per week, the average occupational pension then being paid was £18 per week.[16] (These figures may be compared with average weekly full-time earnings for adult males at that time of about £100.) This does, however, somewhat understate the benefits from occupational pension schemes of the newly retired, for it includes some pensions of long standing (some more than twenty years old) fixed in a period when benefits were less generous. In 1979, for example, the average male employee retiring from the public sector on pension could expect £28 from his occupational scheme, while for the private sector the figure was £20 a week. In addition, many employees could expect lump sums on retirement: in 1979 these averaged £4,000–£5,000.

It is sometimes suggested that pension schemes have merely substituted for other forms of individual savings, and that this increase in pension entitlement represents merely a diversion of old age savings from their traditional channels. This is implausible. All the evidence we have encountered in the course of this study suggests a high degree of liquidity preference by members of the schemes, a preference which the requirements of the scheme often deliberately frustrated. Leavers who were offered returns of contributions or retirees offered lump sums preferred to take their money rather than leave it in the scheme. Insurance companies advised their salesmen who encountered the (rare) employer who suggested offering staff a free choice between a salary rise and an equivalent employer's contribution to a pension fund to break off negotiations, as it was obvious what the staff preferred. Not surprisingly, then, the imperfect studies of savings behaviour which have been made suggest that occupational pension schemes do significantly increase overall savings, rather than merely replacing other channels of savings.[17] It is also clear that they have spread wealth more equally. The degree to which employees accrue pension wealth does, it is true, increase sharply with income so that pension saving is biased towards the better-off.[18] Yet this saving is more equally distributed than other forms of asset-holding, so that the decline in the inequality of wealth-holding in British society has been accelerated by the spread of pensioning. In 1936 the top 10% of the population held 88% of total wealth, pension rights being an insignificant portion of this; by 1972 the share of the top 10% in other wealth fell to 71%, but if the more equally distributed pension rights are included the overall fall in their share was to 67%. Thus, improved occupational pensions accounted for nearly a fifth of the modern spread of wealth-holding.[19]

Occupational pension schemes have, then, facilitated the decision to retire by making it easier for greater numbers of the old to look forward to economic security in retirement. However, there were still many employees, particularly among the unskilled working class, who had no such entitlement. For them retirement was feared rather than welcomed, and they were still forced by economic pressures to continue working.[20] When they could no longer do so, state pensions were their major recourse in old age. It might have been expected that the availability of state pensions in 1909 and the significant improvements in 1928 and 1946 would have produced discrete jumps in retirement, but no such pattern is obviously discernible in Figure 9.1. This is not to say that the state pension changes did not have real effects. For example, when the pension age was reduced in 1928 from seventy to sixty-five and deflation increased the real value of pensions, there was a clear impact on the sixty-five to sixty-nine age-group. Between the Censuses of 1921 and 1931, the proportion of that age-group who were retired more than doubled, from 14% to 30%, whereas retirement in other age-groups increased at a slower pace in the same period.[21] Another factor may have been the unusually high level of unemployment, leading to discrimination against older workers in the period. The impact of this and the reduced pension age was too small, however, to show up in our chart of general trends (Figure 9.1). One reason for the limited impact of the 1928 pensions was that there was no requirement for those drawing the old age pension to retire, and no claw-back of earnings if they chose to continue working. Most of those who reached sixty-five did, in fact, then continue to work.[22] The retirement decision was still typically made with physical or mental capacity, job opportunities, personal inclination, and financial resources and needs rather than the state pensions as the determining factors.

The age of sixty-five as the pension age for men had long been considered ideal, and in 1909 the state pensions at seventy had been justified on financial grounds rather than because it was seriously thought that workers generally were capable of working up to that age. The reduction to sixty-five which took effect in 1928 was, then, generally welcomed. The age of sixty-five, was, however, still considered too high for women, and in 1940 women were awarded state pensions from age sixty, a distinction which has been followed in every further development of the state scheme, including the recent earnings-related provisions. The reasons for this expensive change in the state scheme, first undertaken in time of serious wartime emergency and financial stringency, were complex and confused.[23] Labour interests had been pressing for some time for a reduction in pension ages generally to alleviate unemployment, and more particularly for more generous treatment of men who retired at sixty-five whose wives were younger than they (typically by four years) and were thus ineligible to receive a pension until either their husband died or they reached age sixty-five themselves. Various spinsters' pressure groups were also arguing that working women had two jobs – one in the home and one in employment – and that they therefore deserved to retire earlier. These unlikely arguments won the day in 1940 only because of the immediate need of the government to offer a sweetener to Labour for supporting the war effort. Yet in 1946, with very little discussion of the issue,[24] the lower women's age of sixty was maintained. This was in spite of the fact that Labour's post-war state pension scheme more effectively solved the major problem (the younger wives) by making the joint pension for married couples dependent on the husband's age. Once these decisions had been taken, there was a general feeling that the expectations of women already aroused by the promise of retirement at sixty could not be frustrated by legislative change. The differential, remarkably, was supported even by the Phillips Committee, which in 1953 recommended maintaining a differential while generally raising pension ages to sixty-eight for men and sixty-three for women.[25] (This, like most other recommendations of the Committee, was ignored.) More recently, pressures for greater gender equality have led to demands for the equalization of pension ages, but without any real effect.[26]

The availability of wives' pensions on more generous terms from 1940 increased the incentive for men to retire, and in 1946 an even more powerful incentive emerged when old age pensions were both increased and explicitly transformed into retirement pensions. To secure the increased post-war pensions, men of sixty-five and over henceforward had to retire from full-time work; and if they earned more than £1 a week from part-time work, a new 'earnings rule' claimed back all of it. This explicit retirement condition for state pensions had been favoured by trade unionists as an unemploy-ment palliative, and the wartime Beveridge Report had recommended its adoption.[27] It was, however, held to be less appropriate to the post-war full employment conditions in which it was introduced, and it was therefore partially counter-balanced by an incentive to continue at work. The pension (twenty-six shillings a week for a single person) was increased by two shillings a week for each year of work after the pension age. The benefit for deferment was further raised and the earnings rule further relaxed in later years, as governments attempted to persuade more of the elderly to remain in the work force.[28] Over the following decade about half of those qualifying for state pensions at the normal age chose not to retire immediately, and about a fifth were still working as much as five years after the normal retirement age.[29] The financial advantages in the deferment conditions do not, however, appear to have been widely understood, and were small, so they had little effect.[30] The rise in the real value of the state pension, providing a more powerful incentive to retire, has, however, in recent decades been a potent influence. By the 1970s the mass of the population were retiring at ages very close to those stipulated in the state pension scheme, women retiring a little later, at sixty-one on average, and men a little earlier, at sixty-four.[31] Moreover, only 9% of men in the sixty-five to sixty-nine age-group were by then employed in full-time work: it had become clearly the exception rather than the norm to work much beyond the generally accepted retiring age.[32]

For the small numbers of employees generously covered by occupational schemes around the turn of the century, this pattern of retirement was already becoming familiar; indeed, in some cases, retirement came even earlier. Groups such as civil servants, railway clerks, and policemen could then afford to retire, and they tended to do so far more commonly than their colleagues in employments without adequate pensioning arrangements.[33] Yet while the idea of a 'normal' age of retirement is now clearly established in most employees' minds, such a notion was much less commonly accepted in the nineteenth century. Many early occupational pension schemes specified a relatively young age (fifty-five or sixty was not uncommon) at which pensions could be drawn, but the expectation was that few people would wish to retire at that age, and the pensions were often not such as to provide a strong incentive to do so. Thus, in the Northumberland and Durham miners' scheme (which I have noted as the largest nineteenth-century pension scheme) pensions were available at sixty, but only for those who could provide medical certification of their incapacity to work and prove that earnings from other sources were no more than ten shillings a week. The treasurer of the scheme, clearly reflecting the opinion of members, protested strongly against the idea of compelling retirement at a fixed age, pointing out that while most miners retired between fifty-six and sixty-six, at least one of their members had worked in the pit until he was seventy-seven.[34] In large-scale bureaucracies such as the railways and gas companies, the initiative in setting up and extending pension schemes usually lay with the employer, but, even there, the choice of retirement age for employees could be wide-ranging. In South Metropolitan Gas, for example, with its long-established scheme, 20% of the workmen drawing a pension in 1919 had retired between the ages of fifty-five and fifty-nine, 42% between sixty and sixty-five, 25% between sixty-six and seventy, and 9% between seventy and seventy-eight.[35] There are cases on record of pensions in banks and insurance companies in the early decades of the century being paid to those retiring as late as the age of ninety-eight.[36] The average age of actual retirement for pensioners in fifteen railway pension schemes in the early decades of the present century was sixty-four; and other schemes appear to have had a similar experience.[37] This is identical to the modern average age for retirement, though the spread of ages was undoubtedly greater than it later became.

In the twentieth century it became common to specify a 'normal' age of retirement, and indeed this was usually required by the Inland Revenue as a condition of approval of '1921 Act' trust funds. For men, early schemes often specified a normal or minimum retirement age of sixty. By the 1930s a retirement age of sixty was still accepted as desirable in schemes for male clerical workers and administrative staff, but sixty-five was by then already the most commonly specified.[38] A major reason for manual workers was that the state scheme, with its pension age fixed at sixty-five, encouraged uniformity. Other factors were the improving health standards of workers and the difficulty of financing adequate pensions with young retirement ages. Even when the middle classes were brought into the state scheme in 1946, a wide variety of practice survived for many years, but ultimately the pressures led to the adoption of a normal retirement age of sixty-five, as in the state schemes, almost universally.[39] The largest exceptions were the schemes of the civil service and of similar bureaucracies in the private sector, where a pension age of sixty for clerical and administrative staff had been securely entrenched for many decades. Competition in the labour market and the need to match the generous civil service conditions could still lead to a reversal of the long-run trend to increasing specified retiring ages. For example, Lloyds Bank, which raised its normal retirement age from sixty to sixty-five in 1930, reduced it again to sixty in 1974; and Imperial Tobacco, which raised the age to sixty-five in 1965, reduced it to sixty in 1971. It is, however, too early to discern whether such examples represent a reversal of the earlier long-run trend to higher normal retirement ages.

For women, similar factors have been working to increase the normal pension age specified in schemes.[40] It was quite rare for women to be included in pension schemes at all before the First World War, but, where they were, the normal retirement ages specified were surprisingly low. For example, in Cadburys, where men retired at sixty, the women's normal retirement age was as low as fifty. As late as 1936, when there were 335,000 women in pension schemes, 18% of female manual workers and 37% of female staff had a normal retirement age of fifty-five or less.[41] The reasons for this were obscure, but it is clear that the younger women's pension age was well established even *before* the 1940 decision to reduce it from sixty-five to sixty in the state scheme. Longevity can hardly be an explanation, for working women, like women in general, live longer than men. Nor can the strain of child rearing, for marriage was in most pensionable occupations a ground for dismissal, or at least a ground for exclusion from the pension scheme: we are largely considering a female work force of spinsters in the period before the Second World War. Gender stereotyping – rather than fact – may have a great deal to do with the lower pension age for these women. Managers of female clerical workers, for example, referred to their menopausal symptoms as mentally disabling. Be that as it may, as with men, the power of the state scheme to standardize conditions has been evidenced since the Second World War, and sixty is now the normal retirement age for women in the great majority of pension schemes.[42] The consequence of this, and of their greater longevity, is that the cost of pensioning women can be very considerably greater than the cost of pensioning men.

The specification of a normal age for retirement does not, of course, require an employer to force all workers of that age to retire. As we have seen, there was a wide spread of actual retirement ages in early schemes, and this practice survived for many years.[43] As schemes became more generous, however, the temptations to retire voluntarily at this specified age became greater. Thus the actuary of one railway pension scheme had averred in 1895 that 'you all know that so long as a member can work he will not retire at 60'.[44] But when benefits were improved a few years later to a final salary basis, he had to eat his words as the retirement rate substantially increased.

Employers sometimes welcomed this, but, where they did not, they soon considered providing incentives for their most valuable staff to stay on. Some early schemes had given no extra pension to someone who deferred retirement: the idea was simply that, if he was healthy enough to do so, he was lucky, and should no more expect to draw a pension than he would expect to draw a death benefit if he did not die. However, as funded and insured schemes spread, the accumulating funds were conceived of in terms of 'savings', and it became more natural to think of employees as having to be compensated for not drawing pensions. By the 1940s it was quite common for pensions to be increased by 8% for each year of deferred retirement.[45]

The Inland Revenue, which generally insisted on the specification of a normal retirement age, initially resisted the granting of such deferment rights, on the grounds that it would increase pensions beyond the usual limit of two-thirds of final salary. Just before the Second World War, they extended such regulations to insured schemes, but when wartime conditions made it essential to encourage older workers to remain in the work force, they ceased to enforce this consistently.[46] There was total confusion for a decade after the War about what the Inland Revenue would or would not allow. Some pension increases for deferment were allowed, some people were allowed to draw pensions and also continue working, and some were not allowed to get any benefits from deferment and were forbidden to continue contributing to pension funds.[47] Only in 1953 did it emerge clearly that the Revenue would permit pension increases to compensate for deferred retirement above the usual pension limits, subject to an overriding limit of either forty-five sixtieths of final salary or the actuarially calculated increase.[48] (The latter allowed for the fact that an older retiree would draw his pension later and for fewer years than a normal age retiree.) The Revenue generally discouraged the payment of pensions to those who continued working for the same employer, but (in a glorious piece of logic whose rationale only the dedicated bureaucratic apologist would seek to penetrate) insisted that they be paid rather than deferred if a person upon reaching normal retirement age moved to a new employer. The upshot of this, and of the general labour shortage in post-war conditions of full employment, was that more and more employers offered deferment benefits to employees whom they wanted to retain after normal retiring age; and deferment rights, usually subject to the employer's approval, were increasingly written into the rules of schemes. It was soon quite rare for anyone deferring retirement not to gain some additional pension benefit in consequence.[49] In the civil service, for example, those with an entitlement to a pension and lump sum equivalent to forty-sixtieths of final salary at the normal retirement age of sixty were, from 1949, permitted to increase their pension by up to the equivalent of one-sixtieth for each year of service up to

Table 9.2 *Retirement ages in the UK home civil service, 1975–82*

Age of Retirement	Deferred Retirees 1975–8		Deferred Retirees 1980–2	
	Number	%	Number	%
60	10,373	20	14,781	29
61	3,956	8	14,501	28
62	3,862	8	4,927	10
63	4,051	8	3,493	7
64	12,347	24	5,080	10
65	8,718	17	8,206	16
66	2,050	4	253	0
67	1,462	3	111	0
68	1,103	2	74	0
69	873	2	53	0
70	609	1	36	0
71–5	1,235	2	78	0
	50,639	100	51,593	100

Source: Data supplied to the author by HM Treasury, their reference MFB 8/85 [A/1218]. Figures for 1979 were not available. There were also some deferred retirements before age sixty for some specialist employments with lower retiring ages.

the age of sixty-five. Table 9.2 shows the resulting pattern of deferred retirement, which is typical of modern white-collar employment for generous schemes of this nature.

The deferment provisions took some of the rigidity out of the idea of specifying a normal chronological age of retirement, but they were the easiest adjustments, for the cost, given the actuarial assumptions of most schemes, was nil. Early retirement was more problematical. It was possible to treat it in a parallel way, making an actuarial reduction in pension to allow for the longer period of payment, but that usually produced an unacceptably low pension. Moreover, some schemes were much less generous: they gave only the employee's contributions back to those who retired before the normal age, though some employers made up for this by paying more generous benefits *ex gratia* to employees whom they wished to retire early. By 1956, most public sector schemes already offered better ill-health early retirement pensions based on accrued service (i.e., someone who had worked for thirty rather than the full forty years would receive three-quarters pension), or even more generous provisions. By the 1970s most members of private sector schemes had also gained similar improvements in early retirement benefits, with at least a pension reflecting accrued rights, and, in the more generous schemes, even better pensions, up to the pension that would have been drawn at normal retirement age.[50] Voluntary early retirement, for reasons other than ill-health, was normally only accepted by the Inland Revenue as legitimate if it was no more than ten years before the normal pension age. Employers did sometimes offer this option, typically for five years or less before normal retirement, particularly at times when they were trying to reduce staffing levels as an alternative or supplement to redundancy schemes.

In the 1950s, when there was particular concern at the extent to which increased pensioning might be artificially restricting the labour supply, there were, as we have seen, many criticisms of pension schemes for encouraging discrimination against the old.[51] Some of these criticisms were justified, but most were the results of misunderstanding about the nature of pension schemes. Indeed, in some respects pension schemes provided an extra incentive to employ the old. Those who had reached the normal pension age and accrued full pension rights, for example, were cheaper to employ because no employer's pension contributions were then required, or indeed permitted by the Inland Revenue. The employee would also have a greater incentive to work, since after age sixty-five he paid lower taxes, lower national insurance contributions and eventually got higher state and occupational pension benefits as a result of the deferment provisions. This ought to have meant that older employees were substantially cheaper than younger ones,[52] and thus that they would be employed even if their productivity had fallen off somewhat. In fact, however, employees have increasingly chosen to retire or employers have increasingly compelled them to do so at something near what is now accepted as the normal age of retirement. Can it be that, despite all the adjustments that have been made, there is a strong element of 'ageism', of discrimination by employers against the old, not on grounds of capacity but on grounds of chronological age alone?

The practice which can most clearly be branded as ageism is that of compulsory retirement at some arbitrarily defined, fixed retirement age.[53] This practice was rare in the nineteenth century, and many early pension schemes were extremely flexible about retirement age. This does not, of course, mean that compulsory retirement was then unknown. It was natural for an old employee who could not do his job to be dismissed, and, according to the customs of the trade, locality or firm, he might or might not be offered a light job or an *ex gratia* pension to compensate.[54] Yet it became increasingly common in the twentieth century to require employees to retire at sixty or sixty-five, irrespective of their physical or mental condition. The earliest examples of widespread enforcement of this were for clerical and administrative employees in areas such as the civil service and banks, where mandatory retirement policies were implemented towards the end of the nineteenth century. In almost all such cases, the mandatory policy was backed up by very generous pension provisions. Although many nineteenth-century pension schemes did not include mandatory retirement rules, it was preeminently those same bureaucratically organized employment systems which we have identified as first adopting pension schemes that also first applied mandatory retirement rules. In the civil service, where pensions were payable from age sixty, retirement practices varied between departments in the mid nineteenth century. Civil servants for a time successfully resisted pressure from personnel managers in the Treasury to implement a general mandatory retirement age of sixty-five, but from 1890 this was enforced on senior civil servants, and from 1898 on all grades.[55] Some banks and public utilities, particularly in the last three decades of the century, also began to enforce retirement at ages typically varying between sixty and sixty-five on their clerks. Again, there was opposition from the staff in many cases, though the employers were usually able to buy this off by offering more generous pensions. On the railways, for example, mandatory retirement for clerks was quite generally imposed around the turn of the century, and, in order to win staff acceptance, their employers had to bail out the consequential deficits which emerged in the pension funds. In later decades, too, white-collar employees were more likely than others to have mandatory retirement rules.[56]

How can this pattern be explained? A natural consequence of bureaucracy is that employment practices are enshrined in rules. The spread of mandatory retirement rules may thus in part be a simple consequence of this characteristic of large-scale organizations, which have accounted for a progressively larger share of employment in the course of the twentieth century. Moreover, as greater numbers of employees survived well into their sixties, with improved longevity in the twentieth century, the need to establish clear retirement rules to avoid an excessively aged work force became more insistent. However, the nature of employment contracts in such bureaucracies suggests that the motivation may be more complex than merely the formalization of traditional rules. The whole package of internal labour market institutions, of which we have identified the growth of pension schemes as a part, encouraged long service; but this in itself created strains of a more problematic kind. Employers introducing mandatory retirement often appealed to the needs of younger employees for career progression: the increasing numbers of aged staff were, it was alleged, blocking the promotion prospects of the young. Since such career progression was an important part of the internal labour market incentive structure, particularly for white-collar staff, it was important that such blockages should be removed according to predictable rules. Moreover, job ladders with progressive salary scales also resulted in the older employees being paid rather more than their true output justified. It was difficult to impose salary reductions or demotions on such staff to reflect their declining productivity in old age, particularly given the expectations and hierarchical relationships implicit in such a system. Mandatory retirement, legitimized by more generous pensioning, conveniently allowed bureau-cracies to buy themselves out of the expensive bias towards overpaying older workers implicit in their reward systems. In the twentieth century, such motives were commonly behind the expansion of existing pension schemes or the founding of new ones, and compulsory retirement has thus been closely associated with the spread of pension schemes and modern personnel management practices.[57]

Manual workers were less commonly subjected to mandatory retirement rules; but when they were this often resulted from similar changes in the reward structure. Trade unions had generally attacked the common nineteenth-century practice of employers of gradually reducing the wages of the old in order to reflect their declining productivity, a practice which permitted and encouraged the gradual withdrawal of such workers from the labour force.[58] The unions did so, not because they preferred instantaneous to gradual retirement in principle, but rather because they feared that such practices would undermine union-negotiated pay scales. The unions had varying success in gaining influence over pay scales. Employers resisted union control and in some cases only conceded it on the basis of piece rates which reflected individual worker effort. In the latter type of payment system, older workers found their piece rate earnings declining as they became less productive, and could choose to accept that, or retire voluntarily, perhaps by shifting to less demanding work. Hence, mandatory retirement rules were unnecessary and rarely implemented in these industries.[59] However, in many firms piece work systems declined and union-negotiated hourly rates and new payment systems such as measured day work replaced them, particularly in the post-war period. As they came increasingly to determine the earnings of manual workers, the incentive to employers compulsorily to retire older manual workers also increased. In both manual and non-manual employment in the course of the century, then, mandatory retirement rules have come to be more widely accepted as part of a general package of changes in employment practices.

The development of modern retirement practices has not, of course, been without its critics. Libertarians generally have bemoaned the absence of individual control over the retirement decision.[60] In the inter-war years of high unemployment, there was an increased disposition to view the pensioning of the old, by the state or by employers, as a desirable source of jobs for the young.[61] There was, understandably, a distinct reluctance amongst the old to oblige, at least as long as the state pension remained so inadequate; in fact most of those reaching sixty-five, as we have seen, simply drew the pension but did not retire.[62] By the same token, in the 1950s, when politicians of both parties were exhorting workers not to retire because they were needed in the labour force,[63] they in fact retired in greater numbers as the incentives offered by the improvements in the state scheme and in occupational pension benefits were realized. Because they were locked into already agreed pension structures, moreover, employers were only able to adjust their schemes marginally to discourage retirement.

The evidence on the choice of retirement age by the parties involved shows it to be a complex interactive process which cannot be understood in isolation from the context in which modern practices have developed, or from the incentives for both employers and employees which have been built into this. There are clearly aspects of modern pensioning in which the costs and benefits to society of retiring or continuing at work are *not* reflected in the costs and benefits as perceived at the time of the decision by the individual or his employer. It is the private costs and benefits to these actors which determine the retirement decisions. Some of the gap between private and social costs and benefits is an entirely desirable consequence of the insurance element in pension funds. It is sensible, for example, to share the risks of longevity or widowhood where these cannot be predicted or controlled by the individuals involved. To impose private costs equal to social costs when these benefits are required would, of course, negate many of the achievements of collective risk-sharing which pension schemes encapsulate.

The question remains, however, of whether other practices which are not inherent in rational old age savings, including mandatory retirement at a fixed age, have been explored by employers and employees in a way which has yet definitively produced incentives which are in the best long-term interests of either party. Pensions and mandatory retirement are, as we have seen, so deeply embedded in the whole package of employment practices, particularly those that inhibit gradual reduction in participation paralleled by reduced remuneration, that any real change on this front would imply the overhaul of far more than the pension system alone; it would rather require a rethinking of the whole nature of employment contracts and lifetime work patterns. The last major set of changes in the pensions institution – the extensive modification of pensions to provide an incentive for deferred retirement – occurred in the 1950s, under the pressure of full employment and with employers interested in extending the working lives of their employees. The high levels of unemployment in the 1970s and early 1980s were a less fertile field for the cultivation of new ideas for rebalancing retirement decisions in a more equitable and creative manner.[64]

Epilogue: Contemporary critics and the future of pensions

We knew how to make our predecessors retire. When it comes to forcing our own retirement, our successors must find some method of their own.

C. Northcote Parkinson,
Parkinson's Law, 1958,
p. 122

In the 1980s, the return of mass unemployment on a level not experienced since the 1930s, and the radicalization of politics on both right and left, have changed the focus of the pension debate. Many employees once in pension schemes have been thrown out of both schemes and jobs, with early retirement on pension sometimes used as a means of alleviating the resulting hardship. Between 1979 and 1983, membership of occupational pension schemes declined from 11.8 million to 10.9 million: roughly in line with the fall in employment.[1] The percentage coverage among those full-time employees retaining jobs has remained roughly constant. The coverage of full-time women employees has increased to the same level as that for men, and the coverage of the 'core' work force has shown no signs of receding.[2] More than three-quarters of males over the age of twenty-five are now in occupational pension schemes.[3] Moreover, with improved vesting of pension rights, those who did not maintain stable employment patterns will still accumulate pension rights. Whereas barely a third of retirees drew occupational pensions before compulsory vesting, this proportion is rapidly rising to two-thirds and over. Moreover, women, who form the majority of the old, are now increasingly benefiting from their husbands' schemes through the spread of widows' pensions. Even if occupational pension coverage expands no further, then, the schemes may be expected to make a greater contribution to the well-being of the old than in the past.[4] Meanwhile, pension entitlements for those who are not members of contracted-out occupational schemes – that is, typically, younger workers and part-timers as well as the quarter or so of full-time employees over twenty-five still excluded – are accumulating in the state earnings-related scheme.

There remains a good deal of uncertainty about the future of pension provision. Neither employers nor the state can be relied upon to support present promises. As the proportion of the retired old grows at the beginning of the twenty-first century, some features of schemes may be expected to be called into question, especially if more resources are not created through economic growth, or if the expectations of the working population are not somehow curtailed. Overseas experience already provides some guide to the possibilities. The German Federal government has, for example, recently partly reneged the generous promises in its earnings-related scheme of 1957, arguing that the working population will not tolerate the increased social security contributions necessary to finance full inflation-proofing at a time of European economic recession. In Britain, similarly, when generous promises come to be redeemed, their true value may well depend on the climate of economic growth and expectations at the time.

Initially, recent governments, whether Labour or Conservative, appeared on the surface to have accepted the main features of the 1970s consensus on the state earnings-related scheme. Yet, beneath the surface, the radical wings of both parties have been expressing vociferous discontent with the present pension regime. Debate has focused on the questions of individual pension entitlements and collective or individual control over the funds which now represent the old age savings of so many workers. On the right, there have been increasingly strident calls for further improvements to the vesting of rights for leavers and for the personalization of pensions. This implies a greater choice for individuals in retirement arrangements and greater personal control over the capital resources on which pension entitlements rest. On the left, there has been a new concern to bring pension fund management within the sphere of collective bargaining and union control, with suggestions that the investment of funds should be directed to broader social purposes than those traditionally pursued by their professional investment managers. These developments have taken place, moreover, against an increasingly bleak background of economic recession and public expenditure cuts.[5]

Meanwhile, the pension funds consolidated their position as a financial power in the land. Their assets, just over £40 billion by 1979, have risen to £120 billion in the stock market recovery of 1984, and they were growing at the rate of £13 billion a year. This wealth is more equally distributed than wealth in general, and powerful interest groups in secure, often unionized jobs at the core of the employed work force are the major beneficiaries of this greater equality. Left-wing critics therefore have a less easy target than in the case of other agglomerations of private wealth. After the Labour movement had achieved its major objective of establishing equivalent state earnings-related pensions for excluded groups, then, critical attention focused on the control of the wealth of pension funds rather than on the principle of occupational provision.

It rapidly became evident that the left had a point. Although pension scheme assets were one of the most widespread and significant forms of wealth holding, the beneficiaries have seen their control over it progressively attenuated. Employers were powerful in pension trusts from the beginning, and gradually increased their control as they increased their funding. While early pension schemes often had up to half of the trustees representing the members, this soon became rare.[6] Moreover, the idea that the trustees represented the beneficiaries' interests was no more than a legal fiction. *De facto*, the great bulk of trustee boards and management committees worked in the interests of the employer. Since, as we have seen, they ultimately depended on the continuing willingness of the employer to fund the benefits, this change was perhaps natural, but that it sat uneasily with the trend to increased democratization and participation in modern society was undeniable.

Growing awareness of this factor led some pension schemes to increase member participation voluntarily in the early 1970s. The pension lobbyists prepared advice on voluntary initiatives by employers, and the Occupational Pensions Board recommended greater disclosure of scheme details and greater participation.[7] However, progress was slow until in 1976 the Labour government proposed to compel all pension schemes to have 50% member representation through trade unions.[8] This provoked an outcry, focused particularly on the proposed requirement that trade unions should control the selection of member representatives.[9] The proposals were dropped by a politically insecure government. None the less, in the space of a few years, the pension schemes moved rapidly to protect their position by voluntary action. By the end of the 1970s, the great majority of pension scheme members were in schemes with a substantial degree of member representation.[10]

Activists on the left have been keen that the new powers of members should be used to gain control over the investment strategy of the funds.[11] They have, however, made little headway. Some unions like NALGO actively oppose the idea of directing investment to Socialist purposes, and member representatives generally show the conservative bias of people representing their own interests. Member representation has done much to improve communication and to legitimate the position of pension funds in the employment relationship. Pension managers have sometimes found member representatives useful in helping them to take a more independent line from the employer on policy matters, and the representatives have brought improved shop-floor knowledge to many areas of discretion in individual pension awards. Employers have, however, generally insisted that investment policy should be laid down in only broad terms by the trustees, and interpreted by the management trustees and their professional advisers, rather than by the member trustees. A few union activists have made serious efforts to radicalize investment policies from their position as trustees, but the most flamboyant attempt by Arthur Scargill to achieve this in the National Coal Board pension fund was thwarted by the law on trustees' duties.[12] This is not to deny that the growing investment strength of pension funds has raised real issues about their role in promoting efficient investment behaviour.[13] There is, however, a fundamental weakness in the arguments advanced by the left. If they are to be taken seriously within the context of a continuing capitalist system with private occupational pensions, rather than as intending to subvert that system, then the argument for full employee control of investment policy leads logically to 'money purchase' pensions. Currently, employers are effectively the guarantors of the solvency of pension funds, and their shareholders typically gain or lose more than employees from the quality of investment decisions made. Pension promises are made in the form of defined benefits, usually related to final salary, and employers are willing to take the risk that the assets of the funds will be sufficient to meet these promises. Only if pensions depended instead on defined contributions and investment returns, so that employees rather than shareholders bore the consequences of bad investment decisions, would employers be likely to concede control over the investment policy of the funds. This is unlikely, for, as we have seen, the whole trend of recent policy has been to reduce this money purchase element in pension funds, and unions have shown no inclination to reverse this by advocating such pensions again.[14]

The radical critique of pension funds has also recently found a new home on the right of the political spectrum. The radical right, like the radical left, has been concerned that pension fund money is in a sense 'nobody's money'.[15] Their solution is not greater collective control, but a restoration of individual control over savings through the establishment of personal portable pensions. The culmination of several decades of support for the private pension sector by Conservative radicals such as Margaret Thatcher and Keith Joseph was their disillusionment with the results for personal capitalism.[16] It was thus their think-tank, the Centre for Policy Studies, which in 1983 published a blueprint for the firmer rooting of the pension system in individual property rights.[17] Currently, the nature of the beneficiary's personal interest in a pension scheme is equivocal: if he stays and the employer continues to support the scheme, the rights to income, but not to control of the investments, are much the same as with ordinary property; but if he leaves or if the scheme is wound up or altered, then his rights depend on a complex tangle of requirements in the trust deed and in general legislation. The new CPS proposals were to reduce the conditional element in pension property rights, substituting personal pension accounts over which the holders of the assets would exercise more direct control.

These proposals, like those of the left, ran up against the logic of the pension system as it had evolved in Britain. They, too, would clearly work best on a defined contribution, money purchase basis, for it would be impossible for individuals to persuade any insurance company or other pension provider to pay pensions based on a final salary over which they had no control. Yet this is precisely what employers, who do have control of final salaries, are able to do. As we have seen, most schemes had recently moved to the defined benefit, final salary basis of pension determination. There is no reason, in principle, why well-invested money purchase schemes with appropriate rules should not do just as well as final salary schemes in providing adequate pensions. Yet there were still memories of frustrated expectations in schemes of the old type, and a return to that system appeared unattractive.[18] There were, however, also more substantial, long-run reasons why the proposals from the new right raised eyebrows. In the government, the Treasury was concerned at the tax expenditure implications of any further pension concessions, while the Department of Health and Social Security was worried about proposals which might require an increase in supervisory staff at the Occupational Pensions Board. Employers, already finding the benefits of schemes constrained by the government's legislation to increase leavers' rights, clearly did not welcome the proposal.[19] For employees, too, personal responsibility for pensioning would bring new hazards. Criticism focused on the need to protect consumers from high-pressure salesmanship, and on precisely who would be allowed to sell the new pension contracts. There may indeed be problems of ensuring good decision-making in a competitive, but uncertain and badly informed market such as this, at least initially, would be. An equally serious problem was the higher cost of individual rather than collective provision. Indeed, as we have seen, the insurance companies first moved from individual to collective pension sales in the inter-war years because they perceived the possibilities of economies of scale and reductions in transaction costs.[20] Nothing has changed the logic of that strategy.

Even so, the radical right's solution was sufficiently attractive to Mrs Thatcher's government for Norman Fowler, the Social Services Secretary, to initiate in 1984 a wide-ranging review of provision for retirement, focusing particularly on this issue of personal pensions.[21] Initially, he proposed that any employee should be allowed to opt out of an employer's scheme and receive the national insurance rebate available to contracted-out employees (averaging 4% of earnings) to put into a personal pension plan. This was insufficient to please the radicals, who felt that more of the employers' contributions (averaging 12% of salary) should be available. The proposal was in any case soon dropped, and the government appeared to be settling instead for a less radical solution. The major development, taking effect from 1985, was the strengthening of preservation rights for leavers to include revaluation of up to 5% per annum for inflation and a new option to take an individual, transferable life annuity rather than a deferred pension.[22] The government rejected proposals to compel insurance of funds or increase state control over them, opting rather for improved disclosure and minor adjustments of trust law to strengthen the ability of members collectively to influence schemes.[23] True personal portable pensions seem likely to be largely confined to a third tier of provision, above pensions from the state and from the employer. These 'additional voluntary contributions' ('AVCs') are already permitted in employers' schemes, but have developed only slowly in the few companies which have encouraged them.[24] The pension interests have, however, pushed them strongly as a viable route to attaining a dimension of individual control.

This compromise will not challenge the present basis of the pensions institution as it has grown up over the last half-century in Britain. Preserved rights have, it is true, now been clearly accepted as a major improvement to the system. 'The argument that the pension industry was built up to provide an employee reward system for life-long service no longer cuts much ice', claimed the incoming president of the Institute of Actuaries in 1984.[25] In this sense individual portability has been partly achieved, but AVCs are unlikely to become as important in strengthening individual rights. Indeed, questions are increasingly asked about whether in some companies pensioning is now too generous. Voices are heard suggesting that the pension system, far from requiring topping up, should be cut back. British Airways recently gave its employees the option of poorer pensions for more immediate cash; more than half preferred the cash.[26] Moreover, even the state earnings-related scheme has come under attack as both being too generous and imposing too much of a stranglehold on change in the private pension system. The champions of personal portable pensions, seeing the imminent failure of their plans, have proposed both the abolition of the state scheme and the end of tax reliefs for occupational pensions.[27] In questioning the tax privileges of occupational schemes, the radical right has thus arrived at the same position as Professor Titmuss on the left thirty years earlier. The left, meanwhile, rushed to the defence of the status quo, with the Trades Union Congress urging the retention of the tax privileges for the occupational funds from which so many of their members benefited.[28]

For a time, it appeared that the Chancellor would indeed restrict the tax concessions to funds.[29] The pensions industry therefore breathed a sigh of relief in March 1985 when he made it clear that he would not do so. For the time being, then, political consensus appeared to have survived the opening up of ideological cracks on both left and right. The radicalism of the right was not, however, dead. A few months later, it emerged that the government intended to phase out the state earnings-related pension scheme on which more than half the working population depended for benefits in addition to the flat-rate pension. This promised to throw even more of the weight of old age saving on to the occupational sector. If the history of pensions is a guide, we can be confident that the occupational pensions movement is unlikely to show the same profile in future decades as it does today.[30]

Statistical appendix

The Government Actuary carried out his first comprehensive survey of occupational pension schemes in 1956; further surveys followed in 1963, 1967, 1971, 1975, 1979, and 1983. Table A.1 summarizes the information on pension scheme membership which is available from these surveys.

Table A.1 *Pension scheme membership, 1956–83*

Year	Total all schemes	Total private sector	Total public sector	Total men	Total women	Total manual	Total non-manual
	(all figures in millions)						
1956	8.0	4.3	3.7	6.4	1.6	4.2*	3.8*
1963	11.1	7.2	3.9	9.4	1.7	5.7	5.4
1967	12.2	8.1	4.1	9.9	2.3	5.8	6.4
1971	11.1	6.8	4.3	8.7	2.4	4.7	6.4
1975	11.4	6.0	5.4	8.6	2.8	5.2	6.3
1979	11.8	6.2	5.6	8.5	3.3	n.a.	n.a.
1983	10.4	n.a.	n.a.	n.a.	n.a.	n.a.	n.a.

Note: * Categories are 'waged' and 'salaried', which, at that time, were roughly equivalent to the distinction between 'manual' and 'non-manual'.

Sources: Government Actuary, *Occupational Pension Schemes: A Survey*, 1958
Occupational Pension Schemes: A New Survey, 1966
Occupational Pension Schemes: Third Survey, 1968
Occupational Pension Schemes: 1971: Fourth Survey, 1972
Occupational Pension Schemes: 1975: Fifth Survey, 1978
Occupational Pension Schemes: 1979: Sixth Survey, 1981
Preliminary report of 1983 survey in *Pensions World*, January 1985
(Where initial results were modified in a subsequent survey, the modified results are shown in the table.)

These estimates of coverage are based on sample surveys and it is possible that sampling errors account for some of the differences shown: in particular, the level of membership shown in 1967 may be too high. The original surveys should be consulted for a more detailed breakdown of the statistics, and for data on a wider range of questions. The first three surveys, for 1956, 1963 and 1967, incorporated some questions which were not well formulated, and care should be exercised, particularly in comparing the results of consecutive surveys; but from 1971 the questionnaires have produced plausible, comparable results in consecutive surveys on a wide range of pension scheme issues, ranging from the adoption of final salary schemes to the participation of members in the management of schemes. For more recent years, annual surveys of pension schemes have been conducted by the National Association of Pension Funds (eg. NAPF, *Ninth Annual Survey of Occupational Pension Schemes, 1983*, Croydon, 1983), and these provide useful additional information on the characteristics of schemes. The coverage is, however, more limited than the Government Actuary's surveys: about half of the members of pension schemes, principally those in relatively small schemes, are excluded from the NAPF surveys.

These sources provide no information on the rate of return on the investments of pension funds. Various commercial monitoring services, including those of Cubie, Wood; Phillips & Drew; Bacon & Woodrow; and Wood McKenzie published appraisals from time to time, often including longer-run statistical series for comparison. Table A.2 is reproduced by kind permission of Phillips & Drew, and shows the experience of the average private sector fund (excluding property investments) over the last two decades. Alternative estimates of the size of investment funds and the rate of return can be made from government statistics of national income and of the flow of funds, published annually in the blue books of *National Income and Expenditure*, and in *Financial Statistics*.

In the last three decades, the quality of statistical data on pension schemes has greatly improved. The period before 1956 is, however, a statistical dark age, punctuated only by the Ministry of Labour survey of private sector 'Schemes providing for Pensions for Employees on Retirement from Work' (*Ministry of Labour Gazette*, May 1938, 172–4), which has been extensively drawn on in the text, particularly in Chapter 3. The estimate in the text of coverage increasing from one in twenty of the work force in the first decade of the twentieth century to one in eight around 1936 (compared with one in three by the time of the first Government Actuary's survey in 1956) is extremely approximate, but is supported in Chapter 1, n. 63 and in Chapter 3, n. 36.

Estimates of coverage and representative statistics showing the changing nature of schemes are difficult to identify before 1956. The Registrar of

Table A.2 *Estimated rates of return on private sector pension funds, 1963–84*

| Year | Rates of return (including capital gains and losses) | |
	(1) Money returns	(2) Real returns
	(%)	(%)
1963	+ 11.5	+ 9.6
1964	− 3.2	− 8.0
1965	+ 7.0	+ 2.5
1966	− 0.2	− 3.9
1967	+ 18.8	+ 16.3
1968	+ 25.3	+ 19.4
1969	− 8.4	− 13.1
1970	− 0.5	− 7.5
1971	+ 38.4	+ 29.4
1972	+ 9.3	+ 1.6
1973	− 21.8	− 32.4
1974	− 32.6	− 51.7
1975	+ 75.6	+ 50.5
1976	+ 7.3	− 7.8
1977	+ 41.1	+ 29.0
1978	+ 4.4	− 4.0
1979	+ 6.4	− 10.8
1980	+ 27.8	− 12.7
1981	+ 10.4	− 1.5
1982	+ 34.4	+ 25.8
1983	+ 24.7	+ 20.1
1984	+ 23.7	+ 18.7

Sources: col. (1): Phillips & Drew monitoring service
col. (2): col. (1) less the percentage change in the Retail Price Index for that year

Friendly Societies (in his *Annual Reports* from 1930) published statistical data on the (probably unrepresentative) minority of funds which were registered under the 1927 Validation Act. There were also very occasional statistical surveys of particular questions conducted by the Association of Superannuation and Pension Funds in the 1940s and 1950s. These data have occasionally been quoted in the notes. Copies of these early ASPF statistical publications are difficult to locate, but a complete set is preserved in the library of the National Association of Pension Funds in Croydon.

The statistical darkness for the early years is also less than total in the case of insurance schemes, and Table A.3 shows the growth in such schemes before the fuller estimates produced by the Government Actuary for the contemporary period. Further statistics on insured schemes were published annually by the Life Offices' Association and the Associated Scottish Life Offices in the 1950s, but the definitions used varied from year to year, and their value as a continuous series is thus limited.

Table A.3 *Group life and pensions business, 1934–49*

	Employees covered			Premium income (£m)		
(1)	(2)	(3)	(4)	(5)	(6)
Year	Five major offices*	Legal & General only	Five major offices*	Legal & General only	Prudential only
1934	120,000	92,457	1.3	0.7	n.a.
1936	255,240†	n.a.	n.a.	n.a.	n.a.
1939	366,000	228,941	5.1	2.6	1.1‡
1944	500,100	n.a.	9.1	4.6	1.7§
1949	709,200	355,147	21.5	9.0	5.0

Notes: * = not named by Pingstone, but probably the Legal & General, Prudential, Eagle Star, Standard Life, and Friends Provident
† = not strictly comparable with the rest of this column: probably includes business of other offices and some schemes based on individual endowment policies
‡ = relates to 1938
§ = relates to 1943

Sources: cols. (2) & (4): G. W. Pingstone, 'Group Life and Pension Schemes . . .', *Journal of the Institute of Actuaries*, LXXVII, 1951 (except 1936, which is from the *Ministry of Labour Gazette*, May 1938, 172)
col. (3): G. W. Pingstone, 'The Group Department', *Temple Bar*, June 1959, 7
cols. (5) and (6): company archives

The only long-run, annual series on pension schemes for earlier years are on the numbers of schemes. Table A.4 summarizes the available data. The limitations of these series are discussed further in Chapter 3 (pp. 38–40 above).

Table A.4 *The number of occupational pension schemes, 1917–56*

Year	(1) Number of pension funds approved under the 1921 Finance Act	(2) Number of pension funds registered under the 1927 Validation Act	(3) Number of pension schemes which were members of the ASPF
1917	n.a.	n.a.	11*
1919	n.a.	n.a.	55*
1923	n.a.	n.a.	85
1924	n.a.	n.a.	109
1925	n.a.	n.a.	139
1926	n.a.	n.a.	162
1927	n.a.	n.a.	173
1928	924	45	204
1929	1,085	149	227
1930	1,222	183	254
1931	1,384	207	287
1932	1,481	219	309
1933	1,557	222	327
1934	1,641	237	358
1935	1,755	254	398
1936	1,878	268	416
1937	2,021	281	451
1938	2,156	292	473
1939	2,291	304	488
1940	2,394	303	505
1941	2,424	306	559
1942	n.a.	313	619
1943	n.a.	321	697
1944	n.a.	342	787
1945	n.a.	353	814
1946	n.a.	367	835
1947	n.a.	383	866
1948	n.a.	403	882
1949	n.a.	417	945
1950	n.a.	426	1,037
1951	4,348	432	1,052
1952	4,924	438	1,051
1953	n.a.	436	1,091
1954	n.a.	436	1,077
1955	n.a.	432	1,102
1956	n.a.	426	1,128

Note: * relates to membership of the Conference of Superannuation Funds, the predecessor of the Association of Superannuation and Pension Funds

Sources: col. (1): Letter, Inland Revenue to D. N. Chester, 12 August 1942, in PRO ACT 1/683; *Journal of the Institute of Actuaries*, LXXX, 1954, 141; but cf. LXXX, 439
col. (2): *Annual Reports of the Chief Registrar of Friendly Societies*
col. (3): Association of Superannuation and Pension Funds, archives, and *Annual Reports*

A note on sources

There are no secondary works comprehensively covering the development of occupational pension schemes over the last hundred years. However, there is a very large specialist literature in professional journals of actuaries, insurance brokers, personnel managers and so on which has been extensively drawn on in the writing of this book. Full references to such sources, and to the publications in book form dealing with particular questions in specific years, are given in the notes. However, the narrative and analysis in the text also rest on an extensive survey of archival material which is mainly in the hands of private owners, usually the pension funds themselves. These 'archives' are usually in current use and are not generally open to the public. None the less, permission to use them was generously granted in some cases, subject to basic safeguards for the confidentiality of information on individual members. Where a statement about a particular fund is made in the text without any reference to published sources, the reader may assume the information is based on these archives. The following employers' pension schemes were among those surveyed:

Bank of England
British Steel Corporation
Cadbury–Schweppes
C. & J. Clark
Thomas Cook
Distillers Co.
Electricity Council

Federated Superannuation System for Nurses
Federated Superannuation System for Universities
Fine Cotton Spinners & Doublers (Courtaulds, Northern Spinning
   Division)
Greater London Council
Imperial Group
Lloyds Bank
London Transport
Lucas Industries
Marks & Spencer
Midland Bank
National Westminster Bank
Reckitt & Colman
Rowntree Mackintosh
Shell Group
W. H. Smith & Son
South Western Gas Board
Unilever
Universities Superannuation Scheme

The addresses of these and other pension schemes may generally be found in the current edition of the National Association of Pension Funds *Yearbook* (Croydon, 1985 and annually).

In addition the following pension schemes and related archives were identified in public repositories:

Bryant & May	Rose Lipman Library, Hackney
City of London General Pension Society	Guildhall Library
Gas Light & Coke Co.	Greater London Record Office
Journeyman Boot & Shoemakers' Pension Society	Guildhall Library
London Life Association	Guildhall Library
Merchant Seamen's Pension Fund	Public Record Office
Metropolitan Railway	Greater London Record Office
Nationalized Industries	Public Record Office
Navvies' Old Age Pension Fund	Sion College Library
Northumberland and Durham Miners' Permanent Relief Fund	Tyne and Wear Archives, Newcastle
Railway Companies (pre-1948)	Public Record Office
South Metropolitan Gas Co.	Greater London Record Office
Wallpaper Trade Superannuation Society	Modern Records Centre, Warwick

Other, mainly private archives which provided useful material include those of:

Association of Scientific, Technical and Managerial Staff
Bacon & Woodrow
Clerical, Medical & General Assurance
Confederation of British Industry predecessors (Modern Records Centre, Warwick)
Equitable Life
Industrial Society
Labour Party
Legal & General Group
Life Offices' Association
Management Research Group (Ward Papers, Business History Unit, London)
Metropolitan Life, New York
National Association of Pension Funds
National Federation of Professional Workers (Modern Records Centre, Warwick)
Prudential Group
Trades Union Congress

There is a danger in all work in economic history that the historian's attention is focused too much on success, for the archives of successful institutions are the ones that survive. It was possible to counteract this to some extent through the assistance of the Registrar of Friendly Societies, who kindly provided access to such records of seventy-four pension funds as were in his possession by virtue of their being registered under the 1927 Validation Act. The correct interpretation of the thirty-year rule for access to public records is still uncertain. The Registrar took the view that any funds whose registration was cancelled before 1954 could be opened to us. The result was that we were able to inspect the records of many schemes which had been wound up, as this was the common reason for cancelling registration (indeed, there was no other legal means available to cancel registration).

We were thus able to base our historical generalizations on the experience of over 300 pension schemes for which archival evidence or substantial published material existed. A fuller listing of these schemes is available from the Business History Unit of the London School of Economics.

Notes

Unless otherwise stated the place of publication is London.

1 Savings, work and old age in Victorian Britain

1. Adam Smith, *An Inquiry Into the Nature and Causes of the Wealth of Nations*, 1776 (1937 edition, p. 671).
2. Peter Laslett, *Family Life and Illicit Love in Earlier Generations*, 1977, Chapter 5.
3. M. A. Crowther, 'Family Responsibility and State Responsibility in Britain before the Welfare State', *Historical Journal*, xxv, 1982; David William Thomson, 'Provision for the Elderly in England 1830 to 1908', Ph.D. thesis, Cambridge, 1980; *Report of the Departmental Committee on the Aged Deserving Poor*, Cd 67, 1900 (BPP, x, 1900), Appendix II, p. 11.
4. See, e.g., Lady Bell, *At the Works*, 1907, pp. 110–11.
5. *Report on the Royal Commission on the Poor Laws*, Cd 4499, 1909 (BPP, xxxvii, 1909), p. 178.
6. Thomson, *op. cit.*; Michael Anderson, 'England: Preston in Comparative Perspective', in Peter Laslett, ed., *Household and Family in Past Time*, Cambridge, 1972.
7. Keith Thomas, 'Age and Authority in Early Modern England', *Proceedings of the British Academy*, LXII, 1976.
8. *Censuses of Population, passim*. In 1841, 4.4% of the British population was aged sixty-five or over; in 1901 the proportion was still only 4.7%.
9. In 1901–10 the expectation of life for men aged twenty was forty-three and for women, forty-six (United Nations, *Statistical Yearbook 1959*, New York, 1959, p. 50).

10. Thomas, *op. cit.*

11. In 1881, 73.6% of males aged sixty-five and over were working; in 1891, 65.6%; and in 1901, 61.4%. The proportions of females were similar after allowance is made for lower female labour force participation (C. H. Feinstein, R. C. O. Matthews and J. C. Odling-Smee, *British Economic Growth, 1856–1973*, Oxford, 1982, pp. 57, 506–64). Earlier censuses did not ask appropriate questions on retirement from former occupations for sufficiently reliable aggregate estimates to be made. This is perhaps itself an indication of the lower incidence and perceived importance of retirement.

12. R. J. Morris, 'The Middle Class and the Property Cycle During the Industrial Revolution', in T. C. Smout, ed., *The Search for Wealth and Stability: Essays in Economic and Social History Presented to M.W. Flinn*, 1979.

13. Barry Supple, *The Royal Exchange Assurance: A History of British Insurance, 1720–1970*, Cambridge, 1970, pp. 221–2.

14. In 1899–1900, 18% of Schedule D and 22% of Schedule E taxpayers claimed the relief. The relief for the 22% of Schedule E taxpayers amounted to 2% of *all* Schedule E income (including those on which relief was not claimed) (*Annual Report of the Commissioners of Inland Revenue on the Inland Revenue*, 1899–1900, Cd 347, 1900 (BPP, XVIII, 1900)), pp. 124–5. In 1903, 22% of taxpaying civil servants claimed the insurance relief, and they claimed it for 5% of their incomes (*Report of the Commission on Superannuation in the Civil Service*, Cd 1744, 1903 (BPP, XXXIII, 1903)), pp. viii–ix. Civil servants, having an excellent pension scheme, might have been expected to spend less on life assurance than others with comparable incomes (above the tax threshold) at this time.

15. 'Annuities IV', *The Economist*, 14 October 1916, 645–6; Supple, *op. cit.*, pp. 257–8; H. J. P. Oakley, 'On the Annuity Business of the British Life Offices and the Valuation Thereof', *Journal of the Institute of Actuaries*, XLIII, 1909.

16. Paul Johnson, 'Credit and Thrift: A Study of Working Class Household Budget Management in Britain, 1870–1939', Ph.D. thesis, Oxford, 1982.

17. Samuel Smiles, *Thrift*, 1875, pp. 17–71; John Martinson, 'Pensions and Voluntary Effort: A Suggestion and an Experiment', in Committee on Old Age Pensions, *Old Age Pensions: A Collection of Short Papers*, 1903, pp. 170–86.

18. See, e.g., Gareth Stedman-Jones, *Outcast London*, Oxford, 1971.

19. See, e.g., Ross McKibbin, 'Working Class Gambling in Britain, 1880–1939', *Past and Present*, No. 82, 1979, for a sympathetic view of the benefits of gambling.

20. 'Provision for Old Age by Trade Societies', *The Labour Gazette*, July 1893, 64, August 1893, 89, November 1893, 168, December 1893, 199, January 1894, 24.

21. Bentley B. Gilbert, 'The Decay of Provident Institutions and the Coming of Old Age Pensions in Great Britain', *Economic History Review*, XVII, 1965.

22. This account is based on the records of the Society, 1862–1938, in the Tyne and Wear County Archive Department (ref. 919/31). See also the remarks of the fund's general treasurer in giving evidence to the Ryland Atkins Committee, Cmd 411, 1919 (BPP, XXVII, 1919), qq. 5448ff.

23. Cf. p. 32 below for its subsequent demise.

24. See p. 11 below.

25. See, e.g., Michael R. Hain, 'Industrial Work and the Family Life Cycle, 1889–

1900', in Paul Uselding, ed., *Research in Economic History*, IV, Greenwich, Connecticut, 1979, pp. 279–356. See also pp. 129–30 below.

26. Bell, *op. cit.*, p. 109; T. A. B. Corley, *Quaker Enterprise in Biscuits: Huntley & Palmers of Reading, 1822–1972*, 1972, p. 100.

27. Long-run trends in these factors are discussed in Chapter 9 below.

28. Evidence of William Marshall (managing clerk, Vickers) to Royal Commission on the Poor Laws and Relief of Distress (*Minutes of Evidence*, Cd 5066, 1910 (BPP, XLVIII, 1910) qq. 87722, 87952); W. Beveridge, *Unemployment: A Problem of Industry* 1919, p. 211; Keith Middlemass and John Barnes, *Baldwin: A Biography*, 1969, p. 9.

29. *Report of the Departmental Committee on the Aged Deserving Poor*, Cd 67, 1900 (BPP, X, 1900), Appendix II, p. 11.

30. Michael Anderson, 'The Impact on the Family Relationships of the Elderly of Changes Since Victorian Times in Governmental Income-Maintenance', in Ethel Shanas and Marvin Sussman, eds., *Family, Bureaucracy, and the Elderly*, Durham, N.C., 1977; Jill S. Quadagno, *Aging in Early Industrial Society: Work, Family, and Social Policy in Nineteenth Century England*, New York 1982, Chapter 5; Thomson, *op. cit.*

31. A precise quantitative assessment of their thesis is difficult, given the aggregation of poor law expenditure (which was rising with population and living standards) on the aged with that on other paupers. Still, they have produced coherent regional and circumstantial evidence of increasing tightness to support the view in the text.

32. Joseph L. Melling, 'British Employers and the Development of Industrial Welfare c. 1880–1920: An Industrial and Regional Comparison', Ph.D. thesis, 2 vols., Glasgow, 1980; A. E. Musson, *Enterprise in Soap and Chemicals: Joseph Crosfeld & Sons Ltd., 1815–1965*, Manchester, 1965, p. 177; Norman Mutton, 'William Orme Foster', in D. J. Jeremy, ed., *Dictionary of Business Biography*, Vol. 2, 1984; T. A. B. Corley, *op. cit.*, p. 101; D. C. Coleman, *Courtaulds: An Economic and Social History*, Vol. 1, Oxford, 1969, p. 257. Some *ex gratia* pensions could be extremely large for the top men: for instance, the assistant actuary of the Equitable Life Company was in 1817 pensioned on full salary after forty-two years' service (M. E. Ogborn, *Equitable Assurance*, 1962, p. 161). At London Life, William Docker received a pension of £1,700 p.a. between his retirement and his death in 1904: see Minutes of the Meetings of the Court of Directors, Vol. 18, 13 May 1904, p. 439, in Guildhall Library, ref. Ms. 19,636.

33. See, e.g., the remarks of A. J. Hobson (Sheffield) in *Report of the 48th Annual Meeting of the Association of Chambers of Commerce of the United Kingdom*, 1908, p. 147.

34. See, e.g., Sidney Pollard and Paul Robertson, *The British Shipbuilding Industry, 1870–1914*, Cambridge, Mass, 1979, p. 199. For a sensitive description of the gift relationships between employer and employee see Patrick Joyce, *Work, Society and Politics: The Culture of the Factory in Late Victorian England*, Sussex, 1980, especially p. 170.

35. E.g., the 1879 partnership minutes of the Walker lead manufacturers bluntly state 'No pensions to be granted under any circumstances': David J. Rowe, 'A History of the Lead Manufacturing Industry in Great Britain, 1778–1980',

Ph.D. thesis, Newcastle, 1982, 224, 392. See also Rowe, *Lead Manufacturing in Britain: A History*, 1983, p. 201.

36. Captain Michael Peters, 'The Mischief of Pensions', *Gentleman's Magazine*, CCCIII, August and September 1907; Reginald Pound, *Selfridge: A Biography*, 1960, p. 110.

37. Joseph Melling, 'Employers, Industrial Welfare and the Struggle for Workplace Control in British Industry, 1880–1920', in Howard F. Gospel and Craig R. Littler, eds., *Managerial Strategies and Industrial Relations: An Historical and Comparative Study*, 1983, pp. 64–6; Bell, *op. cit.*, p. 121; Bernard W. E. Alford, *W. D. & H. O. Wills and the Development of the U.K. Tobacco Industry, 1786–1965*, 1973, p. 290. For an example of a typical nineteenth-century occupational dividing and savings club (without pension benefits) see the records of the Street Shoemakers' Benefit Society in C. & J. Clark archives, Street.

38. Marios Raphael, *Pensions and Public Servants: A Study of the Origins of the British System*, Paris, 1964.

39. Samuel Johnson, *Dictionary*, 1755.

40. Gerald Rhodes, *Public Sector Pensions*, 1965.

41. On the operation of the civil service scheme see *Report of the Commission on Superannuation in the Civil Service*, Cd 1744, 1903 (BPP, XXXIII, 1903).

42. See Rhodes, *op. cit.*; H. W. Manly and T. G. Ackland, 'On the Superannuation and Pension Funds of Certain Metropolitan Borough Councils . . .', *Journal of the Institute of Actuaries*, XLVI, 1912; P. H. J. H. Gosden, *The Evolution of a Profession*, Oxford, 1972, pp. 132ff. Many of these varied quite sharply from the civil service or armed forces schemes, for example in being funded, or in providing benefits on other than a final salary basis.

43. The first non-statutory superannuation fund in the private sector known to me (and drawn to my attention by John H. Boyes, editor of the *Newcomen Bulletin*) was for lock-keepers on the River Lee. Salary deductions of two shillings a week provided pensions of up to ten shillings a week (minutes of the Committee of Trustees of the River Lee, 8 January 1821, in PRO RAIL 845/9). There were earlier *statutory* schemes for 'private sector' companies such as the East India Company and the Bank of England and for groups like merchant seamen; and there were many earlier examples of *ex gratia* unfunded pensions (see, e.g., M. B. Donald, *Elizabethan Monopolies: The History of the Company of Mineral and Battery Works from 1565 to 1604*, 1961, p. 104).

44. Philip S. Bagwell, *The Railway Clearing House in the British Economy, 1842–1922*, 1968, p. 165.

45. PRO RAIL 1086/2.

46. *Report of the Departmental Committee on Railway Superannuation Funds*, Cd 5349, 1910 (BPP, LVII, 1910). See also A. Hewat, *Widows' and Pension Funds*, 1896.

47. Jon Press, 'The Collapse of a Contributory Pension Scheme: The Merchant Seamen's Fund, 1747–1851', *Journal of Transport History*, V, 1979. For the failure of subsequent attempts to develop a scheme see the papers in PRO MT 9/19, 9/36, 9/178, 9/328, and 9/600.

48. *Report on the Departmental Committee on Railway Superannuation Funds*, Cmd 5349, 1919 (BPP, LVII, 1910).

49. See the evidence of Mr Wilcox (LNWR) in *Evidence to the Departmental Committee on Old Age Pensions*, Cmd 411, 1919 (BPP, XXVII, 1919), qq. 3727, 3907.
50. 'Personal Memorandum for the Unofficial Use of Mr. Lambert in his Discussions on the Financial State of the Provident Fund and the Servants' Pension Fund', May 1894 in PRO RAIL 258/207, Part 1.
51. PRO RAIL 258/207, 258/298.
52. Sterling Everard, *History of the Gas Light & Coke Company*, 1949, pp. 117–22, 176, 197, 207–8, 266–7, 290–1, 324–5; evidence of H. F. Ibbs, accountant to the company, in Cmd 411, 1919, qq. 4335ff.
53. See, e.g., Joseph Melling, 'Industrial Strife and Business Welfare Philosophy: The Case of the South Metropolitan Gas Company from the 1880s to the War', *Business History*, XXI, 1979; see also the company's archives in Greater London Council Archives, class B/S Met G/III.
54. Midland Bank Archives, London Joint Stock Bank Annual Reports and Board Minutes Q 4 (for 16 January 1845 and 1 January 1846).
55. *Bankers' Magazine*, XLIII, September 1883, 857, October 1883, 999, 1029–30, November 1883, 1099–1101, XLIX, January 1884, 24–9.
56. R. S. Sayers, *Lloyds Bank in the History of English Banking*, Oxford, 1957, p. 85; J. R. Winton, *Lloyds Bank, 1918–1969*, Oxford, 1982, p. 41.
57. E. H. Phelps Brown, *The Growth of British Industrial Relations*, 1959, p. 78; Supple, *op. cit.*, pp. 385–90. At the Royal Exchange, the scheme was formalized only in terms of levels of benefit. Technically, pensions often remained *ex gratia* in the Royal Exchange and elsewhere. The Royal Exchange scheme was not funded, by the balance-sheet reserve method, until 1890.
58. *Royal Commission on the Civil Service, Minutes of Evidence*, Cd 1745, 1903 (BPP XXXIII, 1903), qq. 5147, 5151, evidence of H. W. Manly, Actuary and Secretary, Equitable Life.
59. 4 and 5 Will. IV c. 24.
60. J. D. Scott, *Siemens Brothers, 1858–1958*, 1958, p. 248; Phelps Brown, *op. cit.*, p. 78. For a discussion of the aims of German company welfarism see Eugene M. McCreary, 'Social Welfare and Business: The Krupp Welfare Programme, 1860–1914', *Business History Review*, XLII, 1968. France also seems to have developed pension schemes unusually early: see Peter N. Stearns, *Old Age in European Society: The Case of France*, 1977, pp. 52–8, 145. See also Max Horlick and A. M. Skolnik, *Private Pension Schemes in West Germany and France*, Washington, 1971.
61. Coats founded their scheme in 1895, Colmans and Wills in 1899.
62. The Statistical Department of the Board of Trade prepared a list of pension schemes for internal use in 1912, but that does not appear to have survived. These early statistical efforts were later described as 'half-hearted' and 'entirely dropped during the War': see E. C. Ramsbottom, memorandum of 27 June 1923, in PRO LAB 2/1576, file 583/1929.
63. In 1907–8, the railway funds included 91,126 staff members and 190,133 manual workers: *Report of the Departmental Committee on Railway Superannuation Funds*, Cd 5349, 1910 (BPP, LVII, 1910). The Northumberland and Durham Miners' Permanent Relief Society had 142,092 members in 1901 (1911 Valuation Report, ref. 919/36 in Tyne and Wear County Archives Department).

There were 107,782 established civil servants in 1902 (*Return Showing the Total Number of Persons in the Established Civil Service . . .* 1902 (BPP, LXXXIII, 1902), p. 61). There were 122,500 in the navy in 1902 (*Navy Estimates for the Year 1902/ 3 . . .*, 1902 (BPP, LIX, 1902)) and 284,378 in the army (*General Annual Report on the British Army for the year 1902*, Cd 1496, 1903 (BPP, XXXVIII, 1903), Part 2, p. 4.), but these numbers were exceptionally high in the aftermath of the South African War and many of those serving were not pensionable. There were more than 100,000 other public sector workers (e.g., teachers, policemen, local government employees) in pension schemes at the turn of the century. The other several dozen private sector pension schemes known to be in existence around 1900 rarely had more than 1,500 members. See also the listings in 'Old Age Pensions: Tables and Memoranda', Cd 3618, 1907 (BPP, LXVII, 1907). The total population in employment in 1900 was 18,020,000 (C. H. Feinstein, *National Income, Expenditure and Output of the United Kingdom, 1855–1965*, Cambridge, 1972, p. T125).

64. See n. 36 above.

2 Rival pioneers of collectivism: pensions, the state and employers (1899–1927)

1. There is a large literature on the coming of state old age pensions in Britain. The text draws particularly on the following: R. V. Sires, 'The Beginning of British Legislation for Old Age Pensions', *Journal of Economic History*, XIV, 1954; D. Collins, 'The Introduction of Old Age Pensions in Great Britain', *Historical Journal*, VIII, 1965; J. H. Treble, 'The Attitude of the Friendly Societies Towards the Movement in Great Britain for State Pensions, 1878–1908', *International Review of Social History*, XV, 1970; Bentley B. Gilbert, 'The Decay of Provident Institutions and the Coming of Old Age Pensions in Great Britain', *Economic History Review*, XVII, 1965; Patricia M. Williams (now Thane), 'The Development of Old Age Pension Policy in Great Britain, 1878–1925', Ph.D. thesis, London, 1970; Patricia Thane, 'Noncontributory vs. Insurance Pensions, 1878–1908', in Thane, ed., *Origins of British Social Policy*, 1978.

2. For a sensitive discussion of the factors behind the change in labour attitudes, see Patricia Thane, 'The Working Class and State Welfare in Britain, 1880–1914', *Historical Journal*, XXVII, 1984.

3. *Statement Showing for Certain Areas in England and Wales the Number of Old-Age Pensioners . . .*, Cd 7015, 1913 (BPP, LV, 1913), Part I.

4. *Ibid.*, p. 3; A. H. Halsey, *Trends in British Society Since 1900*, 1972, p. 385.

5. Williams, *op. cit.*, p. 252; Charles Booth, *Old Age Pensions and the Aged Poor*, 1899, pp. 37, 70.

6. The pension was raised to seven shillings and sixpence in 1916 and to ten shillings in 1920. In 1910, five shillings was 22% of average weekly wage earnings; ten shillings was only 15% of average wage earnings at the inflation peak of 1920, but after the deflation of the 1920s was 21% again by 1925 (calculated from data in E. H. Phelps Brown and Margaret H. Browne, *A Century of Pay*, 1968, pp. 444–6). However, pensioners may have experienced more favourable price increases than others: the Phelps Brown and Hopkins index of consumer prices (heavily weighted by food and clothing) rose from

1058 in 1909 to 2591 in 1920, falling to 1708 in 1925. Taking into account this, and the wartime imposition of rent control, pensioners may have been considerably better off in 1925 than when pensions were first introduced, and they had certainly roughly maintained parity with the working population after a devastating fall in living standards during the wartime inflation.

7. Williams, *op. cit.*, Chapters 13 and 14; Martin Gilbert, *Winston S. Churchill*, vol. 5, *1922–1939*, 1976, pp. 65–91; David Dilks, *Neville Chamberlain*, Cambridge, 1984, vol. 1, pp. 412–13, 422–37.
8. *Old Age Pensions: Tables and Memorandum*, Cd 3618, 1907 (BPP, LXVIII, 1907).
9. The 1937 Pensions Act extended coverage on a voluntary basis to those earning up to £400 p.a., providing full pensions after only ten years' contributions, but it was less widely taken up than expected. For coverage in the early 1940s, see *Social Insurance and Allied Services*, Cmd 6404, 1942 (BPP, VI, 1942–3, p. 195).
10. Fifty-five percent of pensioners remained at work at age sixty-five and the proportion was still $12\frac{1}{2}$% at seventy-five (*ibid.*, p. 197). See also *H.C. Deb.*, 5th Series, Vol. 329, col. 2147, 1 December 1937.
11. Bentley B. Gilbert, *British Social Policy, 1914–1939*, 1970, p. 253.
12. Calculated from data in Halsey, *op. cit.*, pp. 402–3. This was, to some extent, counterbalanced by a reduction in poor law expenditure, though precise statistics on the portion of poor law expenditure devoted to the aged are not available.
13. A City of London memorial, with 2,000 signatures of bankers, merchants, railway chairmen, and members of Lloyd's urged the postponement of the 1908 legislation. The National Confederation of Employers' Organizations asked the Cabinet to postpone the 1924 legislation (see Gilbert, *op. cit.*, p. 108; Confederation of British Industry Archives, Warwick Modern Records Centre, MSS 200 B/3/2/C645, Part 1).
14. See, e.g., Lord Norton, 'The Interdependence of Capital and Labour', *Financial Review*, LV, July 1908, 17–18.
15. See, e.g., B. S. Rowntree, *Poverty: A Study of Town Life*, 1902; Roy Hay, 'Employers and Social Policy in Britain: The Evolution of Welfare Legislation, 1905–1914', *Social History*, No. 4, 1977.
16. Federation of British Industries Labour Committee, Minutes of Meeting of 10–13 November 1917, in CBI Archives, MSS 200/F/1/1/178.
17. On the development of the actuarial profession, see R. C. Simmonds, *The Institute of Actuaries, 1848–1948*, 1948; A. R. Davidson, *The History of the Faculty of Actuaries in Scotland, 1856–1956*, 1956.
18. The records of the Conference of Superannuation Funds, including J. C. Mitchell's annotated papers, on which this account is based, are now held by the National Association of Pension Funds in Croydon.
19. For examples of lobbying activity, see the records in PRO IR 85/6, IR 75/181, T 172/992, T 172/1400.
20. Royal Commission on the Income Tax, *Minutes of Evidence, with Appendices*, Cmd 288, 1919 (BPP, XXIII, 1919), qq. 4471, 4473, 4480, 4491, 4502.
21. *Report of the Royal Commission on the Income Tax*, Cmd 615, 1920 (BPP, XVIII, 1920), pp. 69–71.
22. PRO IR 171/193.

23. This paragraph draws on the *Annual Reports* of the Association of Superannuation and Pension Funds, now held by the National Association of Pension Funds.

24. Funds could register with the Registrar of Friendly Societies under the Act; but most funds chose the simpler procedure of adopting special clauses which got around the law. Pension trust funds were given blanket exemption from the law against perpetuities – as would have been perfectly feasible in 1927 – in 1970. See also William Phillips, *Pension Scheme Precedents*, 1957, paras. 536–44; *Report of the Departmental Committee on the Effect of the Rule of Law against Perpetuities in its Application to Certain Pension Funds and Funds with Analogous Purposes*, Cmd 2918, 1927 (BPP, XI, 1927). The legal case which gave rise to the doubts was not reported in the usual channels, but an unofficial account appears in *Journal of the Institute of Actuaries*, LVI, 1925, p. 210.

25. Usually employers who eschewed the trust form wished to retain *ex gratia* pensions as a disciplinary measure, as was the case for the Fine Cotton Spinners' and Doublers' Association and the Bank of England.

26. H. H. Edwards and R. Murrell, *Staff Pension Schemes in Theory and Practice*, 1927, pp. 98ff.

27. This is suggested by the low tax-rate which the Inland Revenue charged the funds on refunds of member contributions on withdrawal. This consolidated rate was supposed initially to reflect the average rate of tax which would have been paid by members. At first this was one-third of the standard rate, but in 1931 it was reduced to one-quarter of the standard rate. This is consistent with the fact that only a small proportion of employees paid tax in the inter-war years: in 1920/1, for example, the peak year with low real tax thresholds, there were only 2.1 million schedule E assessments out of a work force of around 20.3 million. The fact that many pension schemes did not bother to get the protection of '1921 Act' status by organizing in trust form is also consistent with many of the beneficiaries' not being income tax payers (see pp. 44–5 below), as is the widespread discontent from non-taxpaying members about the need to pay tax on withdrawal refunds at the consolidated rate. Around half of the members of pension schemes were manual workers (see p. 13 above and pp. 42–4 below), very few of whom paid tax before 1940. The cost of the tax concession was higher than the £100,000 p.a. the Inland Revenue had initially estimated; it was already by 1924 estimated (on what basis is unclear) at £750,000 p.a. (*H.C. Deb.*, 5th Series, Vol. 166, col. 313, Philip Snowden, Chancellor of the Exchequer, 15 July 1924), and was no doubt rising fast. Yet this was small compared with expenditure on pensions (in 1924 employers' contributions alone are estimated to have been £49 million: C. H. Feinstein, *National Income, Expenditure and Output of the United Kingdom, 1855–1965*, Cambridge, 1972, p. T55).

28. Many of the 100 largest manufacturing firms in 1907 (broadly, those employing 3,000 or more people) already had some form of pension provision; cf. the list in Christine Shaw, 'The 100 Largest Manufacturing Employers in 1907', *Business History*, XXV, 1983.

29. Graham L. Reid and D. J. Robertson, eds., *Fringe Benefits, Labour Costs and Social Security*, 1963, p. 77.

30. John Child, 'Quaker Employers and Industrial Relations', *Sociological Review*, XII, 1964; Edward Cadbury, *Experiments in Industrial Organisation*, 1912; Asa Briggs, *Seebohm Rowntree, 1871–1954*, 1961.

31. Personnel management was slow to develop in Britain, partly because of the slow development of managerial hierarchies in general and partly because of the delegation of some labour policy issues to the unusually well-developed British employers' organizations. See Howard F. Gospel, 'Managerial Strategies and Structures', in Gospel and Craig R. Littler, eds., *Managerial Strategies and Industrial Relations: An Historical and Comparative Study*, 1983.

32. Peter B. Doeringer and Michael J. Piore, *Internal Labor Markets and Manpower Analysis*, Lexington, Mass., 1971; Randy Hodson and Robert L. Kaufman, 'Economic Dualism: A Critical Review', *American Sociological Review*, XLVII, 1982; D. T. Mortensen, 'Specific Capital and Labor Turnover', *Bell Journal of Economics*, IX, 1978.

33. Copy of the Distillers Company flysheet kindly provided by Dr R. Weir, University of York.

34. R. H. Selbie, General Manager, Metropolitan Railway, memorandum to the Board, 23 January 1907, in Greater London Council Archives, ref. MET/10/113.

35. Herbert S. Oakley, 'The Humanity Account', *Ways and Means*, II, 1919, 87. See also John B. C. Kershaw, 'The Promotion of Industrial Efficiency and National Prosperity', *The Engineering Magazine*, XXVI, June 1903.

36. See p. 9 above and item 4 in Distiller's preamble in the text.

37. An exception was the Federated Superannuation System for Universities established in 1913, under which insurance policies, paid for jointly by employer and employee, vested entirely in the employee if he left one university for another. This appears to be partly because of the special arguments put forward about the need not to suppress 'academic freedom'.

38. Thirty-eight percent of private sector pension scheme members in 1936 were in non-contributory schemes ('Schemes Providing for Pensions for Employees on Retirement from Work', *Ministry of Labour Gazette*, May 1938, 173). More generally on the absence of withdrawal rights, see pp. 100–4 below.

39. On the effect of final salary schemes, see p. 108 below.

40. Gregory Anderson, *Victorian Clerks*, Manchester, 1976, pp. 34–40; Sterling Everard, *History of the Gas Light & Coke Company*, 1949, pp. 118–19, 122, 197.

41. T. F. Schloss, *Methods of Industrial Remuneration*, 1892, p. 163.

42. Joseph Melling, 'Industrial Strife and Business Welfare Philosophy: The Case of the South Metropolitan Gas Company from the 1880s to the War', *Business History*, XXI, 1979. See, more generally, Melling, 'Employers, Industrial Welfare and the Struggle for Work-Place Control in British Industry, 1880–1920', in Gospel and Littler, *op. cit.*

43. Wayne E. Lewchuk, 'The Role of the British Government in the Spread of Scientific Management and Fordism in the Interwar Years', *Journal of Economic History*, XLIV, 1984.

44. Trades Union Congress, *Annual Report 1888*, p. 46.

45. Trades Union Congress, *Annual Report 1920*, p. 385, *Report 1922*, p. 70, *The Effect of Welfare Work on Trade Unionism*, 1932.

46. A. Creech-Jones, 'Introduction to a Discussion of Superannuation Rights in

Relation to Trade Unions', 12 November 1924, in National Federation of Professional Workers archives, Warwick Modern Records Centre, MSS 239; Management Research Group, 'Pension Schemes for Operative Workers: Report of Inter-Group Directors' Dinner Discussion', 13 January 1937, p. 7, in MRG archives, Business History Unit, London.

47. Eric Wigham, *The Power to Manage: A History of the Engineering Employers' Federation*, 1973, pp. 65, 154, 155–6, 246, 256, 261; A. B. Culley, 'Co-partnership and Pension Schemes', *Copartnership*, June 1920; 'Report of the Subcommittee on Superannuation', February 1921, in National Federation of Professional Workers archives, MSS 239; Clive Jenkins and J. E. Mortimer, *The Kind of Laws the Unions Ought to Want*, Oxford, 1968, pp. 61–6; Melling, in Gospel and Littler, *op. cit.*, pp. 72–84.

48. Alec Spoor, *White Collar Union: Sixty Years of NALGO*, 1967, Chapter 14; *Insurance Guild Journal*, January 1920, quoted in F. D. Klingender, *The Condition of Clerical Labour in Britain*, 1935, p. 47.

49. Arthur W. Petch, *Cooperative Employees and Superannuation Funds*, Manchester, 1930; 'Sixty-Fourth Annual Cooperative Congress', *Ministry of Labour Gazette*, June 1932, 205; J. T. Price, in discussion of Lord Cozens-Hardy, 'Superannuation and Pension Funds in Theory and Practice', Association of Superannuation and Pension Funds, 1938 annual address, pp. 20–1; Percy Redfern, *The New History of the C.W.S.*, 1938, pp. 443–5.

50. *Report of the Departmental Committee on the Superannuation of Local Government Employees*, Ministry of Health, 1927, pp. 21–3.

51. Solicitors advising early schemes gave contradictory advice. For a discussion of the effects of the Truck Acts and Shop Clubs Act, see articles in *Superannuation*, April 1953 and April 1954; Association of Superannuation and Pension Funds, *Autumn Conference 1956*, pp. 12–13, 22; and Ministry of Labour, *Report of the Committee on the Truck Acts*, 1961, para. 16. The Social Security Act of 1973 clearly removed any doubt by exempting pension schemes from the provisions of the Acts.

52. Edward P. Lazear, 'Why is There Mandatory Retirement?', *Journal of Political Economy*, LXXXVII, 1979.

53. See p. 7 above.

54. *Report of the Departmental Committee on Railway Superannuation Funds*, Cd 5349, 1910 (BPP, LVII, 1910). The problem was less serious than it might have been because deflation in the 1873–96 period had had the opposite tendency of making average and final salaries schemes more nearly equal in pension levels.

55. Government Actuary, *Occupational Pension Schemes: A Survey*, 1958, pp. 16, 23–4.

56. Feinstein, *op. cit.*, p. T55. These estimates are extremely approximate.

57. Those who contracted out of the 1925 state pensions were usually local government employers, and railway, gas and insurance companies; see, e.g., memorandum to P. A. Brown, Government Actuary's Department, from the Ministry of Health, 26 September 1942 in PRO ACT 1/683. Some employers disapproved of contracting out, feeling they should not deprive their workers of state benefits; see Association of Superannuation and Pension Funds, *Annual Report 1925*. For some later problems caused by contracting out and the state's

generous compensation for it, see *Report by the Ministry of National Insurance*, Cmd 6738, 1946 (BPP, XX, 1945–6).

58. *Evidence to the Departmental Committee on Old Age Pensions*, Cmd 411, 1919 (BPP, XXVII, 1919), qq. 3968, 4399, 4407, 4411, 5229.

3 The insurance challenge (1927–56)

1. *Social Insurance and Allied Services*, Cmd 6404, 1942 (BPP, V, 1942–3), p. 283; Dorothy Cole and John Utting, *The Economic Circumstances of Old People*, 1962, p. 73; Government Actuary, *Occupational Pension Schemes: A Survey*, 1958, p. 17.
2. José Harris, *William Beveridge: A Biography*, Oxford, 1977, p. 101.
3. C. G. Hanson, A. E. Musson and P. Thane, 'Craft Unions, Welfare Benefits, and the Case for Trade Union Law Reform 1867–1875: An Exchange', *Economic History Review*, XXIX, 1976, pp. 617–35; Mr Wilcox (LNWR) in *Evidence to the Departmental Committee on Old Age Pensions*, Cmd 411, 1919, (BPP, XXVII, 1919), q. 3761.
4. Northumberland and Durham Miners' Permanent Relief Fund archives, Tyne and Wear County Archives Department. For another case see R. C. B. Lane, 'The Dissolution of a Superannuation Society', *Journal of the Institute of Actuaries*, LXXV, 1949.
5. *The Times*, 1, 3, 4, 5, 7 and 8 July 1950.
6. *Report of the Committee on the Economic and Financial Problems of the Provision for Old Age*, Cmd 9333, 1954 (BPP, VI, 1954–5), p. 12.
7. J. Johnston and G. W. Murphy, 'The Growth of Life Assurance in the United Kingdom Since 1880', *Transactions of the Manchester Statistical Society*, 1956–7, 5, 22. For consumer spending, see C. H. Feinstein, *National Income, Expenditure and Output of the United Kingdom, 1855–1965*, Cambridge, 1972, p. T8.
8. Paul Johnson, 'Credit and Thrift: A Study of Working Class Household Budget Management in Britain, 1870–1939', Ph.D. thesis, Oxford, 1982, pp. 21–2; Johnston and Murphy, *op. cit.*
9. *Report on the Committee on Industrial Assurance*, Cmd 4376, 1933 (BPP, XIII, 1932–3), pp. 4–5. See also *Social Insurance and Allied Services*, Cmd 6406, 1942 (BPP, V, 1942–3), p. 115.
10. PRO IR 10/85, 63/49 and 63/51; evidence of William Schooling, 8 May 1919, Royal Commission on Income Tax, *Evidence with Appendices*, Cmd 288, 1919 (BPP, XXIII, 1919), qq. 965–1236; evidence of M. C. Furtado, 5 December 1919, in *idem*, qq. 27362–951.
11. The Life Offices' Association and Associated Scottish Life Assurance Offices had by then became effective lobbyists: see, e.g., PRO T 172/969 Parts I and II and IR 63/49, and LOA archives. Their most effective spokesman was Geoffrey Marks of National Mutual; for his vigorous dissentient view on the concessions to pension funds see *Report of the Royal Commission on Income Tax*, Cmd 615, 1920 (BPP, XVIII, 1920), p. 144.
12. PRO T 172/969, Part II; and Royal Commission on Income Tax, *Evidence, With Appendices*, Cmd 288, 1919 (BPP, XXIII, 1919), V, qq. 16543–17143. In the Second

World War, moreover, the companies also negotiated a lower composite rate of tax for their investment funds which again gave them an edge in the savings market.

13. *Report of the Departmental Committee on the Business of the Industrial Assurance Companies and Collecting Societies*, Cmd 614, 1920 (BPP, XVIII, 1920); J. G. Sinclair, *Evils of Industrial Assurance*, 1932; Industrial Life Offices, *Industrial Life Assurance Explained: A Reply to Criticisms*, 1944.

14. *Journal of the Institute of Actuaries*, LI, 1919, 336.

15. On American developments, see R. Carlyle Buley, *The Equitable Life Assurance Society of the United States, 1859–1964*, New York, 1967, Vol. 2, pp. 770–800, 881–915. On British awareness, see Joseph Burn and Frank Percy Symmons, 'Practical Points in Connection with the Formation and Valuation of Pension Funds, with a Note on Group Assurances', *Journal of the Institute of Actuaries*, XLIX, 1915; P. H. McCormick, 'Group Insurance', *Journal of the Institute of Actuaries*, LI, 1919.

16. Forty-nine out of fifty-two companies selling group policies were parties to the Life Offices' Association Group Insurance Tariff Agreement in 1928: see LOA archives.

17. Burn and Symmons, *op. cit.*; W. J. H. Whittall, 'Notes on Some Recent Developments of Pension Problems in America', *Journal of the Institute of Actuaries*, LI, 1918; Whittall, 'Note on a Fundamental Question Underlying the Pension Problem with a Reference to the School Teachers' Superannuation Act, 1918', *Journal of the Institute of Actuaries*, LI, 1919; Harold Dougharty, *Notes on Deposit Pension Schemes*, 1919; W. J. H. Whittall, Sir William J. Collins and Henry L. Hopkinson, *Pensions for Hospital Officers and Staff: Report of a Subcommittee of the Executive Committee of King Edward's Hospital Fund for London*, 1919; G. S. W. Epps, 'Superannuation Funds: Notes on Some Postwar Problems . . .', *Journal of the Institute of Actuaries*, LII, 1921; A. D. Besant, 'Notes on Some Actuarial Aspects of the Local Government and Other Officers' Superannuation Act, 1922', *Journal of the Institute of Actuaries*, LVI, 1923; Cyril F. Warren, 'An Investigation into the Mortality Experienced by Pensioners of the Staffs of Banks and Insurance Companies, with a Note on the Mortality Experience of Deferred Annuitants', *Journal of the Institute of Actuaries*, LVII, 1926; H. H. Edwards and R. Murrell, *Staff Pension Schemes in Theory and Practice*, 1927; H. Dougharty, *Pension, Endowment and Life Assurance Schemes*, 1927; James Bacon and Guy Woodrow, 'Some Remarks on Superannuation and Pension Funds in Great Britain', *Transactions of the 8th International Congress of Actuaries 1927*, I, pp. 346ff.; Bernard Robertson and H. Samuels, *Pension and Superannuation Funds: Their Formation and Administration Explained*, 1928; Harry Freeman, 'Notes on a Short Method of Valuation of Pension Funds', *Journal of the Institute of Actuaries*, LXI, 1930.

18. Burn and Symmons, *op. cit.*, p. 195.

19. 'Rules and Regulations for Insurance on the Lives of Officers and Clerks in the Alliance Bank Ltd.', 1881, printed booklet in National Westminster Bank Archives, D 469.

20. Barry Supple, *The Royal Exchange Assurance: A History of British Insurance, 1720–1970*, Cambridge, 1970, pp. 204, 280, 451; H. Dougharty, *Pension,*

Endowment, Life Assurance and Other Schemes, for Employees of Commercial Companies, 1927; W. F. Gardner, 'Staff Benefit Schemes', *Journal of the Institute of Actuaries Students' Society*, III, 1928; 'Pensions for Professional Men', *British Medical Journal*, II, 15 July 1911, 127; Herbert S. Oakley, 'The Humanity Account', *Ways and Means*, II, 1919, 86–7; M. E. Ogborn, *Equitable Assurance*, 1962, pp. 245, 256; C. C. H. Drake, 'Life Offices and Staff Pension Schemes', *Journal of The Insurance Institute of London*, XXII, 1928–9; A. W. Tarn and C. E. Byles, *The Guardian Royal Exchange Co. Ltd., 1821–1921*, 1921, p. 56; John Dummelow, *1899–1949* [Metropolitan–Vickers], Manchester, 1949, pp. 89–90; Clerical, Medical & General Archives, collection of pension literature; London Life Association Archives, Guildhall Library, minutes of LLA Court of Directors, 6 November 1918, Vol. 21, p. 35 and 5 December 1928, Vol. 24, p. 126; R. E. Underwood, contribution to discussion in *Journal of the Institute of Actuaries*, LVII, 1926, p. 152.

21. LOA archives, Case 45; Metropolitan Life Archives, New York; Clerical, Medical & General Archives, Actuary's Memorandum, March 1929; Louis I. Dublin, *A Family of Thirty Million: the Story of the Metropolitan Life Insurance Company*, New York, 1943, pp. 181–83; Marquis James, *The Metropolitan Life: A Study in Business Growth*, New York, 1947, pp. 266–7; T. A. E. Layborn, 'Pensions' – the Past and the Future', *The Policy Holder*, 24 February 1966; letter from T. A. E. Layborn, *Pensions*, July 1980, 49; E. A. Ridge, 'Pensions Administration: A Retrospect', *Legal & General Annual Conference Proceedings*, privately printed 1966, pp. 85ff.; T. A. E. Layborn, typescript autobiography, pp. 20ff.; *Statist Insurance Section*, 14 July 1928, iii; Hugh Butler *et. al.*, *The United Kingdom: An Industrial, Commercial and Financial Handbook*, U.S. Department of Commerce, Trade Promotion Series No. 94, Washington, 1930, p. 705; Legal & General Archives, Policy Registers, Kingswood.

22. N. C. Turner, 'Group Insurance and Group Pension Schemes', *Journal of the Institute of Actuaries Students' Society*, III, 1931; M. C. Polman, 'Group Life and Pension Schemes Including Valuation Problems', *Journal of the Institute of Actuaries Students' Society*, V, 1939; A. G. Simons, 'Group Life and Pension Schemes', *Journal of the Institute of Actuaries*, LXXI, 1943; Gordon Pingstone, 'Group Life and Pension Schemes Including Group Family Income Benefit Schemes', *Journal of the Institute of Actuaries*, LXXVII, 1951.

23. H. M. Trouncer, Presidential Address, 27 October 1930, *Journal of the Institute of Actuaries*, LXII, 1931, 7; James Bacon and Guy Woodrow, 'Some Remarks on Superannuation and Pension Funds in Great Britain', *Transactions of the 8th International Congress of Actuaries, 1927*, Vol. 1, 346.

24. 'Staff Pension Schemes', Clerical, Medical & General sales pamphlet, 1929. For the FSSU, see p. 161 n. 37 below.

25. *Sunday Express*, 30 March 1930, 1.

26. Layborn, typescript autobiography, *passim*; *Daily Herald*, 21 January 1932, 1b; *Belfast Telegraph*, 15 February 1935, 5c; *Financial News*, 25 February 1935, 9f, 4 March 1935, 8f, 11 March 1935, 9f, 18 March 1935, 9f, 25 March 1935, 9f; *Sunday Express*, 13 September 1936, 15c, 24 October 1937, 5c; *Daily Telegraph*, 9 January 1937, 8f.

27. Legal & General Insurance, Board Minutes, 29 November 1932, 27 June 1933, 1

August 1933, 15 August 1933, 29 August 1933. This approximately doubled Legal & General's presence in the market – see Quinquennial Investigation, in Board Minutes, 9 April 1937. For dollar estimates, see Metropolitan Life, Board Minutes, 26 September 1933.

28. H. S[amuels], 'Some Legal Points for Works Managers: Pension Funds and Compensation', *Industrial Welfare and Personnel Management*, February 1932, 75; J. H. Robertson, 'Superannuation Schemes', *Industrial Welfare and Personnel Management*, December 1932, 577. There was a lively and continued debate between insurance salesmen and consulting actuaries on their 'impartiality' and rival pension products in many journals throughout the 1930s.

29. L. Hannah, *The Rise of the Corporate Economy*, 2nd edn, 1983, pp. 90ff.

30. Bacon and Woodrow, *op. cit.*; Bacon & Woodrow archives. Lists of consulting actuaries willing to take on pension fund work were regularly prepared and circulated by the Association of Superannuation and Pension Funds.

31. See the description of the Prudential's scheme in 'Pension Schemes for Small Firms', *Industrial Welfare and Personnel Management*, March 1930, 103.

32. Estimates of group pension market share and growth derived from Pingstone, *op. cit.*; G. W. Pingstone, 'The Group Department', *Temple Bar*, June 1959, 7; Legal & General Archives; Prudential archives; John Butt, 'Life Assurance in War and Depression: The Standard Life Assurance Company and its Environment, 1914–39', in Oliver M. Westall, ed., *The Historian and the Business of Insurance*, Manchester, 1984, pp. 166–8; and Government Actuary, *Occupational Pension Schemes: A Survey*, 1958, p. 5. See also Statistical Appendix, p. 148 below.

33. Feinstein, *op. cit.*, p. T125.

34. Hannah, *op. cit.*; P. Mathias, *Retailing Revolution*, 1967, pp. 284, 387.

35. Feinstein's estimates (*op. cit.*, pp. T55–6) of the growth of employer contributions (which include *ex gratia* pensions) are very approximate. His picture of consistent growth in the 1930s is confirmed by data on ordinary contributions for a sample of funds, but lump sum and special grants (which then formed around two-fifths of all employer contributions) are more markedly cyclical than his estimates imply until after the War (*Annual Reports of the Registrar of Friendly Societies*, 1930–9). The growth in pension payments and accumulated funds in the same schemes is continuous and smooth (*ibid.*). The Association of Superannuation and Pension Funds conducted surveys of the member funds in 1943–5 and 1954 which are also consistent with a picture of growth. Earlier surveys of pensioning are rare. For some regional evidence see A. L. Bowley and M. H. Hogg, *Has Poverty Diminished?*, 1925, pp. 25–6, 81–2, 108, 131, 165–6.

36. 'Schemes Providing for Pensions for Employees on Retirement from Work', *Ministry of Labour Gazette*, May 1938, 172–4. On the conduct of the 1936 Inquiry see the papers in PRO LAB 2/1576, LAB 17/122, ACT 1/624. Some confirmation of the data in the 1936 survey is provided by later local surveys suggesting 12–15% coverage in Coventry, Blackburn and Bristol (Charles Madge, 'War Time Saving and Spending – A District Survey', *Economic Journal*, L, 1940, 331; Madge, 'The Propensity to Save in Blackburn and Bristol', *Economic Journal*, L, 1940, 416).

37. Government Actuary, *Occupational Pension Schemes: A Survey*, 1958.

38. For the situation in 1900, see p. 13 above. For later years, see the sources listed in the previous two notes. Estimates for the public sector in 1936 are from Government Actuary, *Occupational Pension Schemes: 1979: Sixth Survey*, 1981, p. 6, and for the size of the work force from Feinstein, *op. cit.*, pp. T126–7; H. F. Lydall (*British Income and Savings*, Oxford, 1955, p. 116), using alternative survey data on savings, estimates a coverage of 29% of employees in 1952.

39. Moses Abramowitz and Vera F. Eliasberg, *The Growth of Public Employment in Great Britain*, Princeton, 1957, p. 25.

40. Sir Norman Chester, *The Nationalization of British Industry 1945–51*, 1975, pp. 825–43.

41. Chester, *loc. cit.*; for evidence of TUC discontent at the Labour government's prevarication, see PRO, PIN, 19/169.

42. Chester, *op. cit.*, pp. 839–40; *International Management Research Association Bulletin*, No. 332, 16 July 1957 (MRG Archives, Business History Unit, London); A. S. V. Skilton, 'Pension Problems of Nationalized Industries', *Superannuation*, No. 17, July 1957.

43. Gerald Rhodes, *Public Sector Pensions*, 1965; A. C. Robb, 'The Development of Public Sector Superannuation Schemes', *Journal of the Institute of Actuaries*, LXXVI, 1950; G. E. Norton, 'The Superannuation Schemes of Local Authorities', address to Association of Superannuation and Pension Funds, 1935; G. V. Blackstone, *A History of the British Fire Service*, 1957, Chapter 22.

44. See p. 116 below.

45. Rhodes, *op. cit.*, pp. 82–3.

46. The generalizations on the private sector in 1936 and 1956 are based on the sources in nn. 36 and 37 above.

47. The 1936 survey showed 814,000 'manual wage earners' and 803,000 'administrative, clerical, sales, etc. staffs' in private sector schemes; the 1956 survey showed 2,350,000 'wage earning' and 1,950,000 'salaried' employees in pension schemes. The categories are not identical, though for the purposes of the comparisons implied in the text they may be taken to be so.

48. W. J. Reader, *Imperial Chemical Industries: A History*, Vol. 2, *The First Quarter Century 1926–1952*, Oxford, 1975, pp. 66–70.

49. Management Research Group, 'Pension Schemes for Operative Workers: Report of Inter-Group Directors' Dinner Discussion', 13 January 1937, in MRG archives; F. V. Brilles and R. Mountjoy, 'Pension Funds for Manual Workers', *Superannuation*, No. 15, November 1956; 'Pensions in the U.K., and Especially Pensions for Operatives', minutes of Industrial Management Research Association meeting, 27 September 1949, MRG archives.

50. J. H. H. Nuttall, 'Caveat!', *Superannuation*, circular letter No. 170, April 1953, circular letter No. 178, April 1954, 12, No. 16, March 1957, 18–19; A. E. Bromfield, 'Pension Schemes: Famous Law Cases', *Journal of the Chartered Insurance Institute*, LII, 1955, 39–42; Ministry of Labour, *Report of the Committee on the Truck Act*, 1961, p. 10; Association of Superannuation and Pension Funds, *Autumn Conference 1956*, pp. 12–13, 22. The 1973 Social Security Act removed lingering doubts about whether compulsion was illegal by making it clear that neither the Truck Acts nor the widely ignored Shop Clubs

Act of 1902 applied to pension funds. As late as 1971, 0.8 million of the 9.7 million employees who were not in pension schemes were eligible for membership of schemes but were voluntarily choosing not to join them (Government Actuary, *Occupational Pension Schemes: 1971: Fourth Survey*, 1972, pp. 9–10), but the great majority of pension schemes are now compulsory for the classes of workers to which they apply. See also Chapter 2, n. 51 above.

51. Layborn, typescript autobiography; *Financial News*, 28 March 1936, 2; Legal & General Archives, policy registers; *The Times*, 17 November 1939, 13.

52. Alan Bullock, *Life and Times of Ernest Bevin*, Vol. 1, 1960, pp. 380–1, 458, 604–65.

53. *Daily Herald*, 21 January 1932, 1; Legal & General, board minutes, 16 February 1932; *Pensions for Millers: Report by the Trustees of the Pension Scheme*, privately printed, 1937; L. H. Green, 'Labour Problems in the British Flour Milling Industry', in Frank E. Gannett and B. F. Catherwood, eds., *Industrial and Labour Relations in Great Britain*, New York, 1939; 'The Group Pension Scheme in the Flour Milling Industry', *Ministry of Labour Gazette*, March 1932, 83.

54. For one exception, see the papers of the Wallpaper Trade Superannuation Society 1928–62, in Warwick Modern Records Centre, MSS 39w, though in fact one firm dominated this industry.

55. Bullock, *op. cit.*, p. 605; Layborn, typescript autobiography, 28–9; W. E. Minchinton, *The British Tinplate Industry: A History*, Oxford, 1957, p. 291; Sir Arthur Pugh, *Men of Steel: By One of Them*, 1951, pp. 498, 505, 511, 513, 516–18; *The Times*, 5 May 1936, 18e, 3 June 1936, 5g; *South Wales Evening Post*, 23 April 1936, 5f, 2 May 1936, 4c; *News Chronicle*, 19 May 1936; records of the tinplate industry discussions in Warwick Modern Records Centre, MSS 36/T15.

56. See p. 17 above.

57. In March 1939, 276,500 out of three million old age pensioners were receiving poor law assistance ('Memorandum on Old Age Pensions', 11 January 1940, in PRO CAB 67/4).

58. See p. 126 below.

59. Quoted in Bullock, *op. cit.*, p. 605.

60. The average pension paid by insurance companies in 1956 was nearly £2 per week (Government Actuary, *Occupational Pension Schemes: A Survey*, 1958), but pensions of less than ten shillings a week were the norm for many manual workers with only ten or twenty years' accumulated entitlement.

61. Undated memo prepared for the Phillips Committee, *circa* 1953, in PRO LAB 10/1275; J. T. Price, M. P., in *Superannuation*, No. 13, March 1956, 12; 'Pensions in the U.K., and Especially Pensions for Operatives', minutes of Industrial Management Research Association meeting, 27 September 1949, MRG archives.

62. Eric B. Nathan, 'Pension Funds and the War', *Industrial Welfare and Personnel Management*, April 1940, 141. Employers' contributions as a proportion of total labour costs temporarily fell during the War: Feinstein, *op. cit.*, p. T54.

63. 'What Are the Postwar Prospects for Life Assurance?', *The Policy*, 29 July 1943, 534; Legal & General archives, Memoranda on Procedure 1939–1945; but cf. minutes of the Inner Circle meeting, 7 January 1943, in LOA archives.

64. *Truth*, 31 October 1941, 365; *Post Magazine*, 11 April 1942, 222; Pingstone, *op. cit.*, pp. 346–7; 'Pension Schemes', *Post Magazine and Insurance Monitor*, 30 October 1948. The leading firm of pension brokers in the 1950s built their business on 'top hat' schemes and non-contributory endowment business, stressing the tax advantages to potential clients: see Anon., 'The Story of Noble Lowndes', 1959, unpublished typescript kindly lent by Mr M. Pilch of Noble Lowndes.

65. Association of Superannuation and Pension Funds, *Autumn Conference 1952*, p. 31; F. W. Bacon, M. D. W. Elphinstone and B. Benjamin, 'The Growth of Pension Rights and Their Impact on the National Economy', *Journal of the Institute of Actuaries*, LXXX, 1954, 141, 161; T. A. E. Layborn, 'New Thoughts on Pensions and Group Schemes', *Journal of the Insurance Institute of London*, XL, 1952, 83.

66. *H.C. Deb.*, 5th Series, Vol. 579, col. 72, 5 December 1957, Vol. 585, cols. 18, 99–100, 25 and 31 March 1958.

4 The state: partner or competitor? (1940–78)

1. For discussions on proposed surveys of pension schemes prior to the 1936 survey, see PRO LAB 2/1576, File 583/1928. On the early work of the Government Actuary's Department, see 'The Government Actuary's Department', *Journal of the Institute of Actuaries*, LXXX, 1954.

2. See p. 20 above.

3. Social Security Act, 1973, Section 69. By 1956, only 6% of all scheme members were in schemes registered under the 1927 Validation Act (Government Actuary, *Occupational Pension Schemes: A Survey*, 1958, p. 17).

4. Ministry of Health, *Report of the Departmental Committee on the Superannuation of Local Government Employees*, 1927, p. 35; Association of Superannuation and Pension Funds, *Annual Report 1925*.

5. See p. 20 above.

6. See p. 5 above. The high rates of taxes on annuities derived from the fact that, despite decades of lobbying from the insurance industry, both the interest elements and the capital elements (the latter of which had usually been taxed already) were subject to income tax. The device of the split annuity was being developed to reduce the problem, and in 1956 the government conceded that annuities bought out of already taxed income should be subject to tax only on the interest element; see p. 50 below.

7. See, e.g., *H.C. Deb.*, 5th Series, Vol. 439, cols. 2369–98, 9 July 1947.

8. *The Tax Treatment of Retirement Benefits: A Report Submitted to the Chairman of the Board of Inland Revenue by the Federation of British Industries, the Association of British Chambers of Commerce, the Life Association and the Association of Superannuation Funds, February 1948* (copy in National Association of Pension Funds archives, circular letter No. 124). The document also contains the best account of current practice in an annex. For a coherent defence of the report, see Frank Bower, 'Taxation of Retirement Benefits', Association of Superannuation and Pension Funds, *Autumn Conference 1949*.

9. The '1921 Act' schemes were thereafter (until 1970) known as 'Section 379' schemes, and insurance schemes as 'Section 388' schemes.

10. *Report of the Committee on the Taxation Treatment of Provisions for Retirement*, Cmd 9063, 1954 (BPP, XIX, 1953–4).

11. A flood of tendentious and self-serving evidence from professional bodies asserted that professional incomes had declined since the pre-war period and that it was no longer possible for those without inherited wealth to aspire to self-employed professional positions. In fact, the opposite was generally the case: those careers were increasingly open to the talents.

12. *Report of the Committee on the Taxation Treatment of Provisions for Retirement*, Reservation, pp. 152–63.

13. *Final Report of the Royal Commission on the Taxation of Profits and Income*, Cmd 9474, 1955 (BPP, XXVII, 1955–6), p. 23.

14. See, e.g., the remarks of A. G. Simon, Chairman of the Life Offices' Association, reported in *Policy Holder*, 25 March 1954, 199; and the discussion in Association of Superannuation and Pension Funds, *Autumn Conference 1954*, pp. 3–36.

15. Anthony Barber, *H.C. Deb.*, 5th Series, Vol. 685, col. 102, 28 November 1963; cf. *Report of the Committee on the Taxation Treatment of Provisions for Retirement*, p. 126; *Financial Times*, 19 April 1956, 9a; *Daily Mail*, 13 August 1956, 2f. On the alternative of self-investment by the self-employed, see H. F. Lydall, *British Incomes and Savings*, Oxford, 1955, p. 136.

16. Despite subsequent rises in the contribution limits to 15% and then 17.5% of earnings; see, e.g., R. Moyse, 'The First Quarter Century of Personal Pension Plans', *Law Society Gazette*, 3 March 1982, 266–7, 7 April 1982, 435–6; *Investors Chronicle and Stock Exchange Gazette*, 10 November 1967, 500. The introduction of loanback facilities and the withdrawal of life insurance premium relief in the 1980s also weighted the advantages in favour of old age provision for the self-employed by these means.

17. T. H. Acklam, 'Practical Suggestions for Improving Outdated Pension Schemes', *Industrial Welfare*, October 1964, 265; Government Actuary, *Occupational Pension Schemes: 1971: Fourth Survey*, 1972, 33.

18. At the Legal & General alone, the need to rewrite schemes absorbed the attention of hundreds of staff for more than four years. As the Life Offices' Association had pointed out, all of this would have been avoided if the legislation had been more sensibly drafted. In self-administered schemes, also, the setting up of 'disapproved' sections to provide lump sums created additional expenses.

19. See the remarks of C. A. Poyser in Association of Superannuation and Pension Funds, *Autumn Conference 1952*, pp. 40–1, and of the Solicitors' Law Clerks Pension Fund in the Association's *Autumn Conference 1955*, p. 11. The Federated Superannuation System for Universities is another example of the conservative tendencies inherent in the old approval system.

20. Government Actuary, *Occupational Pension Schemes: 1979: Sixth Survey*, 1981, p. 2.

21. J. A. Kay and M. A. King, *The British Tax System*, Oxford, 1978, pp. 59–60.

22. This was to be seen, for example, when arbitrary limits on inflation-proofing contributed to the failure of schemes to develop sane and equitable standards; see p. 114 below.

23. C. H. Feinstein, *National Income, Expenditure and Output of the United Kingdom, 1855–1965*, Cambridge, 1972, pp. T126–7.
24. See p. 129 below.
25. PRO LAB 8/1764; and the papers of the National Advisory Committee on the Employment of Older Men and Women, in LAB 8/2006; and of the Committee of Enquiry into the Reasons for Retiring or Continuing at Work, in PIN 46/56. See also *H.C. Deb.*, 5th Series, Vol. 518, cols. 337–48, 21 July 1953.
26. See, e.g., Harold Watkinson, 'Pension Schemes and the Older Worker', Association of Superannuation and Pension Funds, *Autumn Conference 1953*; Watkinson, 'Age of Retirement', *Journal of the Corporation of Insurance Brokers*, Winter 1952–3, pp. 19–20. Seventy-five thousand copies of a booklet, 'Age and Employment', were published in 1953. For an optimistic assessment of the impact of the campaign, see *Second Report of the National Advisory Committee on the Employment of Older Men and Women*, Cmd 9628, 1955 (BPP, XVII, 1955–6).
27. *Social Insurance and Allied Services*, Cmd 6404, 1942 (BPP, V, 1942–3): see also José Harris, *William Beveridge: A Biography*, Oxford, 1977, especially Chapters 16 and 17.
28. See p. 17 above.
29. Association of Superannuation and Pension Funds archives, circular letter no. 107, 14 January 1946, 'National Insurance Bill', p. 4. The 1925 Pensions Act had permitted contracting out of the basic state pension for Crown employees, and employees of local authorities and statutory companies (such as railways and gas companies).
30. Alan Deacon, 'An End to the Means Test: Social Security and the Attlee Government', *Journal of Social Policy*, XI, 1982.
31. *Report of the Committee on the Economic and Financial Problems of the Provisions for Old Age*, Cmd 9333, 1954 (BPP, VI, 1954–5). See also R. C. K. Ensor, 'The Problem of Quantity and Quality in the British Population', *Eugenics Review*, XLII, 1950 for comments on earlier fears about old age dependency prompted by the 1949 Royal Commission on Population.
32. In money terms, the pension was £1.30 in 1946, £1.62½ in 1953, £3.37½ in 1963, and £23.30 in 1979.
33. Calculated from data in *Annual Abstract of Statistics*, *passim*.
34. The National Federation of Old Age Pension Associations, founded in 1940, was a relatively ineffective lobbyist.
35. A. T. Haynes and R. J. Kirton, 'Income Tax in Relation to Social Security', *Journal of the Institute of Actuaries*, LXXII, 1944–6.
36. See p. 52 above.
37. On Titmuss's views, see his papers (especially file 29) deposited in the British Library of Political and Economic Science, Archives Department. See also the sources in nn. 25 above and 38 below, and his articles in *The Times*, 29 December 1953, 7f and 30 December 1953, 7f; and 'Pension Systems and Population Change', *Political Quarterly*, XXVI, 1955. However, the clearest public statement of the Titmuss group's blueprint was Brian Abel-Smith and Peter Townsend, *New Pensions for Old*, Fabian Research Series no. 171, 1955.
38. See, e.g., the papers of the Social Services Subcommittee in Labour Party

archives, especially refs. 110, 200, 260, 493; and Trade Union Congress archives, file T 1249, Social Insurance and Industrial Welfare Committee Minutes, 1956–9.

39. *National Superannuation: Labour Policy for Security in Old Age*, 1957. See also Philip Williams, *Hugh Gaitskell: A Biography*, 1979, p. 525; Hugh Heclo, *Modern Social Politics in Britain and Sweden: From Relief to Income Maintenance*, New Haven, 1974, pp. 261–83.

40. Life Offices' Association, *Retirement Pensions*, 1957; Life Offices' Association, *The Pension Problem*, 1957; Arthur Seldon, *Pensions in a Free Society*, Institute of Economic Affairs, 1957; Associated British Chambers of Commerce, *National Superannuation: A Critical Review of the Proposals of the Labour Party*, 1958.

41. See the papers in LOA archives. Arthur Seldon, who was in close touch with LOA views, echoed this view publicly in a later Institute of Economic Affairs pamphlet, *Pensions for Prosperity*, 1960, p. 42. By the mid 1960s, Keith Joseph was publicly advocating this view as Conservative spokesman on pensions.

42. Lord Boyd-Carpenter, *Memoirs*, 1980, pp. 129–48; *Provision for Old Age: The Future Development of the National Insurance Scheme*, Cmd 538, 1958 (BPP, XXIV, 1957–8); *The Economist*, 18 October 1958, 204–7; John Boyd-Carpenter, 'Pensions – The Next Ten Years', Association of Superannuation and Pension Funds, *Autumn Conference 1961*, pp. 1–19. Lord Boyd-Carpenter and Mr R. J. Kirton of the Life Offices' Association provided additional information on the discussions leading to the 1961 scheme in interview.

43. T. E. J. Holland, of Norwich Union Insurance, quoted in *East Anglian Daily Times*, 1 March 1960, 5c.

44. It is now, in principle, possible to work out whether scheme members gained or lost from contracting out. A major factor in the calculation is the rate of inflation in the period 1961–75 and the inflation-proofing granted by the scheme, since the state benefits, though not originally index-linked, were index-linked by Barbara Castle in 1975. It is noteworthy, if hardly surprising, that none of the professional advisers in the early 1960s was able to identify at that time the crucial factors in determining the profitability of contracting out; the more flexible of them did at least see that it would depend on unforecastable and uncontrollable monetary or political factors.

45. In 1958, the government had expected 2.5 million contracted-out employees; in fact, the number soon rose to twice that. By 1967, 30% of employees in private sector schemes and 70% in public sector schemes were contracted out (Government Actuary, *Occupational Pension Schemes: Third Survey*, 1968, pp. 12–13). There were many guides to the contracting-out decision published at the time; for one of the sanest, see R. W. Abbott, 'Growth of State Pensions and their Effect on Occupational Schemes', *The Accountant*, 4 June 1960, 687–91.

46. For exceptions see Government Actuary, *Occupational Pensions: A New Survey*, 1966, p. 11.

47. This and the following paragraphs are based on papers in the Life Offices' Association archives, the National Association of Pension Fund archives, the Trades Union Congress archives, the Labour Party archives, and the Legal & General archives. Most of the relevant files are still currently in use or

considered confidential and are not open to general public inspection. I am grateful to the owners for permission to inspect them, subject to their viewing the use to be made of the information. No changes to the typescript of this book were required by any of these, though this should not be taken to imply that the owners of the files approved of the author's interpretation. See also Life Offices' Association, *Progress by Partnership*, 1969; National Association of Pension Funds, *The Future Relationship of State and Occupational Funds*, 1968; Tony Lynes, *Labour's Pension Plan*, Fabian Tract 396, 1969; Stewart Lyon, contribution to discussion on 'The Future Relationship of State and Occupational Pensions', National Association of Pension Funds, *Conference Report, November 1968*, pp. 12ff. Some points of interpretation were helpfully elucidated in interviews with C. S. S. Lyon, R. J. W. Crabbe, and the late F. M. Redington, who played a major part in the negotiations on behalf of the Life Offices' Association. For indications of the views of the civil servant most closely involved, see J. A. Atkinson, 'The Developing Relationship between the State Pension Scheme and Occupational Pension Schemes', *Social and Economic Administration*, XI, 1977.

48. Thomas Wilson, ed., *Pensions, Inflation and Growth: A Comparative Study of the Elderly in the Welfare State*, 1974, p. 354.
49. *National Superannuation and Social Insurance: Proposals for Earnings Related Social Security*, Cmnd 3883, 1969 (BPP, LIII, 1968–9); *National Superannuation and Social Insurance: Explanatory Memorandum*, Cmnd 4222, 1969 (BPP, XXVII, 1969–70); Richard Crossman, 'White Paper on National Superannuation and Social Insurance', National Association of Pension Funds, *Conference Report, February 1969*, pp. 2ff.; R. H. S. Crossman, 'The Politics of Pensions', Eleanor Rathbone Lecture, Liverpool, 1972.
50. However, like all pension schemes (which in their nature pay survivors), it redistributed income away from the poor, with their limited life expectancy. There was also some countervailing redistribution to the better-off in the benefits formula, based on revalued average salary: see p. 108 below.
51. 'STOP Organizes Thoughtful Attack on Crossman Pensions', *Policy Holder*, 22 May 1970, 886.
52. *Strategy for Pensions: The Future Development of State and Occupational Provision*, Cmnd 4755, 1971 (BPP, I, 1970–1); see also *Social Security Bill: Explanatory Memorandum*, Cmnd 5142, 1972 (BPP, XXXIII, 1972–3). For C. S. S. Lyon's serious doubts about the wisdom of the Joseph scheme, see his 'The Implications of the White Paper for Insured Schemes', in British Institute of Management, conference on the 'Pensions White Paper', 17 October 1971.
53. *Better Pensions: Proposals for a New Pensions Scheme Fully Protected Against Inflation*, Cmnd 5713, 1974 (BPP, XVI, 1974); *H.C. Deb.*, 5th Series, Vol. 873, cols. 5 208–17, 7 May 1974; Barbara Castle, *The Castle Diaries 1974–6*, 1980, pp. 150–60, 362, 394–5.
54. But cf. p. 144 below.
55. See p. 79 below.
56. In 1979, only 1.3 million out of 11.6 million occupational pension scheme members were not contracted out (Government Actuary, *Occupational Pension Schemes: 1979: Sixth Survey*, 1981, p. 5).

57. R. Hemming and J. A. Kay, 'Contracting Out of the State Earnings Related Pension Scheme', *Fiscal Studies*, II, 1981.
58. See pp. 111, 120–1 below.
59. R. W. Abbott (Bacon & Woodrow), letter to *The Times*, 7 November 1961, 13f.
60. H. H. Leedale, 'The Transference of Pension Rights – Getting Round the Taxation Problems', National Association of Pension Funds, *Autumn Conference Report, November 1967*, p. 4.
61. *Report of the Committee on the Economic and Financial Problems of Provision for Old Age*, Cmd 9333, 1954 (BPP, VI, 1954–5); Institute of Actuaries and Faculty of Actuaries, *National Pensions: An Appeal to Statesmanship*, 1959, p. 10; National Joint Advisory Council, *The Preservation of Pension Rights*, Ministry of Labour, 1966, p. 49.
62. *Solvency, Disclosure of Information and Member Participation in Occupational Pension Schemes*, Cmnd 5904, 1975 (BPP, XXXIV, 1974–5); *Equal Status for Men and Women in Occupational Pension Schemes*, Cmnd 6599, 1976 (BPP, XLV, 1975–6); *Occupational Pension Scheme Cover for Disabled People*, Cmnd 6849, 1977 (BPP, XLV, 1976–7); *Improved Protection for the Occupational Pension Rights and Expectations of Early Leavers*, Cmnd 8271 (BPP, VIII, 1980–1); *Greater Security for the Rights and Expectations of Members of Occupational Pensions Schemes*, Cmnd 8649, 1982 (BPP, XII, 1981–2). See also H. M. Langley, The Work of the Occupational Pensions Board: A Personal View by the Secretary to the Board', *Pensions Review*, Autumn 1984, 2–3.

5 Competition and professionalization: the maturing of the pension market (1956–79)

1. Figure 5.1 and statistics in the related paragraphs are based on the surveys by the Government Actuary, particularly his *Occupational Pension Schemes: 1979: Sixth Survey*, 1981. For data on the total work force see C. H. Feinstein, *National Income, Expenditure and Output of the United Kingdom, 1855–1965*, Cambridge, 1972, pp. T126–7; Central Statistical Office, *Economic Trends: Annual Supplement 1981*, 1980, p. 99.
2. For the USA see Alicia H. Munnell, *The Economics of Private Pensions*, Washington, DC, 1982, p. 53; for Europe see Thomas Wilson, ed., *Pensions, Inflation and Growth: A Comparative Study of the Elderly in the Welfare State*, 1974, pp. 70, 129, 177, 255; Occupational Pensions Board, *Greater Security for the Rights and Expectations of Members of Occupational Pension Schemes*, Cmnd 8649, 1982 (BPP, XII, 1981–2), pp. 12, 80.
3. For evidence of the uncertainty generated by expectations of state pensions, see, e.g., L. J. E. Beeson, 'Some Industrial Relations Aspects of Pension Funds', National Association of Pension Funds, *Conference Report, May 1967*, pp. 5ff.
4. In particular they were unwilling to shoulder the risks of final salary schemes, preferring money purchase schemes. See, for instance, E. Brunet, 'Small Firms Face Ever Greater Difficulties', *The Times*, 10 May 1975, 18b.
5. G. L. Reid and D. J. Robertson, eds., *Fringe Benefits, Labour Costs and Social Security*, 1965, pp. 73–4; Gordon A. Hosking and R. C. B. Lane, *Superannuation Schemes*, 1948, Chapter 36.

6. As in earlier paragraphs, the statistics here relate to 1979. However, fuller surveys of the reasons for exclusion were made in 1967, 1971 and 1975, and many of the inferences made in the text above derive from the report in Government Actuary, *Occupational Pension Schemes: 1975: Fifth Survey*, 1978.

7. None the less, a smaller proportion of women were members of schemes. This was partly because women employees were concentrated in categories excluded for non-gender reasons, e.g., because they were part-time or casual workers or more likely to leave before reaching a qualifying age or completing a qualifying period of service. Cf. p. 138 below, for the later improvement in coverage.

8. The 1979 *Sixth Survey* did not separately analyse the treatment of manual workers. The inferences in the text are compatible with the data for 1979 but are based on data in the *Fifth Survey* for 1975.

9. See p. 44 above.

10. Surveys by the Government Actuary between 1956 and 1967 showed manual workers as the majority of private sector scheme members; but non-manual workers then overtook them and the absolute numbers of manual workers appeared to decline precipitately from 4.1 million in 1967 to 2.75 million in 1975. Some of this apparent decline may be due to sampling bias, some of it to the transfer of steel workers to the public sector, and some to the decline in the numbers of manual workers in the work force as a whole. The decline in numbers of non-manual employees in private sector pension schemes was less marked: from 4.0 million in 1967 to 3.25 million in 1975. Separate figures for manual and non-manual employees are not available for 1979, but private sector scheme membership as a whole had by then increased again.

11. See p. 55 above.

12. F. V. Brilles and R. Mountjoy, 'Pension Funds for Manual Workers', *Superannuation*, No. 15, November 1956; Management Research Group, 'Pension Schemes for Operative Workers: Report of Inter-Group Directors' Dinner Discussion', 13 January 1937, in MRG archives. An Association of Superannuation and Pension Funds survey of 902 member schemes in 1954 (ASPF archives, circular letter No. 244) found that the schemes founded after the War were more likely than earlier ones to have separate schemes for manual workers. By 1975 60% of manual workers in schemes were in separate schemes. See Government Actuary, *Occupational Pension Schemes: 1975: Fifth Survey*, p. 10.

13. T. A. E. Layborn, 'New Thoughts on Pensions and Group Schemes', *Journal of the Insurance Institute of London*, XL, 1952. See also pp. 47–8 above.

14. See the discussion in National Association of Pension Funds, *Conference Report*, May 1965, p. 25, May 1966, pp. 35–6, Autumn 1967, p. 18.

15. See, e.g., Industrial Welfare Society, *Employee Benefit Schemes*, 1949, p. 15. See also p. 109 below.

16. British Institute of Management, *Toward Single Status*, 1975; Incomes Data Services, *Harmonization of Conditions*, No. 273, 1983; W. Brown, *The Changing Contours of Industrial Relations*, Oxford, 1982.

17. Competitive industries such as construction or clothing manufacture were the least likely to offer pensions: see, e.g., *Department of Employment Gazette*, February 1971, 156. In many firms it was the production and marketing

managers who appreciated the competitive conditions and opposed the improvement of pension benefits when these were proposed by personnel managers. This was the case, for example, in Clarks, the shoemaking company.

18. See p. 103 below.
19. See pp. 111 and 120–1 below.
20. See p. 50 above.
21. See pp. 57–8 above.
22. A. B. Atkinson and A. J. Harrison, *Distribution of Personal Wealth in Britain*, Cambridge, 1978, p. 159.
23. See p. 135 below.
24. See p. 11 below.
25. Government Actuary, *Occupational Pension Schemes: 1979: Sixth Survey*, 1981, p. 37.
26. The early schemes had a low funding rate because the benefits were on a less generous basis, but also because the chances of drawing them (given heavier mortality) were less; one of the reasons for the rise in cost in the twentieth century is increased longevity.
27. Government Actuary, *Occupational Pension Schemes: 1979: Sixth Survey*, pp. 33–7.
28. Government Actuary, *Occupational Pension Schemes: A Survey*, 1958, p. 6; Government Actuary, *Occupational Schemes 1979: Sixth Survey*, p. 17.
29. See p. 35–8 above.
30. Obituary of Duncan C. Fraser in *Journal of the Institute of Actuaries*, LXXVIII, 1952, 384–6; Obituary of W. J. H. Whittall, *Journal of the Institute of Actuaries*, LXII, 1931, 325; Obituary of George King, *Journal of the Institute of Actuaries*, LXIV, 1933, 241ff.; Bacon & Woodrow archives; V. A. Burrows (R. Watson & Sons), 'Some Actuarial and Financial Aspects of Superannuation Schemes', Association of Superannuation and Pension Funds, 6 May 1937 address.
31. See, e.g., the debate between T. A. E. Layborn (of Bowring & Layborn, insurance brokers) and R. W. Abbott (of Bacon & Woodrow, consulting actuaries) in Association of Superannuation and Pension Funds, *Autumn Conference 1952*; S. W. Singleton, 'The Transfer From a Life Office Fund to a Privately Administered Fund', *Superannuation*, No. 24, November 1959; Prudential Corporation archives, files on 'Consulting Actuaries 1948–64'; 'Pensurer', 'A Self-Administered Fund and an Insured Scheme', *Policy Insurance Weekly*, 2 September 1954, 618–22; J. C. S. Hymans, 'Pension Schemes II: Private Fund or Insured Scheme', *The Accountant*, 10 December 1950, 588.
32. On the growth of the consulting business of actuaries and others see Pam Spooner, 'Pension Consultants: Growth of a New Industry', *Investors Chronicle*, 6 March 1981, 30–1.
33. H. E. Raynes, 'Factors Controlling the Rate of Interest on Long-Term Investments', *Journal of the Institute of Actuaries*, LXVI, 1935; C. H. L. Brown and J. A. G. Taylor, 'Some Observations on the Rate of Interest as Affecting Pension Funds', *Journal of the Institute of Actuaries*, LXIX, 1938.
34. Denis Weaver, 'Pension Fund Investments', *Superannuation*, April 1950 (circular letter No. 141). Insurance company actuaries were also relatively

conservative about investment policies before 1950. See, for instance, Nicholas Davenport, 'Keynes in the City', in Milo Keynes, ed., *Essays on John Maynard Keynes*, 1975, pp. 224–9.

35. See G. Ross Goobey's remarks in Association of Superannuation and Pension Funds, *Autumn Conference 1950*, pp. 17–18 and *Autumn Conference 1956*, pp. 20ff.; and his articles 'Pension Fund Investment', *Superannuation*, No. 11, April 1955; 'A Pension Fund's Policy: An Interview with the Manager of the Imperial Tobacco Company's Pension Fund', *The Financial Times*, 8 December 1958, 6c; see also Harold Wincott, 'The Cult of the Equity with Particular Reference to Institutional Investing', *Superannuation*, No. 26, October 1961.

36. *Report of the [Wilson] Committee to Review the Functioning of Financial Institutions*, Cmnd 7937, 1980, p. 89. See also Table A.2 in the Statistical Appendix, p. 146 below.

37. Brian P. Whitehouse, *Partners in Property: A History and Analysis of the Provision of Institutional Finance for Property Development*, 1964, pp. 92, 108–9; T. A. Roberts, 'Investment in Property', in National Association of Pension Funds, *Conference Proceedings*, May 1969.

38. *Report of the [Wilson] Committee*, p. 463.

39. 'Solving the Investment Problem', *Superannuation*, No. 17, July 1957; *Industrial Management Research Association Bulletin*, No. 332, 16 July 1957; 'A Unit Trust with an Excellent Record', *Investors Chronicle and Money Market Review*, 4 November 1960, 473.

40. See, e.g., Throgmorton Management in *Industrial Management Research Association Bulletin*, No. 349, 8 July 1958; *Manchester Guardian*, 30 July 1958, 8b.

41. At the beginning of 1984 Warburgs advised 220 clients with funds valued at £4,850 million, Schroders 123 clients with funds of £4,550 million, Phillips & Drew 128 clients with funds of £3,500 million and Barclays 55 clients with funds of £3,000 million (*The Financial Times*, Supplement, 21 February 1984, i).

42. This was the practice of the Philips and Ford pension funds, for instance.

43. This account is based on the archives of the Prudential, the Legal & General, and the Life Offices' Association.

44. Between 1956 and 1963 the proportion of members in the private sector in insured schemes rose from 53% to 60% (Government Actuary, *Occupational Pension Schemes: A New Survey*, 1966, p. 9).

45. In 1963 88% of all schemes were insured, but this proportion varied from 97% of those with twelve or fewer members to only 34% in schemes with 1,000 or more members (*ibid.*, p. 10).

46. 'New Thinking in Occupational Schemes', *The Financial Times*, 25 February 1971, Supplement, ii.

47. F. W. Bacon, M. D. W. Elphinstone and B. Benjamin, 'The Growth of Pension Rights and Their Impact on the National Economy', *Journal of the Institute of Actuaries*, LXXX, 1954, 158; Government Actuary, *Occupational Pension Schemes: 1979: Sixth Survey*, 1981, pp. 17–18.

48. This can be seen, generally, in the proceedings of the annual conference of the Association of Superannuation and Pension Funds.

49. For a fuller discussion of the effects of inflation on fund finances, see Richard

Hemming and John Kay, 'The Future of Occupational Pension Provision in Britain', in Michael Fogarty, ed., *Retirement Policy: the Next Fifty Years*, 1982.
50. See pp. 108–11 below.
51. K. Muir McKelvey, 'Valuation Surplus', National Association of Pension Funds, *Autumn Conference, December 1966*.
52. For a fuller discussion of some of the critical problems with modern actuarial practice, see R. Hemming and J. A. Kay, *The Economic Basis of Pension Funding*, Oxford, forthcoming.
53. Based on material in the archives of the Life Offices' Association and Legal & General.
54. Margaret Stone, 'Pension Funds Feeling the Pinch', *The Times*, 14 March 1975, 19. For annual fluctuations in investment returns, see Statistical Appendix, Table A.2, p. 146 below.
55. R. Hemming and J. A. Kay, 'Real Rates of Return', *Fiscal Studies*, II, 1981.
56. G. A. Hosking, *Pension Schemes and Retirement Benefits*, 4th edn, rev. by K. Muir McKelvey, p. 128; Henley Centre for Forecasting, *The Pensions Dilemma*, 1976; Barry Riley, 'Pension Fund Investment', *The Financial Times* Supplement, 21 February 1984, I.
57. Janette Rutterford, 'Index-Linked Gilts', *National Westminster Bank Quarterly Review*, November 1983.

6   Accident and design in the evolution of pensions

1. E.g., the sources quoted in Chapter 4, nn. 40 and 41 above.
2. See pp. 140–1 below.
3. For examples of changing member sophistication over the redistributive effects of final salary schemes see, e.g., pp. 107–11 below; for member participation generally, see pp. 140–1 below.
4. J. Hyman and T. Schuller, 'Employee Participation in the Management of Pension Schemes', University of Glasgow, Centre for Research in Industrial Democracy and Participation, 1983; Mary Strachan Cousins, 'A Study of Sixteen Pension Schemes', *Personnel Management*, XXXVIII, 1956, 19.
5. See, e.g., the file on the 1927 Validation Act, 36–7, in Bacon & Woodrow archives.
6. Lord Sinclair, *H.L. Deb.*, 5th Series, Vol. 207, cols. 38–43, 21 January 1958.
7. R. J. W. Crabbe and C. A. Poyser, *Pension and Widows' and Orphans' Funds*, Cambridge, 1953, p. 2.
8. See pp. 43–4 above.
9. R. R. Nelson and S. G. Winter, *An Evolutionary Theory of Economic Change*, Cambridge, Mass., 1982.
10. See pp. 31–2 above.
11. See pp. 92–3 below.
12. A. Kaye-Butterworth (North Eastern Railway) in *Evidence to the Board of Trade Committee on Railway Superannuation Funds*, Cd 5484, 1911 (BPP, XXIX, Part I, 1911), qq. 1451–5; O. H. Jones (Cadburys) in *Appendix to the Report of the Departmental Committee on Old Age Pension, Including Evidence*, Cmd 411, 1919 (BPP, XXVII, 1919), qq. 3913, 4023.

13. Many of the criticisms which Musson and Hanson have levelled at working-class schemes for old age savings in the nineteenth century can be applied to employer-run pension schemes in the twentieth. Cf. Chapter 3, n. 3 above.
14. See p. 72 above.

7 *Pensions in Peril? Securing, solvency and vesting*

1. This can be deduced from the statistics on withdrawal rates and death rates in any pension scheme, until preservation of benefits became more common in the 1970s and after. It is also clear (on any reasonable assumptions about membership, age structures, membership turnover, and member and pensioner death rates) from a comparison of the numbers of people who are members of schemes, and the number of those who are drawing pensions decades later. In 1936, for example, 1.6 million people were members of private sector occupational pension schemes and in the subsequent two decades membership climbed sharply to 4.3 million in 1956; but there were less than 0.1 million pensioners in 1936, only 0.3 million in 1956, and 1.2 million in 1979 (plus at the latter date 0.2 million widows and dependants drawing pensions); see 'Schemes Providing for Pensions for Employees on Retirement from Work', *Ministry of Labour Gazette*, May 1938, 172, 174; Government Actuary, *Occupational Pension Schemes: 1979: Sixth Survey*, 1981, pp. 6, 12.
2. On widows' benefits, see pp. 117–21 below.
3. James J. McLauchlan, 'The Fundamental Principles of Pension Funds: Inaugural Address', *Transactions of the Faculty of Actuaries*, IV, 1908, 198, 201. Of 1,000 males entering at age twenty, he expected 784 to withdraw, 90 to die and only 126 to survive as members drawing a pension. Cf. Royal Exchange Assurance's experience in 1840–99, when half the staff left before retirement, just over one-third retired on pension, and less than one-sixth died in service (Barry Supple, *The Royal Exchange Assurance: A History of British Insurance, 1720–1970*, Cambridge, 1970, p. 385).
4. Life expectancy data for 1978 in United Nations, *Demographic Yearbook 1982*, New York, 1984, p. 402. Cf. Chapter 1, n. 9.
5. Tony Lynes, *French Pensions*, LSE Occasional Papers in Social Administration, No. 21, 1967, especially pp. 48–9. The consequence in France was the introduction of the so-called 'répartition' system of pensioning, backed by the state but organized by groupings of employers, and relying for the payment of pensioners on pay-as-you-go levies on current workers.
6. W. Andrew Achenbaum, *Old Age in the New Land*, Baltimore, Md., 1978, pp. 128–9. A forthcoming history of American pensions by Dr Steven A. Sass explores the parallels with the British railway system.
7. On the modern US pension system, see Alicia H. Munnell, *The Economics of Private Pensions*, Washington, D.C., 1982; Zvi Bodie and John B. Shoven, eds., *Financial Aspects of the United States Pension System*, Chicago, Ill., 1983. For a UK perspective of US regulation, see Occupational Pensions Board, *Solvency, Disclosure of Information and Member Participation in Occupational Pension Schemes*, Vol. 3, *Overseas Practice*, 1975, p. 75. On the problems of the US

system of federal insurance guarantees of the solvency of occupational funds, see 'Jumping Ship', *The Economist*, 10 July 1982, 40.

8. Association of Superannuation and Pension Funds, *Annual General Meeting, June 1949*, p. 3.

9. Occupational Pensions Board, *op. cit.*, p. 16.

10. *The Times*, 25 March 1936, 9d. Usually existing pensioners were more secure than current contributors in the winding up of a fund, though the precise position depended on the rules and trust deed. See also D. McCulloch, 'When the Company Goes Bust: Questions Raised by the Rolls-Royce Issue', *The Times*, 13 February 1971, 9a; Eric Brunet, 'Pensions: The Right to the Facts when a Scheme is Wound Up', *The Times*, 15 March 1975, 18c. On the dissolution of a friendly society pension scheme, cf. R. C. B. Lane, 'The Dissolution of a Superannuation Society', *Journal of the Institute of Actuaries*, LXXV, 1949.

11. For instance, Beagle Aircraft was cited as a case of bankruptcy of the employer leading to default on pension benefits in union evidence to the Occupational Pensions Board (ASTMS Research Department paper supplied to the author by Mr Bryan Freake). See also C. G. Lewin, 'Termination of Pension Schemes', *Pensions World*, February 1985, 70–2.

12. John Plender, *That's the Way the Money Goes: The Financial Institutions, and the Nation's Savings*, 1982, pp. 27–9. For other examples of public sector deficits, see, e.g., *The Times*, 22 April 1935, 9d, 2 December 1935, 11c, 4 December 1935, 9d.

13. On the origins of self-regulation, see Supple, *op. cit.*, pp. 130–45.

14. The trust deed usually specified an order of precedence in meeting liabilities in the event of winding-up: typically current pensioners first, then deferred annuitants currently employed, then early leavers' deferred annuities, and finally return of surplus to the employer. The Inland Revue initially permitted the latter only in the event of winding-up, but in 1983 appeared to have relaxed the rule to permit actuarially determined surpluses to revert to the employer. This caused some concern (e.g., letter from John Garnett, director, Industrial Society, *The Financial Times*, 29 December 1983, 9c), and there were fears of take-over bids for firms to strip assets from pension funds, following similar developments in the United States (e.g., *Evening Standard*, 13 July 1984, 50). The Inland Revenue have since given the impression that they will permit such repayments to employers only in exceptional circumstances and after consultation with the members whose interests are affected.

15. *Parke* vs. *'The Daily News' and Others*, All England Law Reports 1962, Part 15, pp. 929–48. Section 46 of the 1980 Companies Act (which imposes on the directors the duty of having regard to the interests of employees as well as of shareholders) makes it unlikely that a similar action would now succeed.

16. This has been true recently in cases such as Lucas in the private sector and in some privatized public corporations such as National Freight: see, e.g., S. McLauchlan, *The National Freight Buy-Out*, 1983.

17. '£20 Billion of Pension Funds in Need of Regulation', *The Economist*, 4 November 1978, 109ff.; Association of Superannuation and Pension Funds, *Autumn Conference 1952*, pp. 31–2; R. W. Abbott, 'Pension Schemes: Aims and Achievements', *The Accountant*, 29 January 1955, 118–19; H. W. Carey in

National Association of Pension Funds, *Conference Report May 1969*, pp. 38ff.;
W. J. Hudson, 'The Captive Pension Challenge: What the Offices Need to
Offer', *Life Policy Market*, February 1980, 26.

18. *Evans* vs. *London Co-operative Society Ltd.* (Chancery), Times Law Report, 6
July 1976. For a discussion of the duties of trustees, see Tom Schuller and Jeff
Hyman, 'Trust Law and Trustees: Employee Representation in Pension
Schemes', *Industrial Law Journal*, XII, 1983, 85–7.

19. *Report of the [Wilson] Committee to Review the Functioning of Financial
Institutions*, Cmnd 7937, 1980, p. 95.

20. Mr Gunlake, 'Surplus or Deficit?', Association of Superannuation and Pension
Funds, *Autumn Conference, 1960*, p. 6; K. Muir McKelvey, 'Valuation Surplus',
National Association of Pension Funds, *Autumn Conference, December 1966*,
pp. 16–17.

21. Gunlake, *loc. cit.* For the overestimation of mortality in the teachers'
superannuation scheme, see, e.g., *The Times*, 22 April 1935, 9d.

22. Casual inspection of occupational mortality data suggest that this is not
implausible. See, e.g., Office of Population Censuses and Surveys, *Occupational
Mortality 1970–72 England and Wales*, DS No. 1, 1978. Casual claims of this
kind were also sometimes made by pension experts, e.g., H. Dougharty,
*Penion, Endowment, Life Assurance and Other Schemes, for Employees of ~
Commercial Companies*, 1927, p. 26.

23. Gunlake, *op. cit.*, p. 5; Gordon Pingstone, 'Group Life and Pension Schemes
Including Group Family Income Benefit Schemes', *Journal of the Institute of
Actuaries*, LXXVII, 1951, 355–60.

24. On widows' pensions, see pp. 117–21 below.

25. p. 78 above.

26. G. S. W. Epps, 'Superannuation Funds: Notes on Some Postwar Problems . . .',
Journal of the Institute of Actuaries, LII, 1921. See also the correspondence
between the Great Western Railway and the Pension Society Committee in
PRO, RAIL 258/436.

27. For instance, in a sample of 156 registered funds with 193,000 members in 1934,
deficiencies of actuarial valuation (in 56 of the funds) were 20% of total funds
(*Report of the Chief Registrar of Friendly Societies*, 1934 (BPP, IX, 1934–5), p.
30).

28. See p. 74 above.

29. Government Actuary, *Occupational Pension Schemes: A Survey*, 1958, p. 24.

30. Richard Hemming and John Kay, 'The Future of Occupational Pension
Provision in Britain', in Michael Fogarty, ed., *Retirement Policy: The Next Fifty
Years*, 1982, pp. 114–19.

31. See p. 101 below.

32. F. M. Redington, Presidential Address, *Journal of the Institute of Actuaries*,
LXXXV, 1959, 6.

33. Including *ex gratia* pensions, unfunded rights probably exceeded funded rights,
at least until the 1960s. See J. Revell, *The Wealth of the Nation: The National
Balance Sheet of the United Kingdom, 1957–61*, Cambridge, 1967, pp. 374, 396.
See also n. 27 above and other *Reports of the Chief Registrar of Friendly
Societies*.

34. See the quotation which heads this chapter.

35. Government Actuary, *Occupational Pension Schemes: A Survey*, 1958, pp. 24–5.
36. Circular letter No. 107, 11 March 1946, 7, in Association of Superannuation and Pension Funds archives.
37. See pp. 31–2 above.
38. *Report of the [Wilson] Committee to Review the Functioning of Financial Institutions*, Cmnd 7937, 1980, p. 533 implies the acceptance of full funding, as does an examination of recent practices in major funds.
39. See p. 96 above.
40. *Report of the [Wilson] Committee*, p. 325; L. C. B. Gower, *Review of Investor Protection: A Discussion Document*, 1982, p. 129.
41. Occasionally employees could recover their pension rights by suing for wrongful dismissal: see, e.g., T. A. E. Layborn, 'Modern Developments in Pension Schemes', Association of Superannuation and Pension Funds, *Autumn Conference 1952*, p. 9. However, as Layborn pointed out, employers could remove this right by minor changes in the trust deed. Unfair dismissal procedures before industrial tribunals now provide a new remedy.
42. W. J. H. Whittall, 'Note on a Fundamental Question Underlying the Pension Problem with a Reference to the School Teachers' Superannuation Act, 1918', *Journal of the Institute of Actuaries*, LI, 1919, 248; John C. Mitchell, 'Pension Schemes for Office Staffs', Association of Superannuation and Pension Funds address, 1935, p. 8.
43. For a survey of the situation after the Second World War, see A. S. Owen, 'Pension Schemes and Funds: The Problem of Transfers of Employment', *Journal of the Insurance Institute of London*, XLI, 1952–3, reprinted in *Superannuation*, No. 10, October 1954.
44. See pp. 23–4 and 36–7 above.
45. See pp. 56–8 above.
46. Stanley Parker, *Older Workers and Retirement*, Office of Population Censuses and Surveys, 1980, pp. 17, 27. See also Ken Mayhew, 'Occupational Mobility in Britain', *Oxford Bulletin of Economics and Statistics*, XLIII, 1981.
47. In a survey of 39,000 retiring members of one life office's schemes in 1971–82, only 25% had 30 or more years' service, 21% had 21–30 years, and 29% 11–20 years (Occupational Pensions Board, *Greater Security for the Rights and Expectations of Members of Occupational Pension Schemes*, Cmnd 8049, 1982 (BPP, XII, 1981–2), p. 71, n. 1.)
48. Barry McCormick and Gordon Hughes, 'The Influence of Pensions on Job Mobility', *Journal of Public Economics*, XXIII, 1984. Prior to this study generalizations were based on casual empiricism: opinion was usually that young people and manual workers were not much affected, but that higher-paid employees were. McCormick and Hughes show that the effect on reducing job mobility is in fact greater for manual workers than for higher-paid people. American data also show a significant effect of pension fund membership in reducing job mobility: see B. R. Schiller and R. D. Weiss, 'The Impact of Private Pensions on Firm Attachment', *Review of Economics and Statistics*, LXI, 1979, 369–72.
49. For instance, in a 1966 survey of Shell employees 71% of men endorsed the

statement that pension rights would make them think before leaving their job. A 1984 Gallup survey of 800 people aged between twenty-one and fifty-five on occupational pension schemes, commissioned by the Secretary of State for Social Services, also showed widespread knowledge of the penalty deterrents for leavers, and as many as one in seven of those aged between forty-five and fifty-five claimed to have been put off job changing as a result.

50. 'Loosing the Golden Chains', *The Economist*, 20 June 1964, 1386–7.
51. The public sector figures are an approximation, owing to an obscurity in the presentation of the survey results. See Government Actuary, *Occupational Pension Schemes: A New Survey*, 1966, pp. 45–9, *Occupational Pension Schemes: 1971: Fourth Survey*, 1972, pp. 47–50, *Occupational Pension Schemes: 1979: Sixth Survey*, 1981, pp. 70–3.
52. The National Association of Pension Funds and its predecessors were generally more favourable to transferability and more liberal-minded than the Confederation of British Industry and its predecessors, which more accurately reflected the views of employers on this issue. For examples of employer opposition in private, see minutes of the Fifth Meeting of the National Advisory Committee on the Employment of Older Men and Women, 19 March 1953, OMW (M)5, in LAB 8/2006, and Industrial Management Research Association Archives, report of meeting of 13 December 1949, p. 3 (Business History Unit, London School of Economics, Slip 639, General Meetings, w/10/46–51/17, Group 1). By the 1960s full preservation, it was reckoned, would increase the cost of schemes by 25–35%: see K. M. McKelvey, 'Valuation Surplus', National Association of Pension Funds, *Autumn Conference*, December 1966, p. 34.
53. Basil Taylor, 'Nothing to Lose But Your Pension Rights', *The Listener*, 19 September 1963, 410–11.
54. National Joint Advisory Council, *The Preservation of Pension Rights*, Ministry of Labour, 1966. The report made no recommendations on inflation-proofing or widows' pensions, and the members were unable to agree on whether preservation should be encouraged by legal compulsion, tax incentives or some other means.
55. Association of Superannuation and Pension Funds, *Annual Report 1949*, p. 6; G. A. Hosking and D. G. Lee, 'Should Pension Rights be Transferable?', *Superannuation*, April 1951, circular letter No. 151; A. S. Owen, *op. cit.*; F. H. Spratling, F. W. Bacon and A. E. Bromfield, 'Preservation of Pension Rights', *Journal of the Institute of Actuaries*, LXXXIII, 1957.
56. G. Rhodes, *Public Sector Pensions*, 1965, pp. 81–7. For criticism of government's behaviour as an employer see Association of Superannuation and Pension Funds, *Autumn Conference, 1961*, p. 15.
57. See p. 45 above.
58. Government Actuary, *Occupational Pension Schemes: A New Survey*, 1966, p. 46.
59. R. W. Abbott, 'Preservation of Pension Rights', *British Tax Review*, January–February 1964, 31; *The Economist*, 20 June 1964, 1387; National Association of Pension Funds, *Conference Report 1963*, p. 30; National Joint Advisory Council, *op. cit.*, p. 22.
60. They were taxed at one-quarter of the standard rate, though the majority of

those receiving refunds normally paid tax at the standard rate. There was no longer any justification for this rate, which had been fixed decades earlier as a composite rate to reflect the fact that most pension scheme members were not taxpayers (see p. 160n. 27 below). The Inland Revenue had also placed other barriers in the way of transferability at various dates. For a defence of their position, see H. H. Leedale, 'The Transference of Pension Rights: Getting Round the Taxation Problems', National Association of Pension Funds, *Conference Report 1967.*

61. For younger workers, their own contribution alone, if privately invested, could secure better pensions than the deferred pensions being offered in typical schemes.
62. Companies often discriminated against early leavers by not offering any inflation-proofing, even in cases where they did offer such protection for retiring company pensioners; others offered compensation at a much lower rate; and leavers also lost the inflation compensation implicit in final salary schemes. See also pp. 111–14 below.
63. Arthur Seldon, *Pensions in a Free Society*, 1957, pp. 23–5.
64. H. E. Raynes (Legal & General), in discussion of Owen, *op. cit., Journal of the Insurance Institute of London*, XLI, 1952–3, p. 31.
65. Occupational Pensions Board, *Improved Protection for the Occupational Pension Rights and Expectations of Early Leavers*, Cmnd 8271, 1981 (BPP, VIII, 1980–1), p. 7, and Appendix 5.
66. Joe Irving, 'Pensions: Scandal of the Golden Handcuffs', *The Sunday Times*, 17 May 1981, 63; Roger Hardman, 'Pensions: Part 2: Cutting the Golden Handcuffs', *The Sunday Times*, 24 May 1981, 61.
67. Occupational Pensions Board, *loc. cit.* As the Committee pointed out, over the previous ten years the 5% figure would have limited revaluation to 63% whereas the earnings index had in fact quadrupled. In such inflationary conditions, then, preservation would still be virtually worthless. See also Barry Riley, 'The Lack of Protection From 5 percent', *The Financial Times*, 16 June 1984, 7a.

8 Designing the benefit structure

1. Government Actuary, *Occupational Pension Schemes: 1979: Sixth Survey*, 1981, Chapter 8.
2. See, for instance, Arthur Seldon, *Pensions in a Free Society*, Institute of Economic Affairs, 1957, p. 23.
3. See p. 76 above.
4. R. E. Underwood, 'A "Money-Purchase" Pension Scheme', *Journal of the Institute of Actuaries*, LXIV, 1933.
5. James John McLauchlan, 'The Fundamental Principles of Pension Funds', *Transactions of the Faculty of Actuaries*, IV, 1909, 214–20.
6. Joseph Burn and Frank Percy Symmons, 'Practical Points in Connection with the Formation and Valuation of Pension Funds, with a Note on Group Assurances', *Journal of the Institute of Actuaries*, XLIX, 1915, pp. 119ff.; C. W. Kenchington in *ibid.*, 251.

7. The Inland Revenue successfully opposed lump sum payments by Clayton Aniline to compensate the fund for the extra cost, arguing that it was not an 'ordinary annual contribution'. See Association of Superannuation and Pension Funds, *Annual General Meeting 1950*, pp. 8–9.

8. 'Schemes Providing for Pensions for Employees on Retirement from Work', *Ministry of Labour Gazette*, May 1938, 173. In a survey of 682 self-administered funds in 1954, 35% were average salary, and 35% final salary schemes (Association of Superannuation and Pension Funds, *Statistics*, circular letter No. 244, 1 June 1956, ASPF archives).

9. See, for example, the remarks on the abandonment of the London and South Western Railway 'money purchase' scheme in H. Dougharty, *Pension, Endowment, and Other, Life Assurance Schemes for Employees of Commercial Companies*, 1927, pp. 9–10. Actuaries generally had an initial professional distaste for 'service-salary' schemes, for they introduced further uncertainties into their calculations, requiring effectively a forecast of the shape and height of the salary pyramid and promotion patterns over forty years.

10. *Report of the Committee appointed by the Board of Trade to inquire into the Constitution, Rules, Administration, and Financial Position of the Superannuation and similar funds of Railway Companies*, Cd 5349, 1910 (BPP, LVII, 1910), p. 15.

11. Only 2% of insured schemes in a 1954 survey were on a final salary basis. See Association of Superannuation and Pension Funds, *Statistics*, circular letter No. 244, 1 June 1956, ASPF archives.

12. Government Actuary, *Occupational Pension Schemes: Third Survey*, 1968, pp. 24–6.

13. There may be other advantages to final salary schemes for employers. Among those which have been suggested are the tax advantages of the overfunding they may permit. The high achieved investment returns experienced by funds in the 1960s also led employers into over-optimism about their ability to afford final salary schemes. See National Association of Pension Funds, *The Future Relationship between State and Occupational Pensions*, paras. 40–2.

14. Government Actuary, *Occupational Pension Schemes: 1979: Sixth Survey*, 1981, p. 41. The state earnings-related scheme permitted a 'revalued average salary' formula (i.e. average salary, but with the salary revalued to compensate for inflation) also. It is not clear why trade unions did not press for this, as Labour Party pension planners did for the state scheme to reduce its inegalitarian effects. See n. 16 below.

15. Many of the schemes with accrual rates of one-sixtieths did, however, permit the benefit to be taken in the form of a lump sum of three times the pension and a reduced accrual rate of one-eightieths, which was the minimum which made contracting out possible and retained the tax privileges of lump sums. See pp. 114–17 below.

16. See, e.g., Geraldine Kaye, 'Are Pensions Outmoded?', Gresham Research Lecture, Institute of Actuaries, 26 April 1984 (reported in *Pensions World*, July 1984) for criticism of the hidden cross-subsidies in final salary schemes. The Labour Party's experts discussing the state earnings-related scheme in the 1970s were aware of the problem (and chose a revalued average salary formula which

was biased against the poor, but less so than the final salary formula), but they noted that many unions were not aware of this factor (interviews and unpublished Labour Party policy documents).

17. Though not the 1961 graduated scheme (which was not inflation-proofed until it was retrospectively changed in 1975), or the 1973 Social Security Act scheme of Keith Joseph (which would have strengthened the 'money purchase' principle by basing state earnings-related pensions on it).

18. See p. 62 above. The precise degree of inflation-linking of the guaranteed minimum pension is extremely complex: for an explanation, see Michael O' Higgins, 'Comment on Chapter 3', in Michael Fogarty, ed., *Retirement Policy: The Next Fifty Years*, 1982, pp. 69–70.

19. Letter to GWR from the Subcommittee of the Great Western Railway Pension Society, 17 January 1918, in PRO RAIL 258/436.

20. For instance, Cadburys agreed to increase their contributions to their fund to help compensate pensioners for inflation, and the government took powers to increase the pensions of various categories of state employees, including civil servants and teachers, in the Pensions (Increase) Acts of 1920 and 1924.

21. Association of Superannuation and Pension Funds, *Increased Payments to Existing Pensioners*, circular letter no. 157, 1 November 1951, in ASPF archives. By 1963, 25% of members and 60% of pensioners were in schemes providing some form of post-retirement augmentation (Government Actuary, *Occupational Pension Schemes: A New Survey*, 1966, pp. 37–8.) Many schemes not offering such augmentation were not yet active, and had few or no pensioners.

22. E.g., the remarks of J. A. Mulligan (Courtaulds Pension Funds) in Association of Superannuation and Pension Funds, *Autumn Conference 1960*, p. 51.

23. Leo Pliatzky, *Getting and Spending: Public Expenditure, Employment and Inflation*, Oxford, 1982, p. 155; [Scott] *Inquiry into the Value of Pensions*, Cmnd. 8147, 1981. By 1979, about 85% of occupational pension scheme members in the public sector were entitled to the index-linked benefits specified in the Pensions (Increase) Acts (i.e., full compensation for inflation) and the remainder, although not entitled to them by scheme rules, in practice obtained them. See Government Actuary, *Occupational Pension Schemes: 1979: Sixth Survey*, 1981, p. 58.

24. Government Actuary, *Occupational Pension Schemes: 1979: Sixth Survey*, 1981, p. 57.

25. *Ibid.*, pp. 56–7.

26. Government Actuary, *Civil Service Pay Research: the 1980 Review of the Adjustment for Differences in Superannuation Benefits*, 1980, p. 8.

27. Occupational Pensions Board, *Greater Security for the Rights and Expectations of Members of Occupational Pension Schemes*, Cmnd 8649, 1982 (BPP, XII, 1981–2), p. 54. Cf. pp. 103–4 above.

28. Government Actuary, *Occupational Pension Schemes: 1979: Sixth Survey*, 1981, pp. 57–8.

29. Alan C. Chapman, 'Indexation of Pensions in the Private Sector – One Company's Approach', *Pensions World*, October 1983, pp. 687–9. Rank have committed themselves to paying increases; rather more firms have retrospectively granted full compensation for inflation. Over the highly inflationary five-year period to 1984, Barclays, British Leyland, John Lewis, Marks & Spencer,

RTZ, and Shell paid increases ahead of inflation; while Imperial Group, J. Sainsbury, Unigate and Unilever came close to it, and Woolworth, DRG, Tate & Lyle and the Co-op paid very poor inflation compensation (according to a survey in *Money Magazine*, reported in *The Financial Times*, 30 October 1984, 6f).

30. This myopia is also attested by the typical choice of annuity by individuals investing retirement lump sums: very few take a lower immediate annuity in return for later escalation rather than the initially high, but fixed, annuity contract.

31. See, e.g., *Superannuation*, No. 25, April 1961, 8. They were also curiously reluctant to publicize their policy on advanced funding of inflation-proofing (see, e.g., *Policy Holder*, 14 October 1977, 1807).

32. There was a problem of adverse selection: if a lump sum option were offered, poor lives would tend to accept it and good lives to refuse it, increasing the overall cost of the scheme. This could, however, be minimized by requiring the option to be chosen some years before retirement.

33. The Manchester Corporation Thrift Fund and the Fine Cotton Spinners' & Doublers' Fund, for instance, both established around the turn of the century, did, however, advise beneficiaries on the purchase of annuities if they preferred that. The Federated Superannuation System for Universities, established in 1913, allowed the beneficiary to choose whether to buy an endowment lump sum or a deferred annuity policy.

34. Government Actuary, *Occupational Pension Schemes: 1979: Sixth Survey*, 1981, p. 39.

35. *Second Report of the Royal Commission to Inquire into the Civil Establishments of the Different Offices of State at Home and Abroad*, c 5545, 1888 (BPP, XXVII, 1888), p. 21.

36. Royal Commission on Income Tax, *Evidence, with appendices and index*, Cmd 288, 1919 (BPP, XXII, 1919), q. 4492.

37. Government Actuary, *Occupational Pension Schemes: 1979: Sixth Survey*, 1981, p. 38.

38. This account is based on three unpublished manuscripts by Tony Lynes: 'The Civil Service Deferred Pay Movement'; 'The Commutation of Civil Service Pensions'; and 'The History of Lump Sums'. I am especially grateful to the author for sharing with me the results of his pioneering unpublished research in the public records on these issues. He is not, of course, responsible for the interpretation placed upon the evidence in the text. See also *Report of the Royal Commission on Superannuation in the Civil Service*, Cmd 1744, 1903 (BPP, XIX, 1903).

39. See pp. 47–8 above.

40. See pp. 47–50 above.

41. 'Notes on Retirement and Death Provision for Employees', circular letter No. 186, December 1945, Association of Superannuation and Pension Fund archives, p. 2; W. F. Marples, in discussion, Association of Superannuation and Pension Funds, *Autumn Conference 1948*, p. 16; Messrs Cope and Goobey, in discussion, National Association of Pension Funds, *Regional Conference: Birmingham 1962*, pp. 31–2. See also n. 17 of Chapter 4.

42. Gallup poll, commissioned by Legal & General, 1983.

43. *Ibid.*
44. National Joint Advisory Council, *Preservation of Pension Rights*, Ministry of Labour, 1966, p. 42.
45. *H.C. Deb.*, 5th Series, Vol. 176, col. 313, 15 July 1924, Vol. 185, col. 1202, 22 June 1925.
46. See p. 20 above.
47. Government Actuary, *Occupational Pension Schemes: A Survey*, 1958, p. 24. See also 'Notes on Widows' Pensions', *Superannuation*, No. 14, July 1956; H. A. R. Barnett, 'Widows' Pensions', *Superannuation*, No. 15, November 1956.
48. *Superannuation*, No. 14, July 1956, 12; Government Actuary, *Occupational Pension Schemes: A New Survey*, 1966, p. 41, *Occupational Pension Schemes: Third Survey: 1968*, p. 27. A survey of widows aged sixty-five and over in 1962 showed only 9% received employer pensions (many of which would be from their own employment or special widows' schemes rather than the widow's allocation option). See Peter Townsend and Dorothy Wedderburn, *The Aged in the Welfare State*, 1965, p. 102.
49. R. E. Underwood, 'Widows' and Orphans' Pension Schemes', Association of Superannuation and Pension Funds, *Autumn Conference 1950*, and discussion, pp. 26–7; Association of Superannuation and Pension Funds, *Annual General Meeting 1954*; Gordon A. Hosking, 'Pension Schemes and Inflation', *Superannuation*, No. 14, July 1956, 12.
50. Government Actuary, *Occupational Pension Schemes: 1979: Sixth Survey*, 1981, pp. 62, 67.

9 Retirement: age discrimination or the fruits of prosperity?

1. See the opening quotation to this chapter, and also Jill S. Quadagno, *Aging in Early Industrial Society: Work, Family, and Social Policy in Nineteenth Century England*, New York, 1982 and Chris Phillipson, *Capitalism and the Construction of Old Age*, 1982, for modern critical interpretations of retirement. On the ambivalent attitude of those retiring and its crucial dependence on financial security, see Marion P. Crawford, 'Retirement and Role Playing', *Sociology*, VI, 1972; McKenzie Davey & Associates, 'Survey of Employee Views on Pensions and Retirement', *c.* 1966, pension fund records in the possession of Shell UK Administrative Services. See also n. 20 below.
2. An increasing proportion of those working at sixty-five or over are working only part-time, so the table understates the extent of retirement. However, it is difficult to judge how many of those in 'employment' in the earlier years were really in 'pension jobs' with very little productive output, and hence how much the true labour input of the old has declined.
3. The ratio of the proportion of women aged sixty-five or over who were still in the work force to the proportion of women in the twenty-five to sixty-four age-group who were working fell from 65.2% in 1881 to 43.3% in 1911, 15.9% in 1951 and 12.6% in 1973 (calculated from data in Feinstein, Matthews and Odling-Smee, *loc. cit.*).
4. Ministry of Pensions and National Insurance, *National Insurance Retirement Pensions: Reasons Given for Retiring or Continuing at Work*, 1954; Stanley

Parker, *Older Workers and Retirement*, Office of Population Censuses and Surveys, 1980, p. 28; Rosalind M. Altmann, 'The Incomes of Elderly Men in Britain', Ph.D. thesis, University College London, 1978.

5. United Nations, *Statistical Yearbook 1959*, New York, 1959, p. 60; United Nations, *Demographic Yearbook 1982*, New York, 1984, p. 463.

6. W. F. Marples, FIA, in Association of Superannuation and Pension Funds, *Annual Conference 1948*, p. 23; *Report of the Royal Commission on Population*, Cmd 7695, 1949 (BPP, XIX, 1948–9), p. 114; Malcolm L. Johnson, 'The Implications of Greater Activity in Later Life', in Michael Fogarty, ed., *Retirement Policy: The Next Fifty Years*, 1982.

7. Anthony Trollope, *The Fixed Period*, Leipzig, 1882.

8. Harvey Cushing, *The Life of Sir William Osler*, Oxford, 1925, Vol. 1, pp. 666–70, Vol. 2, p. 196. For the view, in the American context, that the medical profession contributed to increasing 'ageism' see, e.g., Carole Haber, *Beyond Sixty-Five: The Dilemma of Old Age in America's Past*, Cambridge, 1983, Chapter 3.

9. G. Stanley Hall, *Senescence: The Last Half of Life*, New York, 1922; D. Speakman, *Bibliography of Research on Changes in Working Capacity with Age*, Ministry of Labour, 1956; A. T. Welford, *Ageing and Human Skill*, Oxford, 1958.

10. Sir John Collie, *Malingering and Feigned Sickness*, 1917, p. 50.

11. For some turn of the century evidence on the increasing impact of technical change on the aged, see Quadagno, *op. cit.*, 154–62.

12. The tendency of such occupations to have significant over-representation of the aged is evident from successive *Censuses of Population*.

13. *Forty-third Report of the Commissioners of H.M. Inland Revenue for the Year Ended 31 March 1900*, Cd 347, 1900 (BPP, XVIII, 1900), pp. 124–5; *Report of the Commission on Superannuation in the Civil Service*, Cd 1744, 1903 (BPP, XXXIII, 1903), pp. viii–ix; H. F. Lydall, *British Incomes and Savings*, Oxford, 1955, pp. 133–7. See also H. F. Lydall, 'The Life Cycle in Income, Saving and Asset Ownership', *Econometrica*, XXIII, 1955; J. R. S. Revell, 'Assets and Age', *Bulletin of the Oxford University Institute of Statistics*, XXIV, 1962. Direct asset ownership is less common in Britain than in other capitalist countries – see, e.g., Ethel Shanas *et. al.*, *Old People in Three Industrial Societies*, 1968, pp. 358–9, 381, 383.

14. Peter Townsend and Dorothy Wedderburn, *The Aged in the Welfare State*, 1965, pp. 96–8; G. C. Fiegehen and A. R. Gault, 'General Trends in Pensioners' Incomes', paper to SSRC Social Security Workshop, 9 December 1983, prepared in Department of Health and Social Security Economic Advisers' Office, London.

15. Fiegehen and Gault, *op. cit.* Capital gains are not included in pensioners' investment income, nor is any rent for owner-occupied housing imputed.

16. Government Actuary, *Occupational Pension Schemes: 1979: Sixth Survey*, 1981, pp. 38ff. See also R. Layard, D. Piachaud and B. Hayes, 'The Elderly', Chapter 10 in Royal Commission on the Distribution of Income and Wealth, *The Causes of Poverty*, Background Paper No. 5, 1978. Earlier occupational pensions were less generous relative to the state scheme: for instance, Peter

Townsend and Dorothy Wedderburn (*op. cit.*, p. 98) reported a median weekly income for aged British couples in 1962 of £4.95 from state benefits, but for those of sixty-five or over who were still in full-time employment the median income was £10.50; those on employer pensions received an additional £2.20.

17. Louis Dicks-Mireaux and Mervyn King, 'Pension Wealth and Household Savings: Tests of Robustness', *Journal of Public Economics*, XXIII, 1984; Francis Green, 'The Effect of Occupational Pension Schemes on Saving in the United Kingdom: A Test of the Life Cycle Hypothesis', *Economic Journal*, XCI, 1981; R. Hemming and R. Harvey, *Occupational Pension Scheme Membership and Retirement Saving*, Institute for Fiscal Studies Working Paper No. 23, 1981.

18. Rosalind M. Altmann, 'An Analysis of Occupational Pensions in Great Britain', *Applied Economics*, XIV, 1982.

19. A. B. Atkinson and A. J. Harrison, *Distribution of Personal Wealth in Britain*, Cambridge, 1978, p. 158.

20. V. George, *Social Security: Beveridge and After*, 1968, pp. 152–3.

21. *Census of England and Wales, 1931, General Report*, 1950, p. 154.

22. Universal pensions at sixty-five rather than seventy would have cost £27.5 million p.a. rather than £16.3 million p.a. (*Tables Prepared in Connection with the Question of Old Age Pensions, with a Preliminary Memorandum*, Cd 3618, 1907 (BPP, LXVIII, 1907)).

23. *Report of the Committee on Pensions for Unmarried Women*, Cmd 5991, 1939 (BPP, XIV, 1938–9); Sir John Simon (Chancellor of the Exchequer), 'Memorandum on Old Age Pensions', 11 January 1940 in PRO CAB 67/4; minutes of cabinet meeting, 16 January 1940, CAB 65/5 W.M. (40) 15th conclusions, para. 4; *H.C. Deb.*, 5th Series, Vol. 356, cols. 373–7, Vol. 357, col. 1203, 20 February 1940; *Report of the Government Actuary on the Financial Provisions of the Bill Relating to Pensions and Health Insurance*, Cmd 6169, 1940 (BPP, V, 1939–40).

24. Lord Beveridge, 'Social Security under Review', *The Times*, 10 November 1953, 9f.

25. *Report of the Committee on the Economic and Financial Problems of the Provision for Old Age*, Cmd 9333, 1954 (BPP, VI, 1954–5), p. 51. It was a woman member of the committee, Janet Vaughan, who dissented from the majority view that the gender inequality must be maintained (*ibid.*, p. 93).

26. Occupational Pensions Board, *Equal Status for Men and Women in Occupational Pension Schemes*, Cmnd 6599, 1976 (BPP, XLV, 1975–6). The Equal Opportunities Commission have also from time to time called for equalization of pension ages: see, e.g., *The Financial Times*, 31 May 1984, 7a.

27. José Harris, *William Beveridge: A Biography*, Oxford, 1977, p. 394.

28. Hugh Gaitskell raised the deferment benefit by 50% and the earnings limit by 100% (*H.C. Deb.*, 5th Series, Vol. 486, col. 848, 10 April 1951). Later the earnings rule was relaxed further and the claw-back was graduated. The complete abolition of the retirement condition and earnings rule was considered desirable but too expensive: see, e.g., Richard Crossman, 'White Paper on National Superannuation and Social Insurance', National Association of Pension Funds, *Conference Report*, 17 February 1969, Part 1, p. 3.

29. *Annual Reports of the Ministry of National Insurance* (from 1953 *Ministry of Pensions and National Insurance*), 1946–58, *passim*. The statistics are difficult to interpret because of administrative changes and sampling differences.

30. A. Zabalza, C. Pissarides and M. Barton, 'Social Security and the Choice between Full-Time Work, Part-Time Work and Retirement', *Journal of Public Economics*, XIV, 1980, 271–2; A. Zabalza and D. Piachaud, 'Social Security and the Elderly: A Simulation of Policy Changes', *Journal of Public Economics*, XVI, 1981, pp. 157–60. Parker, *op. cit.*, pp. 45–6 shows that very few pensions are in fact now reduced on account of the earnings rule and that there is general misunderstanding about its effects.

31. Government Actuary's Department, 'A Projection of Occupational Pension Schemes to the End of the Century', Appendix 5 to *Report of the [Wilson] Committee to Review the Functioning of Financial Institutions*, Cmnd 7937, 1980, pp. 527, 537.

32. Zabalza *et al.*, *op. cit.*, p. 256.

33. *General Report on the Census of England and Wales, 1911, with Appendices*, Cd 8491, 1918 (BPP, XXXV, 1917–18), especially p. 149.

34. John Errington, in *Old Age Pensions: Appendix and the Report of the Departmental Committee on Old Age Pensions including Evidence*, Cmd 411, 1919 (BPP, XXVII, 1919), qq. 5244–8.

35. Henry Lesser, in *ibid.*, q. 4060. The witness did not explain why his percentages summed to less than 100%.

36. Cyril F. Warren, 'An Investigation into the Mortality Experienced by Pensioners of the Staffs of Banks and Insurance Companies, with a Note on the Mortality Experience of Deferred Annuitants', *Journal of the Institute of Actuaries*, LVII, 1926.

37. The average age of retirement of 6,630 pensioners in these railway schemes was sixty-four: see letter from Bethel Bailey, Chairman of the Association of Superannuated Railway Staffs, to A. Bonar Law, 13 November 1918, in PRO T172/992. This may overstate the average retiring age as it includes only those persons alive in 1918: it is likely that a disproportionate number of those who had died were early retirees. Sixty-three-and-a-half is the average age at which skilled trade unionists retired at the turn of the century (Harris, *op. cit.*, p. 101). Critics of the 1909 state pensions from age seventy generally spoke of sixty-five as the more normal age of retirement, and the reduction to sixty-five in the 1925 Pensions Act was in part a response to this feeling. By the 1950s, men in pension schemes usually retired at sixty-five and women at sixty-one (Government Actuary, *Occupational Pension Schemes: A Survey*, 1958, pp. 7, 11).

38. 'Schemes Providing for Pensions for Employees on Retirement from Work', *Ministry of Labour Gazette*, May 1938, 174.

39. Government Actuary, *Occupational Pension Schemes: 1979: Sixth Survey*, 1981, p. 40.

40. This paragraph is based on unpublished research by Carol Watson and Nuala Zahedieh of the Business History Unit, London School of Economics. See also G. Davis and R. Neale, 'Pensions for Women', in National Association of Pension Funds, *Conference Report, May 1969*, Part 1.

41. 'Schemes Providing for Pensions for Employees on Retirement from Work', p. 174.

42. Government Actuary, *Occupational Pension Schemes: 1979: Sixth Survey*, 1981, p. 40.

43. Government Actuary, *Occupational Pension Schemes: A Survey*, 1958, pp. 7, 11.

44. Mr Hardy, in report of the Annual General Meeting of the Railway Clearing House Superannuation Fund Association, 4 February 1895, in PRO RAIL 1086/2.

45. Gordon Pingstone, 'Group Life and Pension Schemes Including Group Family Income Benefit Schemes', *Journal of the Institute of Actuaries*, LXXVII, 1951, 346.

46. *Ibid.*

47. See the discussion at Association of Superannuation and Pension Funds, *Autumn Conference 1953*, pp. 21, 27.

48. 'Note as to Service after Normal Retiring Age, agreed with the Inland Revenue, Somerset House', *Superannuation*, October 1953, circular letter No. 174, pp. 14–15; Association of Superannuation and Pension Funds, *Annual General Meeting 1953*, pp. 18–19; *Report of the Committee on the Taxation Treatment of Provisions for Retirement*, Cmd 9063, 1954 (BPP, XIX, 1953–4), pp. 29–31.

49. Government Actuary, *Occupational Pension Schemes: 1975: Fifth Survey*, 1978, pp. 57–8.

50. Government Actuary, *Occupational Pension Schemes: 1979: Sixth Survey*, 1981, pp. 48–50. See also John Gaselee, 'Flexibility in Retirement Policy and Employees' Pensions', in Henry Beric Wright, ed., *Solving the Problems of Retirement*, Institute of Directors, 1968, for a bullishly optimistic treatment of the trend to more generous early retirement provision.

51. See p. 52 above.

52. Notionally the average modern scheme would have employer's contributions of $12\frac{1}{2}$%, but for most employees in their fifties the actual cost of pension accruals was substantially higher. The saving to the employer in employing someone without pension contributions is, then, potentially very large.

53. In the USA, the rise of mandatory retirement rules (which occurred at much the same time as in Britain) has been somewhat loosely ascribed to industrialization and urbanization (see, e.g., Carole Haber, 'Mandatory Retirement in Nineteenth Century America: The Conceptual Basis for a new Work Cycle', *Journal of Social History*, XII, 1978), but this hardly fits the chronology of the British case and fails to account for the emergence of these rules in some employments but not in others.

54. See p. 7 above.

55. Tony Lynes, 'Retiring Age and Compulsory Retirement in the Civil Service', unpublished manuscript, London School of Economics.

56. 'Age of Compulsory Retirement from Work', *Ministry of Labour Gazette*, LVII, April 1949; and see, generally, Edward P. Lazear, 'Why is there Mandatory Retirement?', *Journal of Political Economy*, LXXXVII, 1979.

57. Ministry of Pensions and National Insurance, *Reasons Given for Retiring or Continuing at Work*, 1954, pp. 7, 24, 28.

58. Quadagno, *op. cit.*, p. 141; Sir John Bingham in *Report and Resolutions of the Association of Chambers of Commerce of the United Kingdom, 1908*, p. 148.

59. This may explain why pension schemes are less common in, for example, the engineering and building industries, where piecework or other performance-related payment systems are common. For example H. F. Lydall (*British Incomes and Savings*, Oxford, 1955, p. 117) estimated that only 9% of employees in building and 18% in metal and engineering were in contributory pension schemes (compared with 27% in all industries) in the early 1950s.

60. See, for instance, the quotation which heads this chapter.
61. See the report of the paper by Stuart Riddle in *Centre for Economic Policy Research Bulletin*, No. 4, August 1984, 9. I understand that Mr Riddle's forthcoming Ph.D. thesis addresses this question in greater detail. See also R. Skidelsky, *Politicians and the Slump*, 1967, p. 119; *H.C. Deb.*, 5th Series, Vol. 386, cols. 419–74, 21 February 1934; A. Bullock, *The Life and Times of Ernest Bevin*, Vol. 1, 1960, pp. 402–3, 438, 516–17.
62. See p. 128 above.
63. See p. 52 above for Conservative government policy; for a Labour Party view see, e.g., G. Isaacs, MP, 'The Problem of the Employment of Older Men and Women', December 1952, in Labour Party Social Services Sub-Committee paper R183, Labour Party archives.
64. Michael Fogarty, 'The Work Option', in Fogarty, ed., *op. cit.*

Epilogue: Contemporary critics and the future of pensions

1. 'Occupational Pension Scheme Survey 1983', preliminary results of the Government Actuary's survey, *Pensions World*, January 1985.
2. *Ibid.* The coverage of full-time females has risen from 53% in 1979 to 60% in 1983: the latter is about the same as for full-time males. The issue of equality of treatment has none the less remained a live one: see, e.g., Ann McGoldrick, *Equal Treatment in Occupational Pension Schemes: A Research Report*, Equal Opportunities Commission, December 1984.
3. General Household Survey data, 1982 and 1983.
4. For some projections, see John Ermisch, 'Resources of the Elderly – Impact of Present Commitments and Established Trends', in Michael Fogarty, ed., *Retirement Policy: The Next Fifty Years*, 1982; Government Actuary's Department, 'A Projection of Occupational Pension Schemes to the End of the Century', Appendix 5 to *Report of the [Wilson] Committee to Review the Functioning of Financial Institutions*, Cmnd 7937, 1980.
5. 'Cut to Revive', *The Economist*, 26 January 1985, 16.
6. Tony Lynes, 'Pensions in Secret', *New Society*, 16 January 1969, 88–9; Lynes, 'Talking About Pensions', *Industrial Society*, June 1972, 7.
7. Confederation of British Industry, *Guidance on the Provision of Information to Members of Occupational Pension Schemes*, 1973. This was prepared jointly by the CBI, NAPF, LOA, ASLO, the CIB Society of Pension Consultants and the Association of Consulting Actuaries. See also Occupational Pensions Board, *Solvency, Disclosure of Information and Member Participation in Occupational Pension Schemes*, Cmnd 5904, 1975 (BPP, XXIV, 1974–5).
8. *Occupational Pension Schemes: The Role of Members in the Running of Schemes*, Cmnd 6514, 1976 (BPP, XLV, 1975–6).
9. Confederation of British Industry, *Who Should Manage Pension Schemes?*, 1977.
10. Jeff Hyman and Tom Schuller, 'Employee Participation in the Management of Pension Schemes', Centre for Research in Industrial Democracy and Participation, University of Glasgow, typescript, May 1983. See also their 'Trust Law and Trustees: Employee Representation in Pension Schemes', *Industrial Law Journal*, XII, 1983; and Government Actuary, *Occupational Pension Schemes:*

1979: Sixth Survey, 1981, pp. 74ff.

11. R. Minns, *Pension Funds and British Capitalism: The Ownership and Control of Shareholdings*, 1980. See also Harry Freeman, 'Pension Fund Investment: The Trade Union View', *Personnel Executive*, November 1982.
12. *Mineworkers' Pension Scheme Trusts Cowan and Others* vs. *Scargill and Others*, Times Law Report, 18 April 1984, p. 8a.
13. Sir Arthur Knight, *Wilson Revisited: Industrialists and Financiers*, Policy Studies Institute Discussion Paper No. 5, 1982; Margaret Reid, *The Secondary Banking Crisis 1973–75*, 1982.
14. See pp. 106–11 above.
15. The phrase is Lord Vinson's, a chief protagonist of personal pensions.
16. See p. 60 above.
17. Nigel Vinson and Phillip Chappell, *Personal and Portable Pensions for All*, Centre for Policy Studies, 1983. The pressure groups of the libertarian right also proposed individual retirement accounts: see, e.g., Adam Smith Institute, *Social Security*, 1984.
18. See pp. 109–11 above.
19. Gallup Survey, August 1984, commissioned by Legal & General.
20. See pp. 35–7 above.
21. *Personal Pensions: A Consultative Document*, Department of Health and Social Security, 1984.
22. See p. 104 above.
23. Earlier the 1981 Companies Act had also improved the requirements of employer disclosure to shareholders of pension liabilities – see 'A True and Fair View of Old Age', *The Economist*, 21 May 1983, 96.
24. Pam Spooner, 'Additional Voluntary Contributions', *Investors Chronicle*, 6 March 1981, 19–23; Eric Short, 'Mars Set a Shining Example', *The Financial Times*, 26 January 1985, 14.
25. Professor Peter Moore, quoted in editorial, *The Times*, 27 November 1984, 17b.
26. Mary Goldring, 'Could the Pensions Workers Get be Less of a Gamble?', *The Listener*, 4 October 1984, 3.
27. *The Financial Times*, 12 December 1984, 6.
28. 'TUC Tries to Save Pension Tax Relief', *The Financial Times*, 2 January 1985, 4; Keith Harper, 'Unions Threaten Industrial Action on Pensions', *Pensions*, February 1985, 47.
29. Leslie Hannah, 'A Tax Privilege Conundrum for the Chancellor', *The Financial Times*, 12 February 1985, 8; Lex, 'Weighing up the Pensions Risk', *The Financial Times*, 21 January 1985, 30.
30. C. S. S. Lyon, 'The Outlook for Pensioning,' *Journal of the Institute of Actuaries*, cx, 1983.

Index